Beginning Hibernate

Third Edition

T0224275

Joseph B. Ottinger

Dave Minter

Jeff Linwood

Apress·

Beginning Hibernate

ISBN-13 (pbk): 978-1-4302-6517-7

ISBN-13 (electronic): 978-1-4302-6518-4

President and Publisher: Paul Manning
Lead Editor: Steve Anglin
Development Editor: Matthew Moodie
Technical Reviewer: Rohan Walia
Editorial Board: Steve Anglin, Mark Beckner, Ewan Buckingham, Gary Cornell, Louise Corrigan, James T. DeWolf, Jonathan Gennick, Jonathan Hassell, Robert Hutchinson, Michelle Lowman, James Markham, Matthew Moodie, Jeff Olson, Jeffrey Pepper, Douglas Pundick, Ben Renow-Clarke, Dominic Shakeshaft, Gwenan Spearing, Matt Wade, Steve Weiss
Coordinating Editor: Anamika Panchoo
Copy Editor: Carole Berglie
Compositor: SPi Global
Indexer: SPi Global
Artist: SPi Global
Cover Designer: Anna Ishchenko

Distributed to the book trade worldwide by Springer Science+Business Media New York, 233 Spring Street, 6th Floor, New York, NY 10013. Phone 1-800-SPRINGER, fax (201) 348-4505, e-mail orders-ny@springer-sbm.com, or visit www.springeronline.com. Apress Media, LLC is a California LLC and the sole member (owner) is Springer Science + Business Media Finance Inc (SSBM Finance Inc). SSBM Finance Inc is a Delaware corporation.

For information on translations, please e-mail rights@apress.com, or visit www.apress.com.

Apress and friends of ED books may be purchased in bulk for academic, corporate, or promotional use. eBook versions and licenses are also available for most titles. For more information, reference our Special Bulk Sales–eBook Licensing web page at www.apress.com/bulk-sales.

Any source code or other supplementary materials referenced by the author in this text is available to readers at www.apress.com. For detailed information about how to locate your book's source code, go to www.apress.com/source-code/.

Dedicated to recursive dedications found around the globe. And my beloved wife.

Contents at a Glance

About the Authors xv

About the Technical Reviewer xvii

Acknowledgments xix

Introduction xxi

■Chapter 1: An Introduction to Hibernate 4.2 1

■Chapter 2: Integrating and Configuring Hibernate 9

■Chapter 3: Building a Simple Application 19

■Chapter 4: The Persistence Life Cycle 41

■Chapter 5: An Overview of Mapping 69

■Chapter 6: Mapping with Annotations 81

■Chapter 7: JPA Integration and Lifecycle Events 115

■Chapter 8: Using the Session 135

■Chapter 9: Searches and Queries 149

■Chapter 10: Advanced Queries Using Criteria 165

■Chapter 11: Filtering the Results of Searches 175

■Chapter 12: Leaving the Relational Database Behind: NoSQL 183

■Appendix: More Advanced Features 195

Index 205

Contents

About the Authors.. xv

About the Technical Reviewer xvii

Acknowledgments xix

Introduction xxi

■Chapter 1: An Introduction to Hibernate 4.2... 1

Plain Old Java Objects (POJOs) 1

Origins of Hibernate and Object/Relational Mapping 3

Hibernate as a Persistence Solution 4

A Hibernate Hello World Example 5

Mappings 6

Persisting an Object 7

Summary 7

■Chapter 2: Integrating and Configuring Hibernate 9

The Steps Needed to Integrate and Configure Hibernate 9

Understanding Where Hibernate Fits into Your Java Application 10

Deploying Hibernate 10

  Installing Maven 11

Connection Pooling 16

Summary 18

Chapter 3: Building a Simple Application 19

A Simple Application 19

A First Attempt..20

Writing Data..21

Reading Data 24

Updating Data 26

Persistence Contexts...27

Removing Data 27

A Note on Managing Sessions 28

A Note on Transactions 28

Writing Our Sample Application...29

Summary 40

Chapter 4: The Persistence Life Cycle 41

Introducing the Life Cycle..41

Entities, Classes, and Names 42

Identifiers 43

Entities and Associations 44

Saving Entities 51

Object Equality and Identity...54

Loading Entities..56

Merging Entities 58

Refreshing Entities 59

Updating Entities 60

Deleting Entities 61

Cascading Operations 62

Lazy Loading, Proxies, and Collection Wrappers 66

Querying Objects 67

Summary..67

■Chapter 5: An Overview of Mapping 69

Why Mapping Cannot Easily Be Automated 70

Primary Keys 71

Lazy Loading 73

Associations 74

The One-to-One Association 75

The One-to-Many and Many-to-One Association 77

The Many-to-Many Association 78

Applying Mappings to Associations 79

Other Supported Features 79

Specification of (Database) Column Types and Sizes 79

The Mapping of Inheritance Relationships to the Database 79

Primary Key 80

The Use of SQL Formula–Based Properties 80

Mandatory and Unique Constraints 80

Summary 80

■Chapter 6: Mapping with Annotations 81

Creating Hibernate Mappings with Annotations 81

The Cons of Annotations 81

The Pros of Annotations 81

Choosing Which to Use 82

JPA 2 Persistence Annotations 83

Entity Beans with @Entity 84

Primary Keys with @Id and @GeneratedValue 84

Compound Primary Keys with @Id, @IdClass, or @EmbeddedId 87

Database Table Mapping with @Table and @SecondaryTable 93

Persisting Basic Types with @Basic 94

Omitting Persistence with @Transient 95

Mapping Properties and Fields with @Column 95

Modeling Entity Relationships 96

Inheritance 102

Other JPA 2 Persistence Annotations 104

Ordering Collections with @OrderColumn 106

Configuring the Annotated Classes 108

Hibernate-Specific Persistence Annotations 109

@Immutable 109

Natural IDs 110

Summary 114

■Chapter 7: JPA Integration and Lifecycle Events 115

The Java Persistence Architecture 115

The Project Object Model 116

The JPASessionUtil class 117

Testing JPASessionUtil 118

Lifecycle Events 122

External Entity Listeners 126

Data Validation 127

Summary 133

■Chapter 8: Using the Session 135

Sessions 135

Transactions and Locking 138

Transactions 138

Locking 141

Deadlocks 142

Caching 145

Threads 148

Summary 148

■Chapter 9: Searches and Queries 149

Hibernate Query Language (HQL) 149

Syntax Basics 150

    UPDATE 150

    DELETE 150

    INSERT 151

    SELECT 151

Named Queries 152

Logging and Commenting the Underlying SQL 155

    Logging the SQL 155

    Commenting the Generated SQL 156

The from Clause and Aliases 156

The select Clause and Projection 157

Using Restrictions with HQL 157

Using Named Parameters 158

Paging Through the Result Set 159

Obtaining a Unique Result 159

Sorting Results with the order by Clause 160

Associations 160

Aggregate Methods 161

Bulk Updates and Deletes with HQL 162

Using Native SQL 163

Summary 164

■Chapter 10: Advanced Queries Using Criteria 165

Using the Criteria API 165

    Using Restrictions with Criteria 165

    Paging Through the Result Set 169

    Obtaining a Unique Result 169

    Sorting the Query's Results 170

Associations 170

Distinct Results 171

Projections and Aggregates 171

Query By Example (QBE) 173

Summary 174

■**Chapter 11: Filtering the Results of Searches** **175**

When to Use Filters 175

Defining and Attaching Filters 176

    Filters with Annotations...176

    Filters with XML Mapping Documents...177

Using Filters in Your Application 177

A Basic Filtering Example..178

Summary..182

■**Chapter 12: Leaving the Relational Database Behind: NoSQL** **183**

Where Is Hibernate When it Comes to NoSQL? 184

Basic CRUD Operations 184

    The Tests...188

    Testing Create and Read...188

    Testing Updates...189

    Testing Removal 190

    Querying in OGM..190

MongoDB..193

Summary..194

■**Appendix: More Advanced Features** **195**

Managed Versioning and Optimistic Locking 195

Limitations of Hibernate 196

Hand-Rolled SQL 197

    Using a Direct Mapping 197

    Using a View 198

    Putting SQL into an Annotation or Mapping..199

Invoking Stored Procedures 201

Overriding the Default Constructor...202

Summary...203

Index...205

About the Authors

Joseph B. Ottinger is a Principal Engineer at Red Hat. He's been messing around with computers since the 1980s, thinking about systems and architecture through war games and music. He's worked as a developer, architect, consultant, and writer since then, including editing stints at *Java Developer Journal* and TheServerSide.com.

A musician, programmer, artist, writer, father, and husband, his interests tend to range far and wide, through philosophy, history, science, art, basketball, and education.

Jeff Linwood has been involved in software programming since he had a 286 in high school. He got caught up with the Internet when he got access to a UNIX shell account, and it has been downhill ever since.

When he's not playing on the computer, his hobby is running ultramarathons. Jeff is based in Austin, Texas, and helps large companies solve tough problems with content management, search engines, and web application development. Jeff also co-authored *Professional Struts Applications* (Apress), *Building Portals with the Java Portlet API* (Apress), and *Pro Hibernate 3* (Apress).

Dave Minter has adored computers since he was small enough to play in the boxes they came in. He built his first PC from discarded, faulty, and obsolete components; and he considers that to be the foundation of his career as an integration consultant. Dave is based in London, where he helps large and small companies build systems that "just work." He wrote *Beginning Spring 2: From Novice to Professional* (Apress) and co-authored *Building Portals with the Java Portlet API* (Apress) and *Pro Hibernate 3* (Apress)

About the Technical Reviewer

 **Rohan Walia** is a Software Consultant with extensive experience in Client-Server, Web-Based, and Enterprise application development. He is an Oracle Certified ADF Implementation Specialist and Sun Certified Java Programmer. Rohan is responsible for designing and developing end-to-end Java/J2EE applications consisting of various cutting-edge frameworks and utilities. His areas of expertise are Oracle ADF, WebCenter, Spring, Hibernate, and Java/J2EE. When not working, Rohan loves to play tennis, travel, and go hiking.

Acknowledgments

Joseph would like to thank various people for encouraging and enabling him to write this book, and so he will: first, his wife and children for allowing him the time and energy to put into the project; Steve Ebersole, project lead for Hibernate; the Open Source and Standards team at Red Hat; friends like Tracy Snell, Andrew Lombardi, Eugene Ciurana, and Justin Lee for serving as sounding boards and source material; his editors, for putting up with his quirks[1]; bands like Rush, Pink Floyd, and Tool for providing the soundtrack to the book[2]; the letter Z, for allowing itself to go underused throughout the book; his Gibson guitar; Robert Sedgewick, just because Joseph has not had the chance to thank him in print yet; Toby Segaran, because he hasn't had a chance to thank him, either; and lastly, Stan Lee, for giving Joseph a worthwhile impetus to learn to read when he was very young.

---

[1]Quirks like his endless footnotes; when asked, they allowed Joseph to have one footnote for every three pages, to which the response was, "Thanks! Three footnotes maximum for every page, got it!"

[2]A soundtrack you won't hear, nor is it likely to be easily detected unless you listen very well. Listen more than that—no, more than that, too. Keep going. Let me know which song you hear, okay?

Introduction

Hibernate is an amazing piece of software. With a little experience and the power of annotations, you can build a complex, database-backed system with disturbing ease. Once you have built a system using Hibernate, you will never want to go back to the traditional approaches.

While Hibernate is incredibly powerful, it presents a steep learning curve when you first encounter it—steep learning curves are actually a good thing because they impart profound insight once you have scaled them. Yet gaining that insight takes some perseverance and assistance.

Our aim in this book is to help you scale that learning curve by presenting you with the minimal requirements of a discrete Hibernate application, explaining the basis of those requirements, and walking you through an example application that is built using them. We then provide additional material to be digested once the fundamentals are firmly understood. Throughout, we provide examples rather than relying on pure discourse. We hope that you will continue to find this book useful as a reference text long after you have become an expert on the subject.

Who This Book Is For

This book assumes a good understanding of Java fundamentals and some familiarity with database programming using the Java Database Connectivity (JDBC) API. We don't expect you to know anything about Hibernate—but if you buy this book, it will probably be because you have had some exposure to the painful process of building a large database-based system.

All of our examples use open-source software—primarily the Hibernate API itself—so you will not need to purchase any software to get started with Hibernate development. This book is not an academic text. Our focus is, instead, on providing extensive examples and taking a pragmatic approach to the technology that it covers.

To true newcomers to the Hibernate API, we recommend that you read at least the first three chapters in order before diving into the juicy subjects of later chapters. Very experienced developers or those with experience with tools similar to Hibernate will want to skim the latter half of the book for interesting chapters. Readers familiar with Hibernate will want to turn to the appendix for discussion of more arcane topics.

How This Book Is Structured

This book is informally divided into three parts. Chapters 1 through 8 describe the fundamentals of Hibernate, including configuration, the creation of mapping files, and the basic APIs. Chapters 9 through 11 describe the use of queries, criteria, and filters to access the persistent information in more sophisticated ways. Chapter 12 addresses the use of Hibernate to talk to nonrelational data stores, providing an easy "on ramp" to NoSQL.

Finally, the appendixes discuss features that you will use less often or that are peripheral to the core Hibernate functionality. The following list describes more fully the contents of each chapter:

Chapter 1 outlines the purpose of persistence tools and presents excerpts from a simple example application to show how Hibernate can be applied. It also introduces core terminology and concepts.

Chapter 2 discusses the fundamentals of configuring a Hibernate application. It presents the basic architecture of Hibernate and discusses how a Hibernate application is integrated into an application.

Chapter 3 presents an example application, walking you through the complete process of creating and running the application. It then looks at a slightly more complex example and introduces the notion of generating the database schema directly from Hibernate annotations.

Chapter 4 covers the Hibernate lifecycle in depth. It discusses the lifecycle in the context of the methods available on the core interfaces. It also introduces key terminology and discusses the need for cascading and lazy loading.

Chapter 5 explains why mapping information must be retained by Hibernate and demonstrates the various types of associations that can be represented by a relational database. It briefly discusses the other information that can be maintained within a Hibernate mapping.

Chapter 6 explains how Hibernate lets you use the annotations to represent mapping information. It provides detailed examples for the most important annotations, and discusses the distinctions between the standard JPA 2 annotations and the proprietary Hibernate ones.

Chapter 7 explains some of the uses of the Java Persistence API (as opposed to the Hibernate-native API), as well as the lifecycle and validation of persisted objects.

Chapter 8 revisits the Hibernate `Session` object in detail, explaining the various methods that it provides. The chapter also discusses the use of transactions, locking, and caching, as well as how to use Hibernate in a multithreaded environment.

Chapter 9 discusses how Hibernate can be used to make sophisticated queries against the underlying relational database using the built-in Hibernate Query Language (HQL).

Chapter 10 introduces the Criteria API, which is a programmatic analog of the query language discussed in Chapter 9.

Chapter 11 discusses how the Filter API can be used to restrict the results of the queries introduced in Chapters 9 and 10.

Chapter 12 introduces Hibernate OGM, which maps objects to non-relational data stores like Infinispan and Mongodb, among others. It shows some of the uses of Hibernate Search to provide a common search facility for NoSQL, as well as offering full text query support.

Appendix presents a large number of peripheral features that do not warrant more extensive coverage in a beginner-level text. The appendix discusses the basics, with examples, of the support for versioning and optimistic locking, and some of the obscure limitations of Hibernate and various ways that these can be worked around. It also discusses the use of events and interceptors.

Downloading the Code

The source code for this book is available to readers from `www.apress.com`, in the Source Code/Download section. Please feel free to visit the Apress web site and download all the code from there.

Contacting the Authors

We welcome feedback from our readers. If you have any queries or suggestions about this book, or technical questions about Hibernate, or if you just want to share a really good joke, you can email Joseph Ottinger at `joeo@enigmastation.com`, Dave Minter at `dave@paperstack.com`, and Jeff Linwood at `jlinwood@gmail.com`.

CHAPTER 1

An Introduction to Hibernate 4.2

Most significant development projects involve a relational database.[1] The mainstay of most commercial applications is the large-scale storage of ordered information, such as catalogs, customer lists, contract details, published text, and architectural designs.

With the advent of the World Wide Web, the demand for databases has increased. Though they may not know it, the customers of online bookshops and newspapers are using databases. Somewhere in the guts of the application a database is being queried and a response is offered.

Hibernate 4 is a library that simplifies the use of relational databases in Java applications by presenting relational data as simple Java objects, accessed through a session manager, therefore earning the description of being an "Object/Relational Mapper," or ORM. It provides two kinds of programmatic interfaces: a "native Hibernate" interface and the Java EE-standard Java Persistence API.

There are solutions for which an ORM-like Hibernate is appropriate, and some for which the traditional approach of direct access via the Java Database Connectivity (JDBC) API is appropriate. We think that Hibernate represents a good first choice, as it does not preclude the simultaneous use of alternative approaches, even though some care must be taken if data is modified from two different APIs.

To illustrate some of Hibernate's strengths, in this chapter we take a look at a brief example using Hibernate and contrast this with the traditional JDBC approach.

Plain Old Java Objects (POJOs)

In an ideal world,[2] it would be trivial to take any Java object and persist it to the database. No special coding would be required to achieve this, no performance penalty would ensue, and the result would be totally portable. In this ideal world, we would perhaps perform such an operation in a manner like that shown in Listing 1-1.

Listing 1-1. A Rose-Tinted View of Object Persistence

```
POJO pojo = new POJO();
ORMSolution magic = ORMSolution.getInstance();
magic.save(pojo);
```

There would be no nasty surprises, no additional work to correlate the class with tables in the database, and no performance problems.

---

[1]A *relational database* is a collection of sets of data items, each of which is formally described and organized. Rules can be put into place for the data such that it can be validated, and indexes can be created such that the data can be queried and updated quickly and safely.

[2]Well, perhaps an ideal world in which an ORM is used for data access. But in *this* book this can be assumed to be the case.

Hibernate comes remarkably close to this, at least when compared with the alternatives,but there are configuration files to create and subtle performance and synchronization issues to consider. Hibernate does, however, achieve its fundamental aim: it allows you to store POJOs in the database. Figure 1-1 shows how Hibernate fits into your application between the client code and the database.

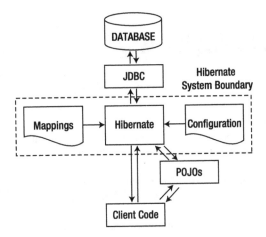

Figure 1-1. *The role of Hibernate in a Java application*

The common term for the direct persistence of traditional Java objects is *object/relational mapping*—that is, mapping the objects in Java directly to the relational entities in a database.

POJOs can be any Java object at all. Hibernate allows you to persist POJOs with very few constraints. Listing 1-2 is an example of a simple POJO that might be used to represent a message. (We'll be modifying this class as we walk through some example code.)

Listing 1-2. The POJO Used in this Chapter's Examples

```
package chapter01.pojo;

public class Message {
    String text;
    public Message() {
    }

    public Message(String text) {
        setText(text);
    }

    public String getText() {
        return text;
    }

    public void setText(String text) {
        this.text = text;
    }
}
```

The sole condescension to Hibernate here is the provision of a default constructor. Hibernate demands that all POJOs to be stored should provide a default constructor;[3] but even that situation can be worked around when third-party classes fail to satisfy this limited requirement (through the use of an Interceptor mechanism in the Hibernate configuration; we will demonstrate this in Appendix A).

Origins of Hibernate and Object/Relational Mapping

If Hibernate is the solution, what was the problem? One answer is that doing things the right way when using JDBC requires a considerable body of code and careful observation of various rules (such as those governing connection management) to ensure that your application does not leak resources. This bit of code from the example JDBC PersistenceTest class shows how much needs to be done to retrieve a list of Message objects:

Listing 1-3. The JDBC Approach to Retrieving the POJO

```java
@Test(dependsOnMethods = "saveMessage")
public void readMessage() {
    Connection connection = null;
    PreparedStatement ps = null;
    ResultSet rs = null;
    List<Message> list = new ArrayList<>();
    try {
        connection = DriverManager.getConnection("jdbc:hsqldb:db1;shutdown=true");

        ps = connection.prepareStatement("SELECT id, text FROM messages");

        rs = ps.executeQuery();
        while (rs.next()) {
            Message message = new Message();
            message.setId(rs.getLong(1));
            message.setText(rs.getString(2));
            list.add(message);
        }

        if (list.size() > 1) {
            Assert.fail("Message configuration in error; table should contain only one."
                +" Set ddl to drop-create.");
        }
        if (list.size() == 0) {
            Assert.fail("Read of initial message failed; check saveMessage() for errors."
                +" How did this test run?");
        }
        for (Message m : list) {
            System.out.println(m);
        }
        // eagerly free resources
        rs.close();
        ps.close();
        connection.close();
```

---

[3]See http://docs.jboss.org/hibernate/orm/4.2/quickstart/en-US/html/ch02.html#hibernate-gsg-tutorial-basic-entity for more details. Short form: Hibernate uses reflection to construct an object before data population. The shortest (and quickest) path to doing that is with a no-argument constructor.

```
    } catch (SQLException e) {
        e.printStackTrace();
        throw new RuntimeException(e);
    } finally {
        try {
            if (rs != null && !rs.isClosed()) {
                rs.close();
            }
        } catch (SQLException ignored) {
        }
        try {
            if (ps != null && !ps.isClosed()) {
                ps.close();
            }
        } catch (SQLException ignored) {
        }
        try {
            if (connection != null && !connection.isClosed()) {
                connection.close();
            }
        } catch (SQLException ignored) {
        }
    }
}
```

Could some of this be trimmed down? Of course. The code to close the resources is very long (and since applications that use JDBC would do this sort of thing a lot, this code begs for refactoring into reusable methods). Using a connection pool instead of DriverManager would also help with this because most, if not all, connection pools automatically release resources on garbage collection. (In this case, though, eager release is still valuable.) You could also use classes like Spring's JDBCTemplate to handle error conditions and connection management.

However, in the end the problem remains: there's a lot of resource management involved, primarily around handling error and termination conditions, and the code itself is very brittle. If we added a field to the database, we would have to find every SQL statement that might need to access that field, and we would modify the code to accommodate it.

We also run into the issue of *types* with this code. This is a very simple object: it stores a simple numeric identifier with a simple string. However, if we wanted to store a geolocation, we'd have to break the location into its multiple properties (longitude and latitude, for example), and store each separately, which means your object model no longer cleanly matches your database.

All of this makes using the database directly look more and more flawed, and that's not before factoring in other issues around object persistence and retrieval.

Hibernate as a Persistence Solution

Hibernate addresses a lot of these issues, or alleviates some of the pain where it can't, so we'll address the points in turn.

First, Hibernate provides cleaner resource management, which means that you do not have to worry about the actual database connections, nor do you have to have giant try/catch/finally blocks. Error conditions may occur such that you do need to handle them, of course; but these are exceptional conditions, not normal ones. (In other words, you're handling exceptions that you actually *should* have to handle, instead of handling every exception that you *might* have to handle.)

Hibernate handles the mapping of the object to the database table, including constructing the database schema for you if you so configure it; it doesn't require one table per object type; you can easily map one object to multiple tables. And Hibernate also handles relationships for you; for example, if you added a list of addresses to a Person object, you could easily have the addresses stored in a secondary table, constructed and managed by Hibernate.

In addition to mapping the object to the database table, Hibernate can handle mappings of new types to the database. The geolocation can be specified as its own table, can be normalized, or can have a custom serialization mechanism such that you can store it in whatever native form you need.

Hibernate's startup takes a little bit longer than direct JDBC code, to be sure. However, system initialization time is usually not a meaningful metric. Most applications have long runtimes and the percentage of time spent in Hibernate initialization is irrelevant to the actual performance of the application; Hibernate's advantages in maintenance and object management more than make up for any time the application spends in configuration. As usual, the right way to consider performance is through testing and analysis of an actual application, as opposed to spitballing anecdotal evidence.

Any Java object capable of being persisted to a database is a candidate for Hibernate persistence. Therefore, Hibernate is a natural replacement for ad hoc solutions (like our JDBC example), or as the persistence engine for an application that has not yet had database persistence incorporated into it. Furthermore, by choosing Hibernate persistence, you are not tying yourself to any particular design decisions for the business objects in your application—including which database the application uses for persistence, which is a configurable aspect.

A Hibernate Hello World Example

Listing 1-4 shows the same test as does Listing 1-3, using Hibernate instead of JDBC. Here, the factory object is initialized on test startup, but it serves the same role as the Connection initialization from the JDBC-based code.

Listing 1-4. The Hibernate Approach to Retrieving the POJO

```java
SessionFactory factory;

@BeforeClass
public void setup() {
    Configuration configuration = new Configuration();
    configuration.configure();
    ServiceRegistryBuilder srBuilder = new ServiceRegistryBuilder();
    srBuilder.applySettings(configuration.getProperties());
    ServiceRegistry serviceRegistry = srBuilder.buildServiceRegistry();
    factory = configuration.buildSessionFactory(serviceRegistry);
}

@Test(dependsOnMethods = "saveMessage")
public void readMessage() {
    Session session = factory.openSession();
    @SuppressWarnings("unchecked")
    List<Message> list = (List<Message>) session.createQuery("from Message").list();

    if (list.size() > 1) {
        Assert.fail("Message configuration in error; table should contain only one."
            +" Set ddl to create-drop.");
    }
    if (list.size() == 0) {
        Assert.fail("Read of initial message failed; check saveMessage() for errors."
            +" How did this test run?");
    }
```

```
for (Message m : list) {
    System.out.println(m);
}
session.close();
```
}

Note that the manual coding to populate the Message object has not been eradicated; rather, it has been moved into an external configuration file that isolates this implementation detail from the main logic.

Also note that we're using the Hibernate Query Language (HQL) to locate the Message. HQL is very powerful, and this is a poor usage of it; we'll dig into HQL quite a bit as we progress.

Some of the additional code in the Hibernate example given in Listing 1-4 actually provides functionality (particularly transactionality and caching) beyond that of the JDBC example.

Mappings

As we have intimated, Hibernate needs something to tell it which tables relate to which objects. In Hibernate parlance, this is called a *mapping*. Mappings can be provided either through Java annotations or through an XML mapping file. In this book, we will focus on using annotations, as we can mark up the POJO Java classes directly. Using annotations gives you a clear picture of the structure at the code level, which seems to be preferred by people writing code.[4] Hibernate also takes a configuration-by-exception approach for annotations: if we are satisfied with the default values that Hibernate provides for us, we do not need to explicitly provide them as annotations. For instance, Hibernate uses the name of the POJO class as the default value of the database table to which the object is mapped. In our example, if we are satisfied with using a database table named Message, we do not need to define it in the source code.

In fact, if our only access is through Hibernate, we don't really even need to know what the table name is; as our example shows, we query based on object type and not the table name. Hibernate automatically constructs the query such that the correct table name is used, even if we were to change the table name to "Messages," for example.

Listing 1-5 shows the Message POJO with annotations for mapping the Java object into the database. It adds an identifier and a toString( ) method to our original POJO; we'd want the ID in any event, but the toString( ) adds convenience as we use the class. (We'll eventually want to add an equals( ) and hashCode( ) as well.)

Listing 1-5. The POJO with Mapping Annotations

```
package chapter01.hibernate;
import javax.persistence.*;

@Entity
public class Message {
    @Id
    @GeneratedValue(strategy = GenerationType.AUTO)
    Long id;
    @Column(nullable = false)
    String text;

    public Message(String text) {
        setText(text);
    }
```

---

[4]Go figure; who knew coders like for things to be code? (Besides coders, I mean.)

```java
    public Message() {
    }

    public Long getId() {
        return id;
    }

    public void setId(Long id) {
        this.id = id;
    }

    public String getText() {
        return text;
    }

    public void setText(String text) {
        this.text = text;
    }

    @Override
    public String toString() {
        return "Message{" +
                "id=" + getId() +
                ", text='" + getText() + '\'' +
                '}';
    }
}
```

Persisting an Object

In the interest of completeness, here's the method used to write a Message into the database with Hibernate. (The JDBC version of this code is present in the downloadable examples, but adds nothing to the knowledge of how to use Hibernate.)

Listing 1-6. Saving a Message Object in Hibernate

```java
@Test
public void saveMessage() {
    Message message = new Message("Hello, world");
    Session session = factory.openSession();
    Transaction tx = session.beginTransaction();
    session.persist(message);
    tx.commit();
    session.close();
}
```

Summary

In this chapter, we have considered the problems and requirements that have driven the development of Hibernate. We have looked at some of the details of a trivial example application written with and without the aid of Hibernate. We have glossed over some of the implementation details, but we will discuss these in depth in Chapter 3.

In the next chapter, we will look at the architecture of Hibernate and how it is integrated into your applications.

CHAPTER 2

■ ■ ■

Integrating and Configuring Hibernate

Integrating Hibernate into a Java application is easy. The designers of Hibernate avoided some of the more common pitfalls and problems with the existing Java persistence solutions, and created a clean but powerful architecture. In practice, this means that you do not have to run Hibernate inside any particular Java EE container or framework. Hibernate only requires Java 6 or later.[1]

At first, adding Hibernate to your Java project looks intimidating: the distribution includes a large set of libraries. To get your first Hibernate application to work, you have to set up the database references and the Hibernate configuration, which might include mapping your objects to the database. You also have to create your POJOs, including any annotation-based mapping. After you have done all of that, you need to write the logic in your application that uses Hibernate to actually accomplish something! But once you learn how to integrate Hibernate with your application, the basics apply for any project that uses Hibernate.

One of the key features of Hibernate's design is the principle of least intrusiveness: the Hibernate developers did not want Hibernate to intrude into your application more than was necessary. This led to several of the architectural decisions made for Hibernate. In Chapter 1, you saw how Hibernate can be applied to solve persistence problems using conventional Java objects. In this chapter, we explain some of the configuration details needed to support this behavior.

The Steps Needed to Integrate and Configure Hibernate

This chapter explains configuration and integration in detail, but for a quick overview, refer to the following list to determine what you need to do to get your first Hibernate application up and running. Then Chapter 3 will lead you through the building of a pair of small example applications that use Hibernate. The first of these examples is as simple as we could make it, so it is an excellent introduction to the following necessary steps:

1. Identify the POJOs that have a database representation.

2. Identify which properties of those POJOs need to be persisted.

3. Annotate each of the POJOs to map your Java object's properties to columns in a database table (covered in more detail in Chapter 6).

4. Create the database schema using the schema export tool, use an existing database, or create your own database schema.

5. Add the Hibernate Java libraries to your application's classpath (covered in this chapter).

---

[1]The runtime requirement of at least Java 6 was confirmed by Steve Ebersole, lead of the Hibernate project. He also specified that JDK 1.7 was required in order to build Hibernate from source.

6. Create a Hibernate XML configuration file that points to your database and your mapped classes (covered in this chapter).

7. In your Java application, create a Hibernate `Configuration` object that references your XML configuration file (covered in this chapter).

8. Also in your Java application, build a Hibernate `SessionFactory` object from the `Configuration` object (covered in this chapter).

9. Retrieve the Hibernate Session objects from the `SessionFactory`, and write your data access logic for your application (create, retrieve, update, and delete).

Don't worry if you don't understand every term or concept mentioned in this list. After reading this chapter, and then following the example in the next chapter, you will know what these terms mean and how they fit together.

Understanding Where Hibernate Fits into Your Java Application

You can call Hibernate from your Java application directly, or you can access Hibernate through another framework. You can call Hibernate from a Swing application, a servlet, a portlet, a JSP page, or any other Java application that has access to a database. Typically, you would use Hibernate to either create a data access layer for an application or replace an existing data access layer.

Hibernate supports the Java Management Extensions (JMX), J2EE Connector Architecture (JCA), and Java Naming and Directory Interface (JNDI) Java language standards. Using JMX, you can configure Hibernate while it is running. Hibernate may be deployed as a JCA connector, and you can use JNDI to obtain a Hibernate session factory in your application. In addition, Hibernate uses standard Java Database Connectivity (JDBC) database drivers to access the relational database. Hibernate does not replace JDBC as a database connectivity layer; Hibernate sits on a level above JDBC.

In addition to the standard Java APIs, many Java web and application frameworks now integrate with Hibernate. Hibernate's simple, clean API makes it easy for these frameworks to support Hibernate in one way or another. The Spring framework provides excellent Hibernate integration, including generic support for persistence objects, a generic set of persistence exceptions, and transaction management. Appendix C explains how Hibernate can be configured within a Spring application.

Regardless of the environment into which you are integrating Hibernate, certain requirements remain constant. You will need to define the configuration details that apply; these are then represented by a `Configuration` object. From the `Configuration` object, a single `SessionFactory` object is created; and from this, `Session` objects are instantiated, through which your application accesses Hibernate's representation of the database.

Deploying Hibernate

There are two sets of components necessary for integration of Hibernate into your application: a database driver and the Hibernate libraries themselves.

The example code for this book uses HSQLDB as a small, embeddable database; this can be found at `http://hsqldb.org/`. This is not to indicate that other databases are of less value than HSQLDB, but it is simply an expedient choice; HSQLDB's sort-of sibling project H2 is also workable, as is Derby; if you have a MySQL or PostgreSQL data server handy, those work as well.

If you're using the Hibernate binary download (from a "release bundle," via `http://www.hibernate.org/downloads`), all of the jars contained in the lib/required directory are mandatory in order to use Hibernate.

Perhaps an easier way to integrate Hibernate is through the use of a build tool, like SBT (http://www.scala-sbt.org/), Gradle (http://www.gradle.org/, used by the Hibernate project itself), or Maven (http://maven.apache.org/), the latter which is arguably the most popular of the build tools, if not the best.[2]

All of these build tools are able to bundle dependencies into a deliverable artifact. They're also able to include dependencies transitively, which means that projects that depend on a given subproject also inherit that subproject's dependencies.

We'll target Maven as a build environment for the rest of the book; users of other build tools are generally able to migrate from Maven fairly easily, and we'll make sure to keep developers who don't use build tools in mind as well.

Installing Maven

There are many ways to install Maven. This is a cursory overview; different operating systems (and different system configurations) can affect the installation procedure, so when you are in doubt, you can refer to http://maven.apache.org/download.cgi#Installation for the actual documentation.

To save you some time, however, you can download Maven from http://maven.apache.org/download.cgi/; you should get the most recent version. UNIX users (including Linux and MacOS users) should download the file ending in tar.gz; Windows users should download the zip file.

In UNIX, untar the file into a directory of your choice; an example of the command that might be run is:

```
mkdir ~/work || cd ~/work; tar xf apache-maven-3.0.5-bin.tar.gz
```

This will create ~/work/apache-maven-3.0.5/, and the mvn executable will be in ~/work/apache-maven-3.0.5/bin; add this to your command path.

For Windows, open the archive and extract it into a known location (for example, C:\tools\). Add the location of mvn.bat (in this example, C:\tools\apache-maven-3.0.5\bin) to your path via the System Properties dialog, and you should be able to run Maven with "mvn" in the command prompt.

Maven uses a project object model, typically written in XML, called "pom.xml". This file describes the project's name and versions and builds configurations (if any), as well as any subprojects and any project dependencies. When Maven is run, it will automatically download any resources it needs in order to complete the build as specified, and then it will compile the project source code; if the project includes tests, it will run the tests and complete the build if (and only if) no test failures occur.

This book uses a parent project that contains global dependencies for the book, and subprojects corresponding to the chapters; much of the operating code is written as a set of tests in the subprojects. Chapter 1, for example, used two methods to write data to and read data from a database; those tests were written as TestNG test classes: chapter01.hibernate.PersistenceTest and chapter01.jdbc.PersistenceTest.

The parent project's configuration file, after Chapter 1 was written, looked like Listing 2-1.

Listing 2-1. The Top-Level Project Object Model for Maven

```xml
<?xml version="1.0"?>
<project xsi:schemaLocation="http://maven.apache.org/POM/4.0.0
        http://maven.apache.org/xsd/maven-4.0.0.xsd"
        xmlns="http://maven.apache.org/POM/4.0.0"
        xmlns:xsi="http://www.w3.org/2001/XMLSchema-instance">
    <modelVersion>4.0.0</modelVersion>
    <groupId>com.redhat.osas.books.hibernate</groupId>
```

---

[2]Arguments about "which build tool is best" are a lot like arguments about relative merits of IDEA, Emacs, Netbeans, Eclipse, and others. Everyone has an opinion, and that opinion is perfectly valid for the one who holds it; however, Maven is generally agreed upon not to be the "best build tool," much like Eclipse is not the "best editor." They're popular. They're common. That's about it.

```xml
    <artifactId>hibernate-parent</artifactId>
    <packaging>pom</packaging>
    <version>1.0-SNAPSHOT</version>
    <modules>
        <module>chapter01</module>
    </modules>
    <name>hibernate-parent</name>

    <properties>
        <project.build.sourceEncoding>UTF-8</project.build.sourceEncoding>
    </properties>

    <dependencies>
        <dependency>
            <groupId>org.testng</groupId>
            <artifactId>testng</artifactId>
            <version>[6.0.12,)</version>
            <scope>test</scope>
        </dependency>
        <dependency>
            <groupId>org.hibernate</groupId>
            <artifactId>hibernate-core</artifactId>
            <version>[4.2.6,4.2.9]</version>
        </dependency>
        <dependency>
            <groupId>org.hsqldb</groupId>
            <artifactId>hsqldb</artifactId>
            <version>[2.2.9,)</version>
        </dependency>
    </dependencies>
    <build>
        <plugins>
            <plugin>
                <groupId>org.apache.maven.plugins</groupId>
                <artifactId>maven-compiler-plugin</artifactId>
                <version>2.3.2</version>
                <configuration>
                    <source>1.7</source>
                    <target>1.7</target>
                    <showDeprecation>true</showDeprecation>
                    <showWarnings>true</showWarnings>
                </configuration>
            </plugin>
        </plugins>
    </build>
</project>
```

This specifies a number of things about the project (such as the Java version), and includes three dependencies: Hibernate itself, the HSQLDB database, and TestNG, the last which is limited to the testing phase (as the "scope" node instructs).

The child projects—in this listing, this is only chapter01—will receive this configuration and its set of dependencies automatically, which means we don't have to repeat ourselves very often.

To build and run this project after installing Maven, you simply have to go to the directory that contains pom.xml, and execute "mvn package"—which will, as stated, download all the required dependencies, build them, and then test the projects in order.

Maven projects have a specific folder layout, although it's configurable; by default, the Java compiler compiles all code found in src/main/java, and the resulting class files are included with src/main/resources in the deliverable artifact. The src/test/java directory contains tests, which are then compiled and run (with src/test/resources and the deliverable artifact in the classpath as well).

Wow, that's a lot of non-Hibernate discussion–and all of it can be found (and subverted) on the websites for each given build environment. In general, you can (and should) use what you like; this book uses Maven because of how common it is, not because it's the One True Build Tool.

Let's look at the actual code we've been running so far and explain it all. That will give you a basis for future discussion, even if you're not going to use it much beyond this chapter.

We've already mentioned the top-level pom.xml file; we're going to start in the chapter02 directory (which is a clone of the chapter01 directory, except with "chapter02" instead of "chapter01"). Our project description file (our pom.xml) is very simple, specifying only the parent project and the current project's name (see Listing 2-2).

Listing 2-2. Chapter 2's Project Object Model

```xml
<?xml version="1.0" encoding="UTF-8"?>
<project xmlns="http://maven.apache.org/POM/4.0.0"
        xmlns:xsi="http://www.w3.org/2001/XMLSchema-instance"
        xsi:schemaLocation="http://maven.apache.org/POM/4.0.0
        http://maven.apache.org/xsd/maven-4.0.0.xsd">
    <parent>
        <artifactId>hibernate-parent</artifactId>
        <groupId>com.redhat.osas.books.hibernate</groupId>
        <version>1.0-SNAPSHOT</version>
    </parent>
    <modelVersion>4.0.0</modelVersion>

    <artifactId>chapter02</artifactId>
</project>
```

Our Message.java is held in src/main/java/chapter02/Message.java. This is the same POJO as in Listing 1-5, except that it's in a different package (chapter02.hibernate instead of chapter01.hibernate). Since everything else is the same, we won't list it here.

Our actual running code is in the src/test directory and consists of two relevant files[3]: src/test/java/chapter02/hibernate/PersistenceTest.java and src/test/resources/hibernate.cfg.xml.

We've already seen the test methods from PersistenceTest.java, but let's take a look at the entire Listing 2-3 so you understand everything in it.

---

[3]There are other classes in the tree, but we no longer care about JDBC in this chapter; they're here because you were promised that chapter02's tree was the same as chapter01's. All of the JDBC stuff is going to be ignored.

Listing 2-3. A Set of Persistence Tests

```java
package chapter02.hibernate;

import org.hibernate.Session;
import org.hibernate.SessionFactory;
import org.hibernate.Transaction;
import org.hibernate.cfg.Configuration;
import org.hibernate.service.ServiceRegistry;
import org.hibernate.service.ServiceRegistryBuilder;
import org.testng.Assert;
import org.testng.annotations.BeforeSuite;
import org.testng.annotations.Test;

import java.util.List;

public class PersistenceTest {
    SessionFactory factory;

    @BeforeSuite
    public void setup() {
        Configuration configuration = new Configuration();
        configuration.configure();
        ServiceRegistryBuilder srBuilder = new ServiceRegistryBuilder();
        srBuilder.applySettings(configuration.getProperties());
        ServiceRegistry serviceRegistry = srBuilder.buildServiceRegistry();
        factory = configuration.buildSessionFactory(serviceRegistry);
    }

    @Test
    public void saveMessage() {
        Message message = new Message("Hello, world");
        Session session = factory.openSession();
        Transaction tx = session.beginTransaction();
        session.persist(message);
        tx.commit();
        session.close();
    }

    @Test(dependsOnMethods = "saveMessage")
    public void readMessage() {
        Session session = factory.openSession();
        @SuppressWarnings("unchecked")
        List<Message> list = (List<Message>) session.createQuery(
            "from Message").list();

        if (list.size() > 1) {
            Assert.fail("Message configuration in error; "
                    + "table should contain only one."
                    + " Set ddl to drop-create.");
        }
```

```
        if (list.size() == 0) {
            Assert.fail("Read of initial message failed; "
                    + "check saveMessage() for errors."
                    + " How did this test run?");
        }
        for (Message m : list) {
            System.out.println(m);
        }
        session.close();
    }
}
```

To begin, note that we're using TestNG to run the tests, which in this case affects our class in a few simple ways.

First, the actual test methods are annotated with @Test; we indicate a dependency between tests with a setting for readMessage(). If saveMessage() were to fail, readMessage() would not be executed, as its execution depends on a successful saveMessage().

Second, there's a mehod annotated with @BeforeSuite method, which is executed before any of the tests are attempted. This gives us a chance to do system initialization. This is where we're setting up Hibernate for usable state–in the JDBC code, we use this same mechanism to load the JDBC driver and create our database schema.[4]

Third, we indicate that failure through the use of Assert.fail(), which should be easy to understand. An exception also indicates a failure, unless we tell TestNG that we *expect* an exception to be thrown (and we can also tell TestNG what specific type of exceptions allow the test to pass).

You're likely to use this construct often because it's easy to integrate into your project build lifecycle (as Maven runs the available tests as part of the build). Also, it gives you a clear order of execution, and also provides an easy way to see what works and what doesn't work. You should feel free to write tests to validate your own understanding of what is being described.

Next, note how the test is constructed.

The test shows the canonically correct way to use Hibernate's native API[5]: first, construct a SessionFactory, which is the entry point to the Hibernate API (much as EntityManager is the entry point for the Java Persistence Architecture); then use the SessionFactory to retrieve short-lived Session objects through which updates, or reads, are performed.

The actual tests mirror the JDBC code fairly well[6] (or vice versa); in both, we acquire a resource through which we "talk to" the database, then we perform an action, then we commit our changes (if any) and clean up. (There are definitely details being skipped; this is the ten-thousand-foot view of the mechanisms in place.)

The last piece of the puzzle is the actual configuration file itself, which is in src/test/resource/hibernate.cfg.xml. See Listing 2-4.

Listing 2-4. The hibernate.cfg.xml, the Hibernate Configuration

```
<?xml version="1.0"?>
<!DOCTYPE hibernate-configuration PUBLIC
        "-//Hibernate/Hibernate Configuration DTD 3.0//EN"
        "http://www.hibernate.org/dtd/hibernate-configuration-3.0.dtd">
```

---

[4]Hmm, we promised that we weren't going to mention the JDBC code any more. Whoops.

[5]Hibernate implements the Java Persistence Architecture as an alternative API. It's a little more generic than the native API, and is configured slightly differently, even though most of the concepts are identical.

[6]Darn it, we keep on coming across that JDBC code that isn't supposed to be mentioned.

```xml
<hibernate-configuration>
    <session-factory>
        <!-- Database connection settings  -->
        <property name="connection.driver_class">
            org.hsqldb.jdbc.JDBCDriver
        </property>
        <property name="connection.url">
            jdbc:hsqldb:db2;shutdown=true
        </property>
        <property name="connection.username">sa</property>
        <property name="connection.password"/>
        <property name="dialect">org.hibernate.dialect.HSQLDialect</property>
        <!-- Echo all executed SQL to stdout  -->
        <property name="show_sql">true</property>
        <!-- Drop and re-create the database schema on startup  -->
        <property name="hbm2ddl.auto">create-drop</property>
        <mapping class="chapter02.hibernate.Message"/>
    </session-factory>

</hibernate-configuration>
```

This file might serve as a boilerplate for every Hibernate configuration. In it, we specify the JDBC driver class; the JDBC URL, user name, and password used to access the database; a *dialect* (which allows Hibernate to correctly produce SQL for each given database); some configuration, such as whether to dump the generated SQL to the console; and what to do for the schema. Lastly, it specifies the classes that should be managed—in this case, only our Message class.

There are a lot of things we can control from this file; we can even use it to specify the mapping of our objects to the database (i.e., ignoring the annotations we've been using so far). You'll see a little more of how to do this in later chapters of this book; it helps quite a bit in mapping existing database schemata[7] to object models.

Most coders will (and should) prefer the annotation-based mappings.

Connection Pooling

As you've seen, Hibernate uses JDBC connections in order to interact with a database. Creating these connections is expensive—probably the most expensive single operation Hibernate will execute in a typical-use case.

Since JDBC connection management is so expensive, you can pool the connections, which can open connections ahead of time (and close them only when needed, as opposed to "when they're no longer used").

Thankfully, Hibernate is designed to use a connection pool by default, an internal implementation. However, Hibernate's built-in connection pooling isn't designed for production use. In production, you would use an external connection pool by using either a database connection provided by JNDI (the Java Naming and Directory Interface) or an external connection pool configured via parameters and classpath.

---

[7]"Schemata" is the plural of "schema." See http://www.merriam-webster.com/dictionary/schema.

■ **Note:** C3P0 (http://www.mchange.com/projects/c3p0/) is an example of an external connection pool. To use it, we would make two changes. First, we need to add c3p0 and Hibernate's c3p0 connection provider as dependencies in the pom.xml. Observe that the version of the hibernate-c3p0 dependency should match the Hibernate version. Listing 2-5 illustrates this connection.

Listing 2-5. Changes for the Object Model to Include c3p0

```
<dependencies>
    <dependency>
        <groupId>org.hibernate</groupId>
        <artifactId>hibernate-c3p0</artifactId>
        <version>[4.2.6,4.2.9)</version>
    </dependency>
    <dependency>
        <groupId>com.mchange</groupId>
        <artifactId>c3p0</artifactId>
        <version>[0.9.2.1,)</version>
    </dependency>
</dependencies>
```

Next, we need to change the Hibernate configuration to tell it to use c3p0. To do this, all we need to do is add any c3p0 configuration property to hibernate.cfg.xml. For example:

```
<property name="c3p0.timeout">10</property>
```

With this line in the configuration, Hibernate will disable its internal connection pool and use c3p0 instead.

However, C3p0 is not the only connection pool; there's also Proxool (http://proxool.sourceforge.net/), which gets mentioned often in the Hibernate documentation.

If you're using Hibernate in a Java EE context–in a web application, for example–then you'll want to configure Hibernate to use JNDI. JNDI connection pools are managed by the container (and thus controlled by the deployer), which is generally the "right way" to manage resources in a distributed environment.

For example, WildFly (http://wildfly.org/) comes preinstalled with an example datasource, named (helpfully) "java:jboss/datasources/ExampleDS". It's an H2 database, so the dialect would need to be changed to org.hibernate.dialect.H2Dialect; the new configuration would look something like what is shown in Listing 2-6.

Listing 2-6. Hibernate, configured to Use JNDI as a Datasource

```
<?xml version="1.0"?>
<!DOCTYPE hibernate-configuration PUBLIC
        "-//Hibernate/Hibernate Configuration DTD 3.0//EN"
        "http://www.hibernate.org/dtd/hibernate-configuration-3.0.dtd">
<hibernate-configuration>
    <session-factory>
        <!-- Database connection settings -->
        <property name="jndi.url">java:jboss/datasources/ExampleDS</property>
        <property name="dialect">org.hibernate.dialect.H2Dialect</property>
        <property name="dialect">org.hibernate.dialect.H2Dialect</property>
```

```
    <!-- Echo all executed SQL to stdout  -->
    <property name="show_sql">true</property>
    <!-- Drop and re-create the database schema on startup  -->
    <property name="hbm2ddl.auto">create-drop</property>
    <mapping class="chapter02.hibernate.Message"/>
  </session-factory>
</hibernate-configuration>
```

Ideally, the java:jboss tree wouldn't be used; you'd use a name scoped to the application component, in the java:comp/env tree.[8]

Summary

In this chapter, we've presented a brief overview of how to use Maven to build and test your projects, as well as how to specify dependencies. We've also shown the usage of TestNG as a simple harness to run code. Lastly, we've explained how to configure Hibernate, starting from acquiring the SessionFactory and concluding with the SessionFactory's configuration, covering the simple JDBC connection management included with Hibernate, the use of a connection pool, and employment of JNDI to acquire database connections.

You should now have enough of a harness in place such that you can focus on *using* Hibernate to help you manage a persistent object model. We will add more detail on this as needed in the example code.

In the next chapter, we're going to build some slightly more complex (and useful) object models to illustrate more of Hibernate's core concepts.

---

[8] See http://www.ibm.com/developerworks/library/j-jndi/?ca=dnt-62 for an article that discusses this concept in some detail, although the implementation specifics are slightly dated.

■ ■ ■

CHAPTER 3

Building a Simple Application

In this chapter, we're going to create the shell of an application, which will allow us to demonstrate a number of concepts common for systems that use Hibernate. We'll be covering:

- Object model design, including relationships between objects

- Operations that view and modify persisted data (inserts, reads, updates, and deletes)

Ordinarily we'd use a service layer to encapsulate some operations, and in fact we will be adding a service layer as we proceed, but at this point we want to see more of how to interact with Hibernate itself. The goal here is not to waste time with a sample application that is "one to throw away." We're definitely not going to be able to have a full and ideal codebase immediately; we'll be modifying this code quite a bit as we proceed, especially in later chapters, but it will be a model for how one might actually use Hibernate in the real world.

Of course, such a statement has a caveat: different applications and architects have different approaches. This is but *one* way to create an application of this sort; others will take different approaches that are just as valid as this one.

Plus, our model will be progressive, meaning that its quality at its genesis will not be very high. We're going to be introducing various new concepts as we proceed; and we'll have plenty of opportunities to go back to previously written code and improve it.

A Simple Application

What we're trying to create is an application that allows peer ranking in various skill areas.

The concept is something like this: John thinks that Tracy is pretty good at Java, so on a scale of 1 to 10, he'd give Tracy a 7. Sam thinks Tracy is decent, but not great; he'd give Tracy a 5. With these two rankings, one might be able to surmise that Tracy was a 6 in Java. Realistically, with such a small sample set you wouldn't be able to gauge whether this ranking was accurate or not, but after twenty such rankings you would have a chance at a truly legitimate peer evaluation.

So what we want is a way for an observer to offer a ranking for a given skill for a specific person. We'd also like a way to determine the actual ranking for each person, as well as a way to find out who was ranked "the best" for a given skill.

If you're looking at these paragraphs with an eye toward application design, you'll see that we have four different types of entities—objects to store—and a few services.

Our entites are: People (which are observers and subjects, thus two entity types that happen to look exactly the same), Skills, and Rankings.

Our relationships look something like this:

A subject—a Person—has zero, one, or many skills. A person's Skills each have zero, one, or many Rankings.
A Ranking has a score ("on a scale of 1 to 10") and an observer (a Person who submits a particular ranking).

A First Attempt

Our first attempt at this project will allow us to write, read, and update Rankings for different subjects, as well as tell us who has the highest average score for a given Skill.

It won't do these things very efficiently at first, but along the way we'll fulfill our desire for (somewhat) agile development practices, and we'll learn quite a bit about how to read and write data with Hibernate.

As usual, we'll be using test-driven development. Let's write some tests and then try to get them to pass. Our first bits of code will be very primitive, testing *only* our data model, but eventually we'll be testing services.

Our data model is shown in Figure 3-1. As you can see, it has three object types and three relationships: Person is related to Ranking in two ways (as subject and observer), and each Ranking has an associated Skill.

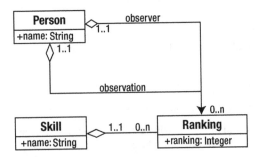

Figure 3-1. *A simple entity relationship diagram*

It's probably worth pointing out that this data model is not ideal. For right now, that's all right—we're trying to build something that gives us a starting point, and we'll factor in our full requirements as we proceed.

We're also admittedly underspecifying our entities. For example, a Person can be more than just a name. (A Person can also be a number, correct?...Oh, wait, that's not as funny as it could be because we're eventually going to add a numeric identifier to every Person as an artificial key.) Perhaps we'll fix this and other issues as we develop our model.

So let's start by designing our objects.

Since our problem description centers on the concept of a Person (as subject and observer), let's start with that. The simplest JavaBean that can represent a Person might look like Listing 3-1:

Listing 3-1. A POJO Representing Our Person Object

```
package chapter03.simple;

public class Person {
    String name;
    public Person() {}
    public void setName(String name) { this.name=name; }
    public String getName() { return name; }
}
```

For the sake of brevity, from here on we're going to ignore simple mutators and accessors (the setName() and getName(), respectively, in the Person class) unless and until we need to include them. We're also going to ignore implementations of toString(), although the sample code has it.

This Person implementation *only* includes the concept of a Person and ignores the other object types. Let's see what they look like, so we can revisit Person and flesh it out, so to speak.

The Skill class looks almost exactly like the Person class, as it should; they could inherit from a common base class, but for right now let's leave them completely separate, as shown in Listing 3-2.

Listing 3-2. A POJO Representing a Person's Skills

```
Package chapter03.simple;

public class Skill {
    String name;
    public Skill() {}
}
```

The Ranking class is a little more complicated, but not by much. Really, all it does is encode one side of the associations shown in the UML. It's worth noting that we don't have to consider database associations at all when we're designing our objects; a Ranking has an attribute matching a subject, so that's what it uses. Take a look at Listing 3-3.

Listing 3-3. A POJO Representing a Ranking of a Person's Skill

```
package chapter03.simple;

public class Ranking {
    Person subject;
    Person observer;
    Skill skill;
    Integer ranking;
    public Ranking() { }
}
```

Writing Data

At this point, we have a fully working data model in Java. We can use this data model with some slight changes to create entities representing the Person types, the Skill types, and Rankings; and we can use the associations to pull data enough to fit our requirements. Creating our data model might look like that shown in Listing 3-4:

Listing 3-4. A Test that Populates a Simple Model

```
package chapter03.simple;

import org.testng.annotations.Test;

public class ModelTest {
    @Test
    public void testModelCreation() {
        Person subject=new Person();
        subject.setName("J. C. Smell");

        Person observer=new Person();
        observer.setName("Drew Lombardo");

        Skill skill=new Skill();
        skill.setName("Java");

        Ranking ranking=new Ranking();
        ranking.setSubject(subject);
```

```
        ranking.setObserver(observer);
        ranking.setSkill(skill);
        ranking.setRanking(8);

        // just to give us visual verification
        System.out.println(ranking);
    }
}
```

However, being able to use the data model isn't the same as being able to persist or query the data model. This is a good start to see how the data model *might* work, but isn't much as far as actually using it.

In order to allow Hibernate to work with our model, we're going to first convert the Person object to an entity by marking it with the @Entity annotation.[1] Next, we mark the name as a column (with @Column) for our data model, and then we're then going to add an artificial key—a unique identifier—to allow us to use something other than a name for a primary key.

We'll describe more about the @Id and @GeneratedValue annotations later; for right now, this marks the attribute as a unique primary key, autogenerated by the database.

The Person object now looks like what's shown in Listing 3-5:

Listing 3-5. The Person Object as a Candidate for Hibernate Persistence

```
package chapter03.hibernate;

import javax.persistence.*;

@Entity
public class Person {
    @Id
    @GeneratedValue(strategy = GenerationType.IDENTITY)
    private Long id;
    @Column
    String name;

    public Person() {
    }
}
```

Now we can create a test that writes an instance into the database. Here's a snippet of code for that purpose. Again, we're going to be refactoring this code quite a bit in future iterations; see Listing 3-6.

Listing 3-6. A Test that persists the Person Entity

```
package chapter03.hibernate;

import org.hibernate.Session;
import org.hibernate.SessionFactory;
import org.hibernate.Transaction;
import org.hibernate.cfg.Configuration;
import org.hibernate.service.ServiceRegistry;
```

---

[1]This seems almost logical.

```java
import org.hibernate.service.ServiceRegistryBuilder;
import org.testng.annotations.BeforeMethod;
import org.testng.annotations.AfterMethod;
import org.testng.annotations.Test;

public class PersonTest {
    SessionFactory factory;

    @BeforeMethod
    public void setup() {
        Configuration configuration = new Configuration();
        configuration.configure();
        ServiceRegistryBuilder srBuilder = new ServiceRegistryBuilder();
        srBuilder.applySettings(configuration.getProperties());
        ServiceRegistry serviceRegistry = srBuilder.buildServiceRegistry();
        factory = configuration.buildSessionFactory(serviceRegistry);
    }

    @AfterMethod
    public void shutdown() {
        factory.close();
    }

    @Test
    public void testSavePerson() {
        Session session=factory.openSession();
        Transaction tx=session.beginTransaction();
        Person person=new Person();
        person.setName("J. C. Smell");

        session.save(person);

        tx.commit();
        session.close();
    }
}
```

This is a near mirror image of our Message example from Chapters 1 and 2, with some important changes.

One change involves initialization; it uses @BeforeMethod and @AfterMethod to initialize and close the SessionFactory after every test. Our configuration tells Hibernate to create the database schema every time we create a SessionFactory; this sequence means that before every test, we're going to reinitialize the database to a known (and empty) state.

The actual test is very simple. It creates a Person, and it does nothing but persist it. We're not even trying to validate that it persists—just that the persistence code runs. Assuming that's the case (and it is), we can also assume the same code works for the Skill object; but the Ranking object—with its associations—needs a little more work.

One of the things we need to think about before writing a Ranking object is how to find one of our objects. For one thing, that sort of ability would help us in the simple persistence test: to validate that not only did the save() method *execute* but that it also actually persisted our data. For another, in the testSavePerson() code, we're creating a Person when we know that Person doesn't exist; with Ranking, however, we fully expect to reuse Person instances as well as Skills.

So we need to create a mechanism by which we can query our database. We'll create a method to return a Person reference from the session, using a query; and we'll revisit the query mechanism in the future to optimize it quite a bit.

Reading Data

Listing 3-7 is the code to look for a Person, given a name. This snippet uses the Hibernate Query Language (HQL), which is loosely related to SQL; we'll see more about HQL in later chapters.

Listing 3-7. A Method to lLcate a Specific Person Instance

```
private Person findPerson(Session session, String name) {
    Query query=session.createQuery("from Person p where p.name=:name");
    query.setParameter("name", name);
    Person person= (Person) query.uniqueResult();
    return person;
}
```

This code declares a reference to org.hibernate.Query, and it builds a rough analog to a SQL select statement. This form of the query selects data from the table created from the Person entity (which may or may not have a table name of "person"), aliased to "p," and limited to objects whose "name" attribute is equal to a named parameter (helpfully called "name").

We then set the parameter value of "name" to the name for which we're searching.

As we're interested in only one possible match at this point (a limitation of our implementation for right now), we return a unique result: a single object. If we have five People with that name in our database, an exception will be thrown; we could fix this by using query.setMaxResults(1), and returning the first (and only) entry in query.list(), but the *right* way to fix it is to figure out how to be very specific in returning the right Person.

If no result is found, a signal value-null-will be returned.

We can now write a findPerson() method that returns an existing Person if one exists by that name, creating a new Person object if none is found; see Listing 3-8.

Listing 3-8. A Method to Save a Person Instance, Given a Name

```
private Person savePerson(Session session, String name) {
    Person person = findPerson(session, name);
    if(person==null) {
        person=new Person();
        person.setName(name);
        session.save(person);
    }
    return person;
}
```

Our first cut at code to build a Ranking (in RankingTest) might then look something like what's shown in Listing 3-9:

Listing 3-9. Saving a Ranking Instance

```
@Test
public void testSaveRanking() {
    Session session = factory.openSession();
    Transaction tx = session.beginTransaction();
    Person subject = savePerson(session, "J. C. Smell");
```

```
        Person observer = savePerson(session, "Drew Lombardo");
        Skill skill = saveSkill(session, "Java");

        Ranking ranking = new Ranking();
        ranking.setSubject(subject);
        ranking.setObserver(observer);
        ranking.setSkill(skill);
        ranking.setRanking(8);
        session.save(ranking);

        tx.commit();
        session.close();
    }
```

The chapter code has this method encoded as it is, but this method also gives us the beginnings of *another* method, one that abstracts all of the repeated code such that we can offer the four important pieces of information and generate data very rapidly.

With that in mind, let's look at queries again. We have shown that queries return single results; let's look at queries that return multiple results, in order, with the understanding that we're *still* very far away from being efficient—or even correct, in many ways.

One of our requirements is to be able to determine the Ranking of a given Person for a given Skill. Let's write another test as a proof of concept.

First, we'll write a method that adds a few more Rankings for J. C. Smell; we've already shown him as having an 8 in Java, let's add a 6 and a 7, which would give him an average Skill of 7, obviously. With that, our test method might look like what is shown in Listing 3-10:

Listing 3-10. A Method to Test Ranking Operations

```
@Test
public void testRankings() {
    populateRankingData();

    Session session = factory.openSession();
    Transaction tx = session.beginTransaction();

    Query query = session.createQuery("from Ranking r "
            + "where r.subject.name=:name "
            + "and r.skill.name=:skill");
    query.setString("name", "J. C. Smell");
    query.setString("skill", "Java");
    int sum = 0;
    int count = 0;
    for (Ranking r : (List<Ranking>) query.list()) {
        count++;
        sum += r.getRanking();
        System.out.println(r);
    }
    int average = sum / count;
    tx.commit();
    session.close();
    assertEquals(average, 7);
}
```

```
private void populateRankingData() {
    Session session = factory.openSession();
    Transaction tx = session.beginTransaction();
    createData(session, "J. C. Smell", "Gene Showrama", "Java", 6);
    createData(session, "J. C. Smell", "Scottball Most", "Java", 7);
    createData(session, "J. C. Smell", "Drew Lombardo", "Java", 8);
    tx.commit();
    session.close();
}
```

This uses a slightly more advanced query: the query walks the attribute tree from the Ranking object to match the subject's name and Skill's name. With the entity references in our object model, it's very easy to do a SQL JOIN without having to know specific database syntax or capabilities; Hibernate takes care of writing all of the SQL for us, and we can use the objects "naturally."

By the way, this isn't a particularly good use of the query facility; we'll be revisiting it quite a bit as we progress, especially in the last section of this chapter, where we use Hibernate's query capability to do all of the work of calculating the average for us.[2]

Updating Data

What if we want to change data? Suppose that Gene Showrama, who in our example code ranked J. C. Smell as a 6 in Java, realizes that he has changed his opinion? Let's see what we have to do to update data.

First, let's take our Ranking average calculation routine and refactor it into a reusable method. (The test code has the refactored method and the original test as shown here.) Next, we'll write our test to update the data, and then recalculate the average, testing it to make sure our data is persisted correctly. See Listing 3-11.

Listing 3-11. A Test Demonstrating Updates

```
@Test
public void changeRanking() {
    populateRankingData();
    Session session = factory.openSession();
    Transaction tx = session.beginTransaction();
    Query query = session.createQuery("from Ranking r "
            + "where r.subject.name=:subject and "
            + "r.observer.name=:observer and "
            +" r.skill.name=:skill");
    query.setString("subject", "J. C. Smell");
    query.setString("observer", "Gene Showrama");
    query.setString("skill", "Java");
    Ranking ranking= (Ranking) query.uniqueResult();
    assertNotNull(ranking, "Could not find matching ranking");
    ranking.setRanking(9);
    tx.commit();
    session.close();
    assertEquals(getAverage("J. C. Smell", "Java"), 8);
}
```

---

[2]It might be an excellent exercise for the reader to revisit this code and write it such that it's more efficient.

What are we doing here? After we populate the data with known values, we're building a query to locate the specific Ranking we want to change (a Ranking on Java for "J. C. Smell," written by "Gene Showrama"). We check to make sure we have a valid Ranking—which we should, as that data was created by our populateRankingData() method—and then we do something very curious.

We set a new Ranking, with ranking.setRanking(9);...and that's it. We commit the current transaction and close the session because we're done with it.

Hibernate watches the data model, and when something is changed, it automatically updates the database to reflect the changes. The transaction commits the update to the database so that other sessions—as contained in the findRanking() method—can see it.

There are a few caveats for this (with workarounds, naturally). When Hibernate loads an object for you, it is a "managed object"—that is, it's managed by that session. Mutations (changes) and accesses go through a special process to write data to the database, or pull data from the database if the session hasn't already loaded it. We refer to this object as being in "persisted state," which leads us to a concept that will become important for us as we use persistence in Java.[3]

Persistence Contexts

There are four states for an object with relation to a session: persistent, transient, detached, or removed.

When we create a new object, it's *transient*—that is, no identifier has been assigned to it by Hibernate, and the database has no knowledge of the object. That doesn't mean the database might not have the data.Imagine if we'd created a Ranking manually for J. C. Smell, from Gene Showrama, on Java. The new Ranking would have an analog in the database, but Hibernate wouldn't know that the object *in memory* was an equivalent to the object representation *in the* database.

When we call save() on a new object, we're marking it as "persistent," and when we query the session for an object, it's also in persistent state. Changes are reflected in the current transaction, to be written when the transaction is committed. We can convert a *transient* object to a *persistent* object by using Session.merge(), which we haven't seen yet (but we will).

A *detached* object is a *persistent* object whose session has been closed or has otherwise been evicted from a Session. In our example of changing a Ranking, when the session is closed, the Ranking object we changed is in *detached* state for the findRanking() call.

A *removed* object is one that's been marked for deletion in the current transaction. An object is changed to *removed* state when Session.delete() is called for that object reference. Note that an object in removed state is removed in the database but not in memory, just as an object can exist in the database without an in-memory representation.

Removing Data

The last thing we want to see is how to delete data or, rather, how to move it into *removed state* with respect to the persistence context—which almost amounts to the same thing. (It's not actually "removed" until the transaction is committed, and even then the in-memory representation is available until it goes out of scope, as we described in the paragraph on "removed state.")

Let's say, for sake of an example, that Gene Showrama has realized that he really doesn't have enough information to offer a valid Ranking for J. C. Smell on Java, so he wishes to delete it. The code for this is very similar to our update: we're going to find the Ranking, and then call Session.delete().

We can refactor our mechanism for finding a Ranking (from the changeRanking() test), which will give us a Ranking in *persistent* state. Then we remove it via the session and commit the change; we can then ask for the new average to see if our changes are reflected in the database.

---

[3]We'll be revisiting this topic in more detail in Chapter 4.

Here's our code, shown in Listing 3-12:

Listing 3-12. Removing a Ranking

```
@Test
public void removeRanking() {
    populateRankingData();
    Session session=factory.openSession();
    Transaction tx=session.beginTransaction();
    Ranking ranking=findRanking(session, "J. C. Smell",
            "Gene Showrama", "Java");
    assertNotNull(ranking, "Ranking not found");
    session.delete(ranking);
    tx.commit();
    session.close();
    assertEquals(getAverage("J. C. Smell", "Java"), 7);
}
```

It's like magic, except that it's not: it's just Hibernate managing the database to reflect the changes we're showing it.

A Note on Managing Sessions

One thing that you may have noticed as we've called findRanking() and savePerson() is that we're establishing a Session (from the SessionFactory) and passing it around quite a bit.

We're doing this to make session management very easy. Remember, the session is our demarcation point for persistence contexts; an object is managed in relation to the *current session*, which makes the "current session" a valuable reference. We want to load our data into the current session so we can use it; if we have other sessions bouncing around, then we're crossing session boundaries as we assign and manipulate data.

Passing the current session around just makes everything simple and clear; it means our transaction boundaries and scopes are easily managed.

A Note on Transactions

We've mentioned "transactions" quite a bit, too, using them with every session reference. So what are they?

A transaction is a "bundled unit of work" for a database.[4]

When you start a transaction, you're saying that you want to see the database as it exists at a certain point in time ("now"), and any modifications affect only the database as it exists from that starting point.

Changes are committed as a whole, so that no other transaction can see them until the transaction completes.

Transactions can be aborted ("rolled back," with the Transaction.rollback() method) such that any changes that have taken place as part of that transaction are discarded. This allows you to guarantee consistency in your data model.

For example, imagine you're creating an order entry system, with an order consisting of an Order object, LineItem objects, and a Customer object. If you were writing an order with seven line items and the sixth line item failed because of invalid data,[5] you wouldn't want an incomplete order to be lingering in the database. You'd want to roll back the changes and offer the user a chance to try again, with correct data.

---

[4]We're going to be revisiting transactions quite a bit in Chapter 4.
[5]Note that Hibernate has validation facilities that make this sort of thing very easy to do; the way this is described here is rather unglamorous.

Naturally, there are exceptions to the definitions of transactions, and Hibernate provides multiple types of transactions (for example, you might have a transaction that allows reads of uncommitted data). Also, different databases might define transactional boundaries in their own ways. Thankfully, this is a pretty important concern for databases, so each one tends to document how transactions are defined. (See http://hsqldb.org/doc/guide/sessions-chapt.html for HSQLDB's documentation of transactions, for example.)

Writing Our Sample Application

What have we seen so far? We've seen:

1. The creation of an object model.

2. The mapping of that object model to a data model.

3. The writing of data from an object model into a database.

4. The reading of data from the database into an object model.

5. The updating of data in the database via our object model.

6. The removal of data from the database via our object model.

With all of this, we're ready to start designing our actual application, armed with the knowledge that our object model works (although efficiency hasn't been considered yet) and with example code to perform most of our tasks as our requirements specify.

We're going to design our application much as we've written our example code; that is, we're going to define an application layer (services), and call that application from tests. In the real world, we'd then write a user interface layer that used the services, just as the tests do.

Just to be clear, our user interactions are:

1. Add a Ranking for a subject by an observer.

2. Update a Ranking for a subject by an observer.

3. Remove a Ranking for a subject by an observer.

4. Find the average Ranking for particular skill for a subject.

5. Find all the Rankings for a subject.

6. Find the highest-ranked subject for a particular skill.

It sounds like a lot, but we've already written much of this code; we just need to refactor it into a service layer for ease of use.

The first thing we want to do is abstract out some basic services—primarily, the acquisition of a session. To do this, we're going to add a new module to our parent project—the "util" module—with a single class, the SessionUtil.

In an application server (such as Wildfly, Glassfish, or Geronimo), the persistence API is accessed through resource injection; the application deployer configures a context for the Java Persistence Architecture, and the application automatically acquires an EntityManager (the JPA equivalent to the session). It's entirely possible (and possibly preferable) to configure Hibernate as the JPA provider; you can then use the Hibernate APIs with a cast to Session.[6]

You can also get this same kind of resource injection via libraries such as Spring or Guice. With Spring, for example, you'd configure a persistence provider, just as you would in a Java EE application server, and Spring would automatically provide a resource through which you could acquire Sessions.

---

[6]Of course, you could *also* just use the raw JPA interface. However, it's much more limited than the Hibernate API.

However, while each of these platforms (Spring, Java EE, and others) are extremely useful and practical (and probably necessary, in Java EE's case), we're going to avoid them for the most part because we want to limit the scope of what we're doing to Hibernate and not get into a discussion of various competing architecture choices.

In the source code, there's a "util" module, apart from the chapter modules. The com.redhat.osas.hibernate.util.SessionUtil class is a singleton that provides access to a SessionFactory—something we've been putting in our test initialization code so far. It looks like what you see in Listing 3-13:

Listing 3-13. A Utility Class for Retrieving a Session

```
package com.redhat.osas.hibernate.util;

import org.hibernate.Session;
import org.hibernate.SessionFactory;
import org.hibernate.cfg.Configuration;
import org.hibernate.service.ServiceRegistry;
import org.hibernate.service.ServiceRegistryBuilder;

public class SessionUtil {
    private final static SessionUtil instance = new SessionUtil();
    private final SessionFactory factory;

    private SessionUtil() {
        Configuration configuration = new Configuration();
        configuration.configure();
        ServiceRegistryBuilder srBuilder = new ServiceRegistryBuilder();
        srBuilder.applySettings(configuration.getProperties());
        ServiceRegistry serviceRegistry = srBuilder.buildServiceRegistry();
        factory = configuration.buildSessionFactory(serviceRegistry);
    }

    public static Session getSession() {
        return getInstance().factory.openSession();
    }

    private static SessionUtil getInstance() {
        return instance;
    }
}
```

The way this class is used is very simple, and can be seen in the test for SessionUtil, as shown in Listing 3-14:

Listing 3-14. A Test for the SessionUtil Class

```
@Test
public void testSessionFactory() {
    Session session = SessionUtil.getSession();
    session.close();
}
```

As you can see, this class does nothing we haven't done so far; it just does it in a class with general visibility. We can add a dependency on this module to other projects and immediately have a clean way to acquire a session—and if need be, we can use this class as an abstraction for acquiring sessions through the Java EE persistence mechanism, or via Spring.

Add a Ranking

The first thing we want to be able to do is add a Ranking. Let's do this first by creating our client code, which will give us an idea of what it is we need to write. See Listing 3-15.

Listing 3-15. A Test to add a Ranking

```
public class AddRankingTest {
    RankingService service=new HibernateRankingService();
    @Test
    public void addRanking() {
        service.addRanking("J. C. Smell", "Drew Lombardo", "Mule", 8);
        assertEquals(service.getRankingFor("J. C. Smell", "Mule"), 8);
    }
}
```

Note that we haven't written our service interface yet, nor its implementation; we're just trying out the API to see how it looks and if it seems to fit what we need to do.

Looking at this code in Listing 3-15, we can fairly easily say that addRanking() logically adds a ranking to J. C. Smell, as observed by Drew Lombardo, about Mule, with a skill level of 8. It'd be easy to confuse the parameters; we'll have to be sure to name them clearly, but even with clear names there's a possibility for confusion.

Likewise, we can say that getRankingFor() fairly clearly retrieves a ranking for J. C. Smell's skill at Mule. Again, the possibility lurks for type confusion; the compiler wouldn't be able to tell us offhand if we called getRankingFor("Mule", "J. C. Smell"); and while we might be able to mitigate this in code, with this structure there's always going to be the possibility for confusion.[7]

It's fair to say that this aspect of the API is clear enough and easily tested; let's get to writing some code.

The test code shown in Listing 3-16 gives us the structure of the RankingService:

Listing 3-16. The RankingService Interface

```
package chapter03.application;

public interface RankingService {
    int getRankingFor(String subject, String skill);

    void addRanking(String subject, String observer, String skill, int ranking);
}
```

Now let's look at the HibernateRankingService, which will reuse much of the code we've written in order to test our data model.

---

[7]How could we address it? Not very easily, that's how. We *could* try to add semantic roles to each attribute–for example, we could mark Drew Lombardo as an observer, and J. C. Smell as a subject. If we used a subject where an observer was expected, then we could programmatically indicate an error condition. However, that doesn't help if Drew is an observer *and* a subject–which is likely to be a normal case.

What we're doing in this class is fairly simple: we have a top-level method (the one that's publicly visible) that acquires a session, then delegates the session along with the rest of the data to a worker method. The worker method handles the data manipulation, and is for the most part a copy of the createData() method from the RankingTest, and uses the other utility methods we'd written for RankingTest, too.

Why are we doing this? Mostly, we're anticipating other methods that might need to use addRanking() in such a way that it participates with an existing session. See Listing 3-17.

Listing 3-17. Public and Private Mechanisms to Add a Ranking

```java
@Override
public void addRanking(String subjectName, String observerName,
                       String skillName, int rank) {
    Session session = SessionUtil.getSession();
    Transaction tx = session.beginTransaction();

    addRanking(session, subjectName, observerName, skillName, rank);

    tx.commit();
    session.close();
}

private void addRanking(Session session, String subjectName,
    String observerName, String skillName, int rank) {
    Person subject = savePerson(session, subjectName);
    Person observer = savePerson(session, observerName);
    Skill skill = saveSkill(session, skillName);

    Ranking ranking = new Ranking();
    ranking.setSubject(subject);
    ranking.setObserver(observer);
    ranking.setSkill(skill);
    ranking.setRanking(rank);
    session.save(ranking);
}
```

This leaves our getRankingFor() method unimplemented; however, just as addRanking() was lifted nearly complete from RankingTest, we can copy the code for getAverage() and change how the Session is acquired, as shown in Listing 3-18.

Listing 3-18. Retrieving a Ranking for a Subject

```java
@Override
public int getRankingFor(String subject, String skill) {
    Session session = SessionUtil.getSession();
    Transaction tx = session.beginTransaction();

    int average = getRankingFor(session, subject, skill);
    tx.commit();
    session.close();
    return average;
}
```

```
private int getRankingFor(Session session, String subject,
                          String skill) {
    Query query = session.createQuery("from Ranking r "
            + "where r.subject.name=:name "
            + "and r.skill.name=:skill");
    query.setString("name", subject);
    query.setString("skill", skill);
    int sum = 0;
    int count = 0;
    for (Ranking r : (List<Ranking>) query.list()) {
        count++;
        sum += r.getRanking();
        System.out.println(r);
    }
    return count == 0 ? 0 : sum / count;
}
```

Just as with the addRanking() method, the publicly visible method allocates a session and then delegates to an internal method, and it's for the same reason: we may want to calculate the average in an existing session. (We'll see this in action in the next section, when we want to update a Ranking.)

The last line in getRankingFor() adds a guard against division by zero, in the case that no rankings for a given skill exist for the subject in question.

For the record, this internal method is still awful. It works, but we can optimize it quite a bit. However, our data sets have been so small that there's been no point. We'll get there.

Now, when we run the test (with mvn package in the top-level directory, or via your IDE, if you're using one), the AddRankingTest passes, with no drama—which is exactly what we want. Even more satisfying, if we want to play around with the internals of HibernateRankingService, we can; we will be able to tell as soon as something breaks because our tests require that things *work*.

Also, if you look *very* carefully—okay, not *that* carefully, because it's rather obvious—you'll see that we've also managed to go down the path of fulfilling another of our requirements: determining the average Ranking for a given subject's Skill. With that said, though, we don't have a rigorous test in place yet. We'll get there.

Update a Ranking

Next, we handle the (not very likely) situation of updating a Ranking. This is potentially very simple, but we need to think about what happens if a pre-existing Ranking doesn't exist. Imagine Drew Lombardo trying to change J. C. Smell's mastery of Mule to 8, when he's not bothered to offer any other Ranking yet.

We probably don't need to think about it *too* much, because in this situation it's likely that we'd just add the Ranking, but other more mission-critical applications may want the extra time spent in thought.

As it is, let's create two tests: one that uses an existing Ranking and another using a nonexistent Ranking; see Listing 3-19.

Listing 3-19. Tests for Updating Rankings

```
@Test
public void updateExistingRanking() {
    service.addRanking("Gene Showrama", "Scottball Most", "Ceylon", 6);
    assertEquals(service.getRankingFor("Gene Showrama", "Ceylon"), 6);
    service.updateRanking("Gene Showrama", "Scottball Most", "Ceylon", 7);
    assertEquals(service.getRankingFor("Gene Showrama", "Ceylon"), 7);
}
```

```
@Test
public void updateNonexistentRanking() {
    assertEquals(service.getRankingFor("Scottball Most", "Ceylon"), 0);
    service.updateRanking("Scottball Most", "Gene Showrama", "Ceylon", 7);
    assertEquals(service.getRankingFor("Scottball Most", "Ceylon"), 7);
}
```

These two tests are very simple.

UpdateExistingRanking() first adds a Ranking, then checks to verify that it was added properly; it updates that same Ranking, then determines if the average has changed. Since this is the only Ranking for this subject and this Skill, the average should match the changed Ranking.

UpdateNonExistentRanking() does almost the same thing: it makes sure that we have nothing for this subject and Skill (i.e., checks for 0, our signal value for "no Rankings exist"), then "updates" that Ranking (which, according to our requirements, should add the Ranking), and then checks the resulting average.

Now let's look at the service's code used to put this into effect, as shown in Listing 3-20.

Listing 3-20. The Code for Updating a Ranking

```
@Override
public void updateRanking(String subject, String observer, String skill, int rank) {
    Session session = SessionUtil.getSession();
    Transaction tx = session.beginTransaction();

    Ranking ranking = findRanking(session, subject, observer, skill);
    if (ranking == null) {
        addRanking(session, subject, observer, skill, rank);
    } else {
        ranking.setRanking(rank);
    }
    tx.commit();
    session.close();
}

private Ranking findRanking(Session session, String subject,
                            String observer, String skill) {
    Query query = session.createQuery("from Ranking r where "
            + "r.subject.name=:subject and "
            + "r.observer.name=:observer and "
            + "r.skill.name=:skill");
    query.setParameter("subject", subject);
    query.setParameter("observer", observer);
    query.setParameter("skill", skill);
    Ranking ranking= (Ranking) query.uniqueResult();
    return ranking;
}
```

It's worth considering that this code could be more efficient for what it does. Since there's no state to be preserved from the record that's been changed, we *could* feasibly delete the record outright if it exists, then add a new record.

However, if the Rankings had a timestamp of sorts—perhaps createTimestamp and lastUpdatedTimestamp attributes—then in this scenario an update (as we do here) makes more sense. Our data model isn't complete yet; we should anticipate adding fields like these at some point.

Remove a Ranking

Removing a Ranking has two conditions to consider: one is that the Ranking exists (of course!) and the other is that it does *not* exist. It might be that our architectural requirements mandate that removal of a Ranking that isn't actually present is an error; but for this case, we'll assume that the removal merely attempts to validate that the Ranking doesn't exist.

Here's our test code, shown in Listing 3-21:

Listing 3-21. Tests that Validate Removing a Ranking

```
@Test
public void removeRanking() {
    service.addRanking("R1", "R2", "RS1", 8);
    assertEquals(service.getRankingFor("R1", "RS1"), 8);
    service.removeRanking("R1", "R2", "RS1");
    assertEquals(service.getRankingFor("R1", "RS1"), 0);
}

@Test
public void removeNonexistentRanking() {
    service.removeRanking("R3", "R4", "RS2");
}
```

The tests should be fairly easy to step through.

The first test (removeRanking()) creates a Ranking and validates that it gives us a known average, then removes it, which should change the average back to 0 (which indicates that no data exists for that Ranking, as already stated).

The second test calls removeRanking() that should not exist (because we don't create it anywhere); it should change nothing about the subject.

It's worth pointing out that our tests are fairly complete, but not as complete as they could be. For example, some of our tests might inadvertently be adding data to the database, depending on how the services are written. While that's not very important for this application, it's worth thinking about how to validate the entire database state after a test is run.

Find Average Ranking for a Subject's Skill

We're nearing the point where we're starting to exhaust the codebase written to test our data model. It's time to verify the code that calculates the average Ranking for a given skill for a given subject. We've already used this code to verify some of our other requirements (all of them so far, in fact), but we've done so with limited data. Let's throw more data at the getRankingFor() method to validate that it's actually doing what it's supposed to do.

Here's our test code, shown in Listing 3-22:

Listing 3-22. A Test that Validates Our Ranking Mechanism

```
@Test
public void validateRankingAverage() {
    service.addRanking("A", "B", "C", 4);
    service.addRanking("A", "B", "C", 5);
    service.addRanking("A", "B", "C", 6);
    assertEquals(service.getRankingFor("A", "C"), 5);
```

```
    service.addRanking("A", "B", "C", 7);
    service.addRanking("A", "B", "C", 8);
    assertEquals(service.getRankingFor("A", "C"), 6);
}
```

We actually don't have any changes for the service—it's using the getRankingFor() method we've already seen.

Find All Rankings for a Subject

What we're looking for here is a list of Skills, with their averages, for a given subject.

We have a few options as to how we can represent this data; do we want a Map, so that we can easily locate what Skill level goes with a Skill? Do we want a queue, so that the Skill levels are ranked in order?

This will depend on the architectural requirements for interaction. At this level (and for this particular application design), we'll use a Map; it gives us the data we need (a set of Skills with their average Rankings) with a simple data structure. Eventually, we'll revisit this requirement and fulfill it more efficiently.

As per usual, let's write our test code, and then make it run properly; see Listing 3-23.

Listing 3-23. Test Code for a Person's Skill Rankings

```
@Test
public void findAllRankingsEmptySet() {
    assertEquals(service.getRankingFor("Nobody", "Java"),0);
    assertEquals(service.getRankingFor("Nobody", "Python"),0);
    Map<String, Integer> rankings=service.findRankingsFor("Nobody");

    // make sure our dataset size is what we expect: empty
    assertEquals(rankings.size(), 0);
}

@Test
public void findAllRankings() {
    assertEquals(service.getRankingFor("Somebody", "Java"),0);
    assertEquals(service.getRankingFor("Somebody", "Python"),0);
    service.addRanking("Somebody", "Nobody", "Java", 9);
    service.addRanking("Somebody", "Nobody", "Java", 7);
    service.addRanking("Somebody", "Nobody", "Python", 7);
    service.addRanking("Somebody", "Nobody", "Python", 5);
    Map<String, Integer> rankings=service.findRankingsFor("Somebody");

    assertEquals(rankings.size(), 2);
    assertNotNull(rankings.get("Java"));
    assertEquals(rankings.get("Java"), new Integer(8));
    assertNotNull(rankings.get("Python"));
    assertEquals(rankings.get("Python"), new Integer(6));
}
```

We have two tests here, of course: the first looks for a subject for whom there should be no data, and it validates that we got an empty dataset in return.

The second validates that we have no data for the subject, populates some data, and then looks for the set of Ranking averages. It then makes sure we have the count of averages we expect, and validates that the Rankings themselves are what we expect.

Again, it's doable to write more complete tests, perhaps, but these tests do validate whether our simple requirements are fulfilled. We're still not checking for side effects, but that's outside of the scope of this chapter.[8]

So let's look at the code for findAllRankings(). As usual, we'll have a public method and then an internal method that participates in an existing Session, as shown in Listing 3-24:

Listing 3-24. Service Methods for Finding Rankings

```
@Override
public Map<String, Integer> findRankingsFor(String subject) {
    Map<String, Integer> results;
    Session session = SessionUtil.getSession();
    Transaction tx = session.beginTransaction();

    results=findRankingsFor(session, subject);

    tx.commit();
    session.close();

    return results;
}

private Map<String, Integer> findRankingsFor(Session session, String subject) {
    Map<String, Integer> results=new HashMap<>();

    Query query = session.createQuery("from Ranking r where "
            + "r.subject.name=:subject order by r.skill.name");
    query.setParameter("subject", subject);
    List<Ranking> rankings=query.list();
    String lastSkillName="";
    int sum=0;
    int count=0;
    for(Ranking r:rankings) {
        if(!lastSkillName.equals(r.getSkill().getName())) {
            sum=0;
            count=0;
            lastSkillName=r.getSkill().getName();
        }
        sum+=r.getRanking();
        count++;
        results.put(lastSkillName, sum/count);
    }
    return results;
}
```

The internal findRankingsFor() method (as with all of our methods that calculate averages) is really not very attractive. It uses a control-break mechanism to calculate the averages as we iterate through the Rankings.[9]

---

[8]One possibility for checking for side effects might be clearing the entire dataset (as we did in the RankingTest code, by closing the SessionFactory down every test), then clearing the data we expected to write and looking for any extraneous data. There are certainly other possibilities, but all of these are out of our scope here.

[9]Pretty much everyone who knows SQL moderately well has probably been fuming about how we're pulling data from the database. That's okay–the way it's being done here *is* pretty lame.

According to the Wikipedia page on control-break (http://en.wikipedia.org/wiki/Control_break), "[w]ith fourth generation languages such as SQL, the programming language should handle most of the details of control breaks automatically." That's absolutely correct, and it's also why I've been pointing out the inefficiency of all of these routines. We're manually doing something that the database (and Hibernate) should be able to do for us—and it *can*. We're just not using that capability yet. We will finally get there when we look at the next application requirement.

In any event, the new tests should be able to pass (perhaps not with flying colors, because the actual underlying services aren't done with an eye for efficiency), which allows us to move to the last (and probably most complicated) requirement.

Find the Highest Ranked Subject for a Skill

With this requirement, we want to find out who is ranked highest for a given Skill; if we have three people Ranked for Java, we want the one whose average score is best. If there are no Rankings for this Skill, we want a null response as a signal value. Off to the tests; let's look at Listing 3-25:

Listing 3-25. The Tests for Finding the Best Person for a Given Skill

```
@Test
public void findBestForNonexistentSkill() {
    Person p = service.findBestPersonFor("no skill");
    assertNull(p);
}

@Test
public void findBestForSkill() {
    service.addRanking("S1", "O1", "Sk1", 6);
    service.addRanking("S1", "O2", "Sk1", 8);
    service.addRanking("S2", "O1", "Sk1", 5);
    service.addRanking("S2", "O2", "Sk1", 7);
    service.addRanking("S3", "O1", "Sk1", 7);
    service.addRanking("S3", "O2", "Sk1", 9);
    // data that should not factor in!
    service.addRanking("S3", "O1", "Sk2", 2);
    Person p = service.findBestPersonFor("Sk1");
    assertEquals(p.getName(), "S3");
}
```

Our first test should be obvious: given a nonexistent Skill, we shouldn't get a Person back. (This follows our established convention that suggests the use of a signal value rather than an exception.)

Our second test creates three subjects, each with Skills in "Sk1," whatever that is. (It's "ability to serve as test data.") S1 has an average of 7, S2 has an average of 6, and S3 has an average of 8. We should therefore expect S3 as the owner of the best Ranking. We're throwing in some outlier data just to make sure that our service is limited to the actual data it's trying to find.

Note that we're not actually returning the Skill's average! For an actual application, that's very likely to be a requirement; it could easily be fulfilled by immediately calling getRankingFor(), but as designed that's a very expensive operation (involving creation of a new Session and a series of database roundtrips). We'll revisit this before too long; here, we're using as few object types as we can.

So let's look at some code in Listing 3-26. And we're finally going to get into a more capable query (and see how we might have been writing some of our other queries more efficiently).

Listing 3-26. Code for Finding the Highest Average for a Given Skill

```
@Override
public Person findBestPersonFor(String skill) {
    Person person = null;
    Session session = SessionUtil.getSession();
    Transaction tx = session.beginTransaction();

    person = findBestPersonFor(session, skill);

    tx.commit();
    session.close();
    return person;
}

private Person findBestPersonFor(Session session, String skill) {
    Query query = session.createQuery("select r.subject.name, avg(r.ranking)"
            + " from Ranking r where "
            + "r.skill.name=:skill "
            + "group by r.subject.name "
            + "order by avg(r.ranking) desc");
    query.setParameter("skill", skill);
    List<Object[]> result = query.list();
    if(result.size()>0) {
        return findPerson(session, (String)result.get(0)[0]);
    }
    return null;
}
```

Our public method follows the convention we've established so far: creating a session and then delegating to an internal method.

The internal method, though, does some things we've not seen yet so far, starting with a different type of query.

Most of our queries have been of the "FROM class alias WHERE condition" form, which is fairly simple. Hibernate is generating SQL that uses a table name and can do joins automatically to iterate over a tree of data ("r.skillname", for example), but the overall form is very simple.

Here, we have an actual SELECT clause. Here's the full query as written in the code:

```
select r.subject.name, avg(r.ranking) from Ranking r where r.skill.name=:skill group by r.subject.
name order by avg(r.ranking) desc
```

This actually returns tuples, which are sets of arrays of objects.

Our "select" clause specifies that the tuple will have two values, pulled from the subject name associated with the Ranking, and a *calculated value* which, in this case, is the average of all of the Rankings in a particular group.

The "where" clause limits the overall dataset to those Rankings where the Skill name matches the parameter.

The "group by" clause means that sets of values are handled together, which in turn means that the average Ranking (the second value of the tuple that the query returns) will be limited to each subject.

The "order by" clause means that Hibernate is going to give us the highest Ranked subjects before the lowest Ranked subjects.

Could we do this programmatically? Of course; that's pretty much what we've seen in most of our code, where we calculate values like the average Skill manually. However, this saves round-trip data time; the database actually performs the calculations and returns a dataset that's exactly large enough to fulfill its role. Databases are normally tuned for efficiency in this kind of calculation, so we're probably saving time as well, provided we're not using an embedded database as we do in this example.[10]

Summary

In this chapter, we've seen how to go from a problem definition to an object model, along with an example of test-driven design to test the model. We've also lightly covered the concepts of object state with respect to persistence and transactions.

We've then focused on the application requirements, building a series of actions through which those requirements could be fulfilled. We've covered how to create, read, update, and delete data, along with using Hibernate's query language to perform a fairly complex query with calculated data.

In the next chapter, we will look at the architecture of Hibernate and the lifecycle of a Hibernate-based application.

---

[10]Even with an embedded database, though, it can be faster; an embedded database can use internal access to the data to which our application code normally has no access, even before we consider the possibility of efficient queries through the use of indexes.

CHAPTER 4

The Persistence Life Cycle

In this chapter, we discuss the life cycle of persistent objects in Hibernate. These persistent objects can be POJOs without any special marker interfaces or inheritance related to Hibernate. Part of Hibernate's popularity comes from its ability to work with a normal object model.

We also discuss the methods of the Session interface that are used for creating, retrieving, updating, and deleting persistent objects from Hibernate.

Introducing the Life Cycle

After adding Hibernate to your application, you do not need to change your existing Java object model to add persistence marker interfaces or any other type of hint for Hibernate. Instead, Hibernate works with normal Java objects that your application creates with the new operator or that other objects create.

For Hibernate's purposes, these can be drawn up into two categories: objects for which Hibernate has entity mappings, and objects that are not directly recognized by Hibernate. A correctly mapped entity object will consist of fields and properties that are mapped, and that are themselves either references to correctly mapped entities, references to collections of such entities, or "value" types (primitives, primitive wrappers, strings, or arrays of these).

Given an instance of an object that is mapped to Hibernate, it can be in any one of four different states: transient, persistent, detached, or removed.

Transient objects exist in memory, as illustrated in Figure 4-1. Hibernate does not manage transient objects or persist changes to transient objects.

Transient Object

Figure 4-1. *Transient objects are independent of Hibernate*

To persist the changes to a transient object, you would have to ask the session to save the transient object to the database, at which point Hibernate assigns the object an identifier and marks the object as being in persistent state.

Persistent objects exist in the database, and Hibernate manages the persistence for persistent objects. We show this relationship between the objects and the database in Figure 4-2. If fields or properties change on a persistent object, Hibernate will keep the database representation up to date when the application marks the changes as to be committed.

Persistent Object

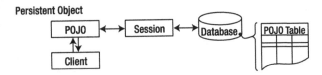

Figure 4-2. *Persistent objects are maintained by Hibernate*

Detached objects have a representation in the database, but changes to the object will not be reflected in the database, and vice versa. This temporary separation of the object and the database is shown in Figure 4-3. A detached object can be created by closing the session that it was associated with, or by evicting it from the session with a call to the session's evict() method. One reason you might consider doing this would be to read an object out of the database, modify the properties of the object in memory, and then store the results some place other than your database. This would be an alternative to doing a deep copy of the object.

Detached Object

Figure 4-3. *Detached objects exist in the database but are not maintained by Hibernate*

In order to persist changes made to a detached object, the application must reattach it to a valid Hibernate session. A detached instance can be associated with a new Hibernate session when your application calls one of the load, refresh, merge, update(), or save() methods on the new session with a reference to the detached object. After the call, the detached object would be a persistent object managed by the new Hibernate session.

Removed objects are objects that are being managed by Hibernate (persistent objects, in other words) that have been passed to the session's remove() method. When the application marks the changes held in the session as to be committed, the entries in the database that correspond to removed objects are deleted.

Versions prior to Hibernate 3 had support for the Lifecycle and Validatable interfaces. These allowed your objects to listen for save, update, delete, load, and validate events using methods on the object. In Hibernate 3, this function moved into events and interceptors, and the old interfaces were removed. In Hibernate 4, the JPA persistence life cycle is also supported, so events can be embedded into the objects and marked with annotations.

Entities, Classes, and Names

Entities represent Java objects with mappings that permit them to be stored in the database. The mappings indicate how the fields and properties of the object should be stored in the database tables. However, it is possible that you will want objects of a particular type to be represented in two different ways in the database. For instance, you could have one Java class for users, but two different tables in the database that store users. This may not be the best database design, but similar problems are common in legacy systems. Other systems that can't be easily modified may depend on the existing database design, and Hibernate is powerful enough to cover this scenario. In this case, how does Hibernate choose which to use?

An object representing an entity will be a normal Java class. It will also have an entity name. By default, the name of the entity will be the same as the name of the class type.[1] You have the option, however, to change this via the mappings or annotations, and thus distinguish between objects of the same type that are mapped to different

---

[1] As we saw in Chapter 3. HQL uses the entity name, not the class name; but because we didn't specify any custom entity names, the class name and the entity name were the same.

tables. There are, therefore, methods in the Session API that require an entity name to be provided to determine the appropriate mapping. If this is omitted, it will either be because no such distinction is needed or because, for convenience, the method assumes the most common case—that the entity name is the same as the class name–and duplicates the function of another, more specific method that permits the entity name to specified explicitly.

Identifiers

An identifier, or identity column, maps to the concept of a primary key in relational databases. A primary key is a unique set of one or more columns that can be used to specify a particular collection of data.

There are two types of identifiers: natural and artificial.

A *natural* identifier is something that the application finds meaningful–a user ID, for example, or a Social Security number[2] or equivalent.

An *artificial* identifier is one whose value is arbitrary. Our code so far uses values generated by the database (identity columns) which have no relation whatsoever with the data associated with that identifier. This tends to yield more flexibility with respect to associations and other such interactions, because the artificial identifier can be smaller than a natural identifier in many cases.

Why would artificial identifiers be better than natural identifiers? Well, there are a few possible reasons. One reason artificial identifiers might be better than natural identifiers is that an artificial identifier might be a smaller type (in memory) than a natural identifier.

Consider a user email. In most cases, user email addresses won't change, and they tend to be unique for a given user; however, the email addresses might be at least ten bytes long (and could be much longer). An integral user ID (a long, or int) might be four or eight bytes long, and no longer.

Another reason is that artificial identifiers won't change with the data's natural life cycle. An email address, for example, might change over time; someone might abandon an old email address and prefer a new one. Anything that relied on that email address as a natural identifier would have to be changed synchronously to allow updates.

Yet another reason is that artificial identifiers are simple. Databases (and Hibernate) allow the use of composite identifiers–identifiers built up from more than one property in an object. However, this means that when you refer to a specific object or row in the database, you have to include *all columns in that identifier*, whether as an embedded object or as a set of individual columns. It's doable, certainly; some data models require it (for legacy or other business reasons, for example). However, for efficiency's sake, most would normally prefer artificial keys.

In Hibernate, an object attribute is marked as an identifier with the @Id annotation, as shown in Listing 4-1.

Listing 4-1. A Typical Identifier Field

```
@Id
public Long id;
```

In Listing 4-1, you see a Long–a "big integer" for HSQL–that's marked as a presumably artificial identifier. This value will need to be assigned before the object with this attribute can be persisted.

In our example code so far, though, we've assigned no identifiers; we've used another annotation, @GeneratedValue, which tells Hibernate that it is responsible for assigning and maintaining the identifier. The mechanism through which this happens depends quite a bit on the Hibernate configuration and the database in use.

---

[2]The U.S. Social Security Administration says that they have enough Social Security numbers to assign unique identification for "several generations." (See http://www.ssa.gov/history/hfaq.html, Q20.) That may be good enough for a natural identifier, although privacy advocates would rightfully complain; also, note that "several generations" might not be enough. Programmers were *absolutely* sure that nobody would still have data with two-digit years in them ... until Y2K, which took a lot of manhours to fix.

There are five different generation possibilities: identity, sequence, table, auto, and none. *Identity* generation relies on a natural table sequencing. This is requested in the @GeneratedValue annotation by using the GenerationType.IDENTITY option, as follows:

```
@Id
@GeneratedValue(strategy=GenerationType.IDENTITY)
Long id;
```

The *sequence* mechanism depends on the database's ability to create table sequences (which tends to limit it to PostgreSQL, Oracle, and a few others). It corresponds to the GenerationType.SEQUENCE strategy.

The *table* mechanism uses a table whose purpose is to store blocks of artificial identifiers; you can let Hibernate generate this for you, or you can specify all of the table's specifics with an additional @TableGenerator annotation. To use artificial key generation via table, use the GenerationType.TABLE strategy.

The fourth artificial key generation strategy is *auto*, which normally maps to the IDENTITY strategy, but depends on the database in question. (It's supposed to default to something that's efficient for the database in question.) To use this, use the GenerationType.AUTO strategy.

The fifth strategy isn't actually a strategy at all: it relies on manual assignment of an identifier. If Session.persist() is called with an empty identifier, you'll have an IdentifierGenerationException thrown.

Entities and Associations

Entities can contain references to other entities, either directly as an embedded property or field, or indirectly via a collection of some sort (arrays, sets, lists, etc.). These associations are represented using foreign key relationships in the underlying tables. These foreign keys will rely on the identifiers used by participating tables, which is another reason to prefer small (and artificial) keys.

When only one of the pair of entities contains a reference to the other, the association is *unidirectional*. If the association is mutual, then it is referred to as *bidirectional*.

■ **Tip** A common mistake when designing entity models is to try to make all associations bidirectional. Associations that are not a natural part of the object model should not be forced into it. Hibernate Query Language often presents a more natural way to access the same information.

In associations, one (and only one) of the participating classes is referred to as "managing the relationship." If both ends of the association manage the relationship, then we would encounter a problem when client code called the appropriate set method on both ends of the association. Should two foreign key columns be maintained–one in each direction (risking circular dependencies)–or only one?

Ideally, we would like to dictate that only changes to one end of the relationship will result in any updates to the foreign key; and indeed, Hibernate allows us to do this by marking one end of the association as being managed by the other (marked by the mappedBy attribute of the association annotation).

■ **Caution** mappedBy is purely about how the foreign key relationships between entities are saved. It has nothing to do with saving the entities themselves. Despite this, they are often confused with the entirely orthogonal cascade functionality (described in the "Cascading Operations" section of this chapter).

While Hibernate lets us specify that changes to one association will result in changes to the database, it does *not* allow us to cause changes to one end of the association to be automatically reflected in the other end in the Java POJOs.

Let's create an example, in chapter04.broken package, of a Message and an Email association, without an "owning object." First, the Message class, as shown in Listing 4-2:

Listing 4-2. A Broken Model, Beginning with Message

```
package chapter04.broken;

import javax.persistence.*;

@Entity
public class Message {
    @Id
    @GeneratedValue(strategy = GenerationType.IDENTITY)
    Long id;

    @Column
    String content;

    @OneToOne
    Email email;

    public Message() {
    }

    public Message(String content) {
        setContent(content);
    }
    // mutators and accessors not included, for brevity
}
```

Listing 4-3 is the Email class, in the same package:

Listing 4-3. A Broken Model's Message Class

```
package chapter04.broken;

import javax.persistence.*;

@Entity
public class Email {
    @Id
    @GeneratedValue(strategy = GenerationType.IDENTITY)
    Long id;

    @Column
    String subject;
```

```
    @OneToOne //(mappedBy = "email")
            Message message;

    public Email() {
    }

    public Email(String subject) {
        setSubject(subject);
    }
    // mutators and accessors not included
}
```

With these classes, there's no "owning relation"; the mappedBy attribute in Email is commented out. This means that we need to update both the Email *and* the Message in order to have our relationship properly modeled in both directions, as the Listing 4-4 test shows:

Listing 4-4. A Common Misconception About Bidirectional Associations

```
@Test()
public void testBrokenInversionCode() {
    Long emailId;
    Long messageId;

    Session session = SessionUtil.getSession();
    Transaction tx = session.beginTransaction();

    Email email = new Email("Broken");
    Message message = new Message("Broken");

    email.setMessage(message);
    // message.setEmail(email);

    session.save(email);
    session.save(message);

    emailId = email.getId();
    messageId = message.getId();

    tx.commit();
    session.close();

    assertNotNull(email.getMessage());
    assertNull(message.getEmail());

    session = SessionUtil.getSession();
    tx = session.beginTransaction();
    email = (Email) session.get(Email.class, emailId);
    System.out.println(email);
    message = (Message) session.get(Message.class, messageId);
    System.out.println(message);
```

```
        tx.commit();
        session.close();

        assertNotNull(email.getMessage());
        assertNull(message.getEmail());
}
```

The final call to message.getEmail()will return null (assuming simple accessors and mutators are used). To get the desired effect, both entities must be updated. If the Email entity owns the association, this merely ensures the proper assignment of a foreign key column value. There is *no* implicit call of message.setEmail(email). This must be explicitly given, as in Listing 4-5.

Listing 4-5. The Correct Maintenance of a Bidirectional Association

```
@Test
public void testProperSimpleInversionCode() {
    Long emailId;
    Long messageId;

    Session session = SessionUtil.getSession();
    Transaction tx = session.beginTransaction();

    Email email = new Email("Proper");
    Message message = new Message("Proper");

    email.setMessage(message);
    message.setEmail(email);

    session.save(email);
    session.save(message);

    emailId = email.getId();
    messageId = message.getId();

    tx.commit();
    session.close();

    assertNotNull(email.getMessage());
    assertNotNull(message.getEmail());

    session = SessionUtil.getSession();
    tx = session.beginTransaction();
    email = (Email) session.get(Email.class, emailId);
    System.out.println(email);
    message = (Message) session.get(Message.class, messageId);
    System.out.println(message);
```

```
    tx.commit();
    session.close();

    assertNotNull(email.getMessage());
    assertNotNull(message.getEmail());
}
```

It is common for users new to Hibernate to get confused about this point. The reason it occurs is that Hibernate is using the actual current state of the entities. In Listing 4-5, when you set the message in the email, but not the email in the message, Hibernate persists the actual relationships in the object model, instead of trying to infer a relationship, even when that relationship would be expected. The extra relationship would be an unexpected side effect, even if it might be useful in *this particular case.*

If we include the mapping (the mappedBy attribute), we get a different result. We're going to modify Message (by moving it to a new package, chapter04.mapped) and Email (by moving it and including the mappedBy attribute, commented out in the prior listing).

The Message code is identical to the "broken" version, except for the package and the entity name (which means Hibernate will use "Message2" as the table name for this type), as shown in Listing 4-6:

Listing 4-6. A Corrected Message Class

```
package chapter04.mapped;

import javax.persistence.*;

@Entity(name = "Message2")
public class Message {
    @Id
    @GeneratedValue(strategy = GenerationType.IDENTITY)
    Long id;

    @Column
    String content;

    @OneToOne
    Email email;

    public Message() {
    }

    public Message(String content) {
        setContent(content);
    }
}
```

The Email code, in addition to changing the entity name and package, adds the mappedBy attribute. This actually adds a column to the Message's database representation, representing the email ID. See Listing 4-7.

Listing 4-7. A Corrected Email Class

```
package chapter04.mapped;

import javax.persistence.*;

@Entity(name = "Email2")
public class Email {
    @Id
    @GeneratedValue(strategy = GenerationType.IDENTITY)
    Long id;
    @Column
    String subject;
    @OneToOne(mappedBy = "email")
    Message message;

    public Email() {
    }

    public Email(String subject) {
        setSubject(subject);
    }
}
```

With the mapping contained in the Message, there are some unexpected results. Our prior test failed to reestablish some relationships, requiring them to be set in both Email *and* Message. Here, we have nearly the same construct, but without the same result.

First, let's see the test code, as shown in Listing 4-8; note that this test is using the chapter04.mapped package, so it's getting the Email and Message classes we just saw:

Listing 4-8. Misleading Behavior

```
@Test
public void testImpliedRelationship() {
    Long emailId;
    Long messageId;

    Session session = SessionUtil.getSession();
    Transaction tx = session.beginTransaction();

    Email email = new Email("Inverse Email");
    Message message = new Message("Inverse Message");

    // email.setMessage(message);
    message.setEmail(email);

    session.save(email);
    session.save(message);

    emailId = email.getId();
    messageId = message.getId();
```

```
    tx.commit();
    session.close();

    assertEquals(email.getSubject(), "Inverse Email");
    assertEquals(message.getContent(), "Inverse Message");
    assertNull(email.getMessage());
    assertNotNull(message.getEmail());

    session = SessionUtil.getSession();
    tx = session.beginTransaction();
    email = (Email) session.get(Email.class, emailId);
    System.out.println(email);
    message = (Message) session.get(Message.class, messageId);
    System.out.println(message);

    tx.commit();
    session.close();

    assertNotNull(email.getMessage());
    assertNotNull(message.getEmail());
}
```

This test passes, even though we didn't set the Email's Message.

That mappingBy attribute is the cause. In the database, the Mapping2 table has a column called "email_id," which is set to the Email's unique identifier when we update the Message's email property. When we close the session and reload, the relationship is set only through that column, which means the relationship is set "correctly" even though we didn't create the relationship properly when we first created the data.

If we were to manage the relationship in the Email entity (i.e., setting the mappedBy attribute in Message.java instead of Email.java), the situation would be reversed: setting the Message's email attribute wouldn't be reflected in the database, but setting the Email's message attribute would.

Here's a summary of the points made:

- You must explicitly manage both ends of an association.

- Only changes to the owner of an association will be honored in the database.

- When you load a detached entity from the database, it will reflect the foreign key relationships persisted into the database.

Table 4-1 shows how you can select the side of the relationship that should be made the owner of a bidirectional association. Remember that to make an association the owner, you must mark the *other* end as being mapped by the other.

Table 4-1. Marking the Owner of an Association

Type of Association	Options
One-to-one	Either end can be made the owner, but one (and only one) of them should be; if you don't specify this, you will end up with a circular dependency.
One-to-many	The *many* end must be made the owner of the association.
Many-to-one	This is the same as the one-to-many relationship viewed from the opposite perspective, so the same rule applies: the *many* end must be made the owner of the association.
Many-to-many	Either end of the association can be made the owner.

If this all seems rather confusing, just remember that association ownership is concerned exclusively with the management of the foreign keys in the database, and things should become clearer as you use Hibernate further. Associations and mappings are discussed in detail in the next few chapters.

Saving Entities

Creating an instance of a class you mapped with a Hibernate mapping does not automatically persist the object to the database. Until you explicitly associate the object with a valid Hibernate session, the object is transient, like any other Java object. In Hibernate, we use one of the save()-or persist(), which is a synonym for save()-methods on the Session interface to store a transient object in the database, as follows:

```
public Serializable save(Object object) throws HibernateException
```

```
public Serializable save(String entityName,Object object) throws HibernateException
```

Both save() methods take a transient object reference (which must not be null) as an argument. Hibernate expects to find a mapping (either annotations or an XML mapping) for the transient object's class; Hibernate cannot persist arbitrary unmapped objects. If you have mapped multiple entities to a Java class, you can specify which entity you are saving (Hibernate wouldn't know from just the Java class name) with the entityName argument.

The save() methods all create a new org.hibernate.event.SaveOrUpdateEvent event. We discuss events in more detail in Appendix A, although you do not have to worry about these implementation details to use Hibernate effectively.

At its simplest, we create a new object in Java, set a few of its properties, and then save it through the session. Here's a simple object, shown in Listing 4-9:

Listing 4-9. A Simple Object for Persistence

```
package chapter04.model;

import javax.persistence.*;

@Entity
public class SimpleObject {
    @Id
    @GeneratedValue(strategy = GenerationType.IDENTITY)
    Long id;
    @Column
    String key;
    @Column
    Long value;

    public SimpleObject() {
    }

    // mutators and accessors not included for brevity
    // equals() and hashCode() will be covered later in this chapter
}
```

Listing 4-10 shows how this object is saved, as shown in chapter04.general.PersistingEntitiesTest, in the testSaveLoad() method:

Listing 4-10. The testSaveLoad() Method as a Test

```
Session session = SessionUtil.getSession();
Transaction tx = session.beginTransaction();

SimpleObject obj = new SimpleObject();
obj.setKey("sl");
obj.setValue(10L);

session.save(obj);
assertNotNull(obj.getId());
// we should have an id now, set by Session.save()
id = obj.getId();

tx.commit();
session.close();
```

It is not appropriate to save an object that has already been persisted. Doing so will update the object, which will actually end up creating a duplicate with a new identifier. This can be seen in PersistingEntitiesTest's testSavingEntitiesTwice() method, which looks like that shown in Listing 4-11:

Listing 4-11. Saving the Same Entity Twice. Don't Do This!

```
@Test
public void testSavingEntitiesTwice() {
    Long id;
    Session session = SessionUtil.getSession();
    Transaction tx = session.beginTransaction();

    SimpleObject obj = new SimpleObject();

    obj.setKey("osas");
    obj.setValue(10L);

    session.save(obj);
    assertNotNull(obj.getId());

    id = obj.getId();

    tx.commit();
    session.close();

    session = SessionUtil.getSession();
    tx = session.beginTransaction();

    obj.setValue(12L);

    session.save(obj);
```

```
        tx.commit();
        session.close();

        // note that save() creates a new row in the database!
        // this is wrong behavior. Don't do this!
        assertNotEquals(id, obj.getId());
}
```

When this test is run, the two identifiers would be expected to be equal but they're not; examining the values yielded equivalent objects, except for the IDs, which were sequentially assigned as the SimpleObject @Id generation specified.

You can, however, update an object with Session.saveOrUpdate(). Listing 4-12 shows another method, testSaveOrUpdateEntity():

Listing 4-12. Updating an Object

```
@Test
public void testSaveOrUpdateEntity() {
    Long id;
    Session session = SessionUtil.getSession();
    Transaction tx = session.beginTransaction();

    SimpleObject obj = new SimpleObject();

    obj.setKey("osas2");
    obj.setValue(14L);

    session.save(obj);
    assertNotNull(obj.getId());

    id = obj.getId();

    tx.commit();
    session.close();

    session = SessionUtil.getSession();
    tx = session.beginTransaction();

    obj.setValue(12L);

    session.saveOrUpdate(obj);

    tx.commit();
    session.close();

    // saveOrUpdate() will update a row in the database
    // if one matches. This is what one usually expects.
    assertEquals(id, obj.getId());
}
```

It wouldn't be advisable to try to match this code construction in production code. The object goes from transient state (when it's created) to persistent state (when it's first saved), then back to transient state (when the session is closed). We then update the object while it's in transient state, and move it *back* to persistent state when we call Session.saveOrUpdate().

Ideally, what you would do is load the object from the session in the first place (as we've done in most of our other examples where we show updates); this means that the updates take place on a persistent object, and we don't actually have to call Session.save() or Session.saveOrUpdate() at all.[3]

Once an object is in a persistent state, Hibernate manages updates to the database itself as you change the fields and properties of the object.

Object Equality and Identity

When we discuss persistent objects in Hibernate, we also need to consider the role that object equality and identity play with Hibernate. When we have a persistent object in Hibernate, that object represents both an instance of a class in a particular Java virtual machine (JVM) and a row (or rows) in a database table (or tables).

Requesting a persistent object again from the *same Hibernate session* returns the same Java instance of a class, which means that you can compare the objects using the standard Java == equality syntax. If, however, you request a persistent object from more than one Hibernate session, Hibernate will provide distinct instances from each session, and the == operator will return false if you compare these object instances.

Taking this into account, if you are comparing objects in two different sessions, you will need to implement the equals() method on your Java persistence objects, which you should probably do as a regular occurrence anyway. (Just don't forget to implement hashCode() along with it.)

Implementing equals() can be interesting. Hibernate wraps the actual object in a proxy (for various performance-enhancing reasons, like loading data on demand), so you need to factor in a class hierarchy for equivalency; it's also typically more efficient to use mutators in your equals() and hashCode() methods, as opposed to the actual fields.

Listing 4-13 is an implementation of equals() and hashCode() for the SimpleObject entity we've been using, generated by IntelliJ IDEA[4] and modified to use accessors:

Listing 4-13. Sample equals() and hashCode() Implementations

```
@Override
public boolean equals(Object o) {
    if (this == o) return true;
    if (!(o instanceof SimpleObject)) return false;

    SimpleObject that = (SimpleObject) o;

    // we prefer the method versions of accessors,
    // because of Hibernate's proxies.
    if (getId() != null ?
        !getId().equals(that.getId()) : that.getId() != null)
        return false;
```

---

[3]We saw this in Chapter 3: chapter03.hibernate.RankingTest's changeRanking() method does an in-place update of a persistent object.
[4]IDEA is an IDE for Java; it has a free community edition and a commercial "ultimate" edition. It can be found at http://jetbrains.com/idea.

```
        if (getKey() != null ?
            !getKey().equals(that.getKey()) : that.getKey() != null)
            return false;
        if (getValue() != null ?
            !getValue().equals(that.getValue()) : that.getValue() != null)
            return false;

        return true;
    }


    @Override
    public int hashCode() {
    int result = getId() != null ? getId().hashCode() : 0;
        result = 31 * result + (getKey() != null ? getKey().hashCode() : 0);
        result = 31 * result + (getValue() != null?getValue().hashCode() : 0);
        return result;
    }
```

The PersistentEntitiesTest's testSaveLoad() method shows off the various possibilities and conditions for equality, as shown in Listing 4-14:

Listing 4-14. Testing Various Combinations of Equality

```
@Test
public void testSaveLoad() {
    Long id = null;

    Session session = SessionUtil.getSession();
    Transaction tx = session.beginTransaction();

    SimpleObject obj = new SimpleObject();
    obj.setKey("sl");
    obj.setValue(10L);

    session.save(obj);
    assertNotNull(obj.getId());
    // we should have an id now, set by Session.save()
    id = obj.getId();

    tx.commit();
    session.close();

    session = SessionUtil.getSession();
    tx = session.beginTransaction();

    // we're loading the object by id
    SimpleObject o2 = (SimpleObject) session.load(SimpleObject.class, id);
    assertEquals(o2.getKey(), "sl");
    assertNotNull(o2.getValue());
    assertEquals(o2.getValue().longValue(), 10L);
```

```
    SimpleObject o3 = (SimpleObject) session.load(SimpleObject.class, id);

    // since o3 and o2 were loaded in the same session, they're not only
    // equivalent - as shown by equals() - but equal, as shown by ==.
    // since obj was NOT loaded in this session, it's equivalent but
    // not ==.
    assertEquals(o2, o3);
    assertEquals(obj, o2);

    assertTrue(o2 == o3);
    assertFalse(o2 == obj);

    tx.commit();
    session.close();
}
```

Note that in this code, o2 and o3 are *equal* (they hold the same reference), while o2 and obj are *equivalent* (the references are different but hold equivalent data). Again, you shouldn't rely on this in production code; object equivalence should always be tested with equals().

Loading Entities

Hibernate's Session interface provides several load() methods for loading entities from your database. Each load() method requires the object's primary key as an identifier.[5]

In addition to the ID, Hibernate also needs to know which class or entity name to use to find the object with that ID. Last, you will need to cast the object returned by load() to the class you desire. The basic load() methods are as follows:

```
public Object load(Class theClass, Serializable id) throws HibernateException
public Object load(String entityName, Serializable id) throws HibernateException
public void load(Object object, Serializable id) throws HibernateException
```

The last load() method takes an object as an argument. The object should be of the same class as the object you would like loaded, and it should be empty. Hibernate will populate that object with the object you requested. While this is similar to other library calls in Java–namely, java.util.List.toArray()-this syntax can be without much of an actual benefit.

The other load() methods take a lock mode as an argument. The *lock mode* specifies whether Hibernate should look into the cache for the object and which database lock level Hibernate should use for the row (or rows) of data that represent this object. The Hibernate developers claim that Hibernate will usually pick the correct lock mode for you, although we have seen situations in which it is important to manually choose the correct lock. In addition, your database may choose its own locking strategy-for instance, locking down an entire table rather than multiple rows within a table. In order of least restrictive to most restrictive, the various lock modes you can use are:

- NONE: Uses no row-level locking, and uses a cached object if available; this is the Hibernate default.

- READ: Prevents other SELECT queries from reading data that is in the middle of a transaction (and thus possibly invalid) until it is committed.

---

[5]As usual, there's more to this than we're discussing here. We'll add more methods to this list as we keep going through Hibernate's capabilities. We're keeping the list small for simplicity's sake.

- UPGRADE: Uses the SELECT FOR UPDATE SQL syntax to lock the data until the transaction is finished.

- UPGRADE_NOWAIT: Uses the NOWAIT keyword (for Oracle), which returns an error immediately if there is another thread using that row; otherwise this is similar to UPGRADE.

- FORCE: Similar to UPGRADE but increments the version for objects with automatic versioning when loaded.

All of these lock modes are static fields on the org.hibernate.LockMode class. (We discuss locking and deadlocks with respect to transactions in more detail in Chapter 8.) The load() methods that use lock modes are as follows:

```
public Object load(Class theClass, Serializable id, LockMode lockMode)
            throws HibernateException

public Object load(String entityName, Serializable id, LockMode lockMode)
            throws HibernateException
```

You should not use a load() method unless you are sure that the object exists. If you are not certain, then use one of the get() methods. The load() methods will throw an exception if the unique ID is not found in the database, whereas the get() methods will merely return a null reference.

Much like load(), the get() methods take an identifier and either an entity name or a class. There are also two get() methods that take a lock mode as an argument. The get() methods are as follows:

```
public Object get(Class clazz, Serializable id)
            throws HibernateException

public Object get(String entityName, Serializable id)
            throws HibernateException

public Object get(Class clazz, Serializable id, LockMode lockMode)
            throws HibernateException

public Object get(String entityName, Serializable id, LockMode lockMode)
            throws HibernateException
```

If you need to determine the entity name for a given object (by default, this is the same as the class name), you can call the getEntityName() method on the Session interface, as follows:

```
public String getEntityName(Object object) throws HibernateException
```

Using the get()and load() methods is straightforward. For the following code sample, we would be getting the Supplier ID from another Java class. For instance, through a web application, someone may select a Supplier details page for the supplier with the ID 1. If we are not sure that the supplier exists, we use the get() method, with which we could check for null, as follows:

```
// get an id from some other Java class, for instance, through a web application
Supplier supplier = (Supplier) session.get(Supplier.class,id);
if (supplier == null) {
    System.out.println("Supplier not found for id " + id);
    return;
}
```

We can also retrieve the entity name from Hibernate and use it with either the get() or load() method. The load() method will throw an exception if an object with that ID cannot be found.

```
String entityName = session.getEntityName(supplier);
Supplier secondarySupplier = (Supplier) session.load(entityName,id);
```

It's also worth pointing out that you can query for an entity, which allows you to look for objects with a specific identifier, as well as sets of objects that match other criteria. There's also a Criteria API that allows you to use a declarative mechanism to build queries. These topics will be covered in later chapters.

Merging Entities

Merging is performed when you desire to have a detached entity changed to persistent state again, with the detached entity's changes migrated to (or overriding) the database. The method signatures for the merge operations are:

```
Object merge(Object object)
```

```
Object merge(String entityName, Object object)
```

Merging is the inverse of refresh(), which overrides the detached entity's values with the values from the database. Listing 4-15 is some example code, from chapter04.general.MergeRefreshTest:

Listing 4-15. Demonstrating the Use and Function of session.merge()

```
@Test
public void testMerge() {
    Long id;
    Session session = SessionUtil.getSession();
    Transaction tx = session.beginTransaction();

    SimpleObject simpleObject = new SimpleObject();

    simpleObject.setKey("testMerge");
    simpleObject.setValue(1L);

    session.save(simpleObject);

    id = simpleObject.getId();

    tx.commit();
    session.close();

    SimpleObject so = validateSimpleObject(id, 1L);

    so.setValue(2L);

    session = SessionUtil.getSession();
    tx = session.beginTransaction();

    session.merge(so);
```

```
        tx.commit();
        session.close();

        validateSimpleObject(id, 2L);
    }

    private SimpleObject validateSimpleObject(Long id, Long value) {
        Session session;
        Transaction tx;// validate the database values
        session = SessionUtil.getSession();
        tx = session.beginTransaction();

        SimpleObject so = (SimpleObject) session.load(SimpleObject.class, id);

        assertEquals(so.getKey(), "testMerge");
        assertEquals(so.getValue(), value);

        tx.commit();
        session.close();

        return so;
    }
```

This code creates an entity (a SimpleObject) and then saves it; it then verifies the object's values (in validateSimpleObject()), which itself returns a detached entity. We update the detached object and merge() it–which should update the value in the database, which we verify.

Refreshing Entities

Hibernate provides a mechanism to refresh persistent objects from their database representation. Use one of the refresh() methods on the Session interface to refresh an instance of a persistent object, as follows:

```
public void refresh(Object object)
            throws HibernateException
```

```
public void refresh(Object object, LockMode lockMode)
            throws HibernateException
```

These methods will reload the properties of the object from the database, overwriting them; thus, as stated, refresh() is the inverse of merge(). Merging overrides the database with the values held by the previously transient object, and refresh() overrides the values in the transient object with the values in the database.

Hibernate usually does a very good job of taking care of this for you, so you do not have to use the refresh() method very often. There are instances where the Java object representation will be out of sync with the database representation of an object, however. For example, if you use SQL to update the database, Hibernate will not be aware that the representation changed. You do not need to use this method regularly, though. Similar to the load() method, the refresh() method can take a lock mode as an argument; see the discussion of lock modes in the previous "Loading Entities" section.

Let's take a look at code in Listing 4-16 that uses refresh()–basically an inverse of the code we saw that demonstrated merge()–and contained in the same test class.

Listing 4-16. Demonstrating the Use and Function of `session.refresh()`

```java
@Test
public void testRefresh() {
    Long id;
    Session session = SessionUtil.getSession();
    Transaction tx = session.beginTransaction();

    SimpleObject simpleObject = new SimpleObject();

    simpleObject.setKey("testMerge");
    simpleObject.setValue(1L);

    session.save(simpleObject);

    id = simpleObject.getId();

    tx.commit();
    session.close();

    SimpleObject so = validateSimpleObject(id, 1L);

    so.setValue(2L);

    session = SessionUtil.getSession();
    tx = session.beginTransaction();

    session.refresh(so);

    tx.commit();
    session.close();

    validateSimpleObject(id, 1L);
}
```

This code is the same as the `merge()` test, with two changes: the first is that it calls `refresh()` rather than `merge()` (surprise!), and the other is that it expects the object's data to revert to the original state from the database, verifying that `refresh()` overrides the transient object's data.

Updating Entities

Hibernate automatically persists changes made to persistent objects into the database.[6] If a property changes on a persistent object, the associated Hibernate session will queue the change for persistence to the database using SQL. From a developer's perspective, you do not have to do any work to store these changes, unless you would like to force Hibernate to commit all of its changes in the queue. You can also determine whether the session is dirty and changes need to be committed. When you commit a Hibernate transaction, Hibernate will take care of these details for you.

---

[6]We've mentioned this a few different times now, along with test code.

The flush() method forces Hibernate to flush the session, as follows:

```
public void flush() throws HibernateException
```

You can determine if the session is dirty with the isDirty() method, as follows:

```
public boolean isDirty() throws HibernateException
```

You can also instruct Hibernate to use a flushing mode for the session with the setFlushMode() method. The getFlushMode() method returns the flush mode for the current session, as follows:

```
public void setFlushMode(FlushMode flushMode)
public FlushMode getFlushMode()
```

The possible flush modes are the following:

- ALWAYS: Every query flushes the session before the query is executed. This is going to be very slow.

- AUTO: Hibernate manages the query flushing to guarantee that the data returned by a query is up to date.

- COMMIT: Hibernate flushes the session on transaction commits.

- MANUAL: Your application needs to manage the session flushing with the flush() method. Hibernate never flushes the session itself.

By default, Hibernate uses the auto flush mode. Generally, you should use transaction boundaries to ensure that appropriate flushing is taking place, rather than trying to "manually" flush at the appropriate times.

Deleting Entities

In order to allow convenient removal of entities from the database, the Session interface provides a delete() method, as follows:

```
public void delete(Object object) throws HibernateException
```

This method takes a persistent object as an argument. The argument can also be a transient object with the identifier set to the ID of the object that needs to be erased.

In the simplest form, in which you are simply deleting an object with no associations to other objects, this is straightforward; but many objects do have associations with other objects. To allow for this, Hibernate can be configured to allow deletes to cascade from one object to its associated objects.

For instance, consider the situation in which you have a parent with a collection of child objects, and you would like to delete them all. The easiest way to handle this is to use the cascade attribute on the collection's element in the Hibernate mapping. If you set the cascade attribute to delete or all, the delete will be cascaded to all of the associated objects. Hibernate will take care of deleting these for you: deleting the parent erases the associated objects.

Hibernate also supports bulk deletes, where your application executes a DELETE HQL statement against the database. These are very useful for deleting more than one object at a time because each object does not need to be loaded into memory just to be deleted, as shown in Listing 4-17.

Listing 4-17. A Bulk Delete Using a Hibernate Query

```
session.createQuery("delete from User").executeUpdate();
```

Network traffic is greatly reduced, as are the memory requirements compared to those for individually issuing a delete()call against each entity identifier.

■ **Caution**   Bulk deletes do not cause cascade operations to be carried out. If cascade behavior is needed, you will need to carry out the appropriate deletions yourself, or use the session's delete() method.

Cascading Operations

When you perform one of the operations described in this chapter on an entity, the operations will not be performed on the associated entities unless you explicitly tell Hibernate to perform them.

For example, the code in Listing 4-18 will fail when we try to commit the transaction, because the Message entity that is associated with the Email entity has not been persisted into the database, so the Email entity cannot be accurately represented (with its foreign key onto the appropriate message row) in its table.

Listing 4-18. A Failed save() due to Cascading

```
Session session = SessionUtil.getSession();
Transaction tx=session.beginTransaction();

Email email = new Email("Email title");
Message message = new Message("Message content");
email.setMessage(message);
message.setEmail(email);

session.save(email);

tx.commit();
session.close();
```

Ideally, we would like the save operation to be propagated from the Email entity to its associated Message object. We do this by setting the cascade operations for the properties and fields of the entity (or assigning an appropriate default value for the entity as a whole). So, the code in Listing 4-18 will perform correctly if at least the PERSIST cascade operation is set for the Email entity's message property. The cascade types supported by the Java Persistence Architecture are:

- PERSIST
- MERGE
- REFRESH
- REMOVE
- DETACH
- ALL

It's worth pointing out that Hibernate has its own configuration options for cascading, which represent a superset of these; however, we're largely following the Java Persistence Architecture specification for modeling, as this will typically be more common by far than the Hibernate-specific modeling.[7]

- CascadeType.PERSIST means that save() or persist() operations cascade to related entities; for our Email and Message example, if Email's @oneToOne includes PERSIST, saving the Email would save the Message as well.

- CascadeType.MERGE means that related entities are merged into managed state when the owning entity is merged.

- CascadeType.REFRESH does the same thing for the refresh() operation.

- CascadeType.REMOVE removes all related entities association with this setting when the owning entity is deleted.

- CascadeType.DETACH detaches all related entities if a manual detach were to occur.

- CascadeType.ALL is shorthand for all of the cascade operations.

The cascade configuration option accepts an array of CascadeTypes; thus, to include *only* refreshes and merges in the cascade operation for a one-to-one relationship, you might see the following:

```
@OneToOne(cascade={CascadeType.REFRESH, CascadeType.MERGE})
EntityType otherSide;
```

There's one more cascading operation that's not part of the normal set, called *orphan removal*, which removes an owned object from the database when it's removed from its owning relationship.

Let's suppose we have a Library entity, which contains a list of Book entities. Listing 4-20 is our entity declarations, omitting constructors, accessors, and mutators:

Listing 4-20. A One-to-Many Relationship for an Orphan Object Demonstration

```
package chapter04.orphan;

import javax.persistence.*;
import java.util.ArrayList;
import java.util.List;

@Entity
public class Library {
    @Id
    @GeneratedValue(strategy = GenerationType.IDENTITY)
    Long id;
    @Column
    String name;
    @OneToMany(orphanRemoval = true, mappedBy = "library")
    List<Book> books = new ArrayList<>();
}
```

---

[7]That's the thing about standards: they're standard.

```
package chapter04.orphan;

import javax.persistence.*;

@Entity
public class Book {
    @Id
    @GeneratedValue(strategy = GenerationType.IDENTITY)
    Long id;
    @Column
    String title;
    @ManyToOne
    Library library;
}
```

Note the use of orphanRemoval in the @OneToMany annotation. Now let's take a look at some test code, which will be fairly verbose since we need to validate our initial dataset, change it, and then revalidate; see Listing 4-21:

Listing 4-21. A Test Showing Orphan Removal

```
package chapter04.orphan;

import com.redhat.osas.hibernate.util.SessionUtil;
import org.hibernate.Session;
import org.hibernate.Transaction;
import org.testng.annotations.Test;

import static org.testng.Assert.assertEquals;

public class OrphanRemovalTest {
    @Test
    public void orphanRemovalTest() {
        Long id = createLibrary();

        Session session = SessionUtil.getSession();
        Transaction tx = session.beginTransaction();

        Library library = (Library) session.load(Library.class, id);
        assertEquals(library.getBooks().size(), 3);

        library.getBooks().remove(0);
        assertEquals(library.getBooks().size(), 2);

        tx.commit();
        session.close();

        session = SessionUtil.getSession();
        tx = session.beginTransaction();

        Library l2 = (Library) session.load(Library.class, id);
        assertEquals(l2.getBooks().size(), 2);
        Query query = session.createQuery("from Book b");
```

```java
        List books = query.list();
        assertEquals(books.size(), 2);

        tx.commit();
        session.close();
    }

    private Long createLibrary() {
        Session session = SessionUtil.getSession();
        Transaction tx = session.beginTransaction();

        Library library = new Library();
        library.setName("orphanLib");
        session.save(library);

        Book book = new Book();
        book.setLibrary(library);
        book.setTitle("book 1");
        session.save(book);
        library.getBooks().add(book);

        book = new Book();
        book.setLibrary(library);
        book.setTitle("book 2");
        session.save(book);
        library.getBooks().add(book);

        book = new Book();
        book.setLibrary(library);
        book.setTitle("book 3");
        session.save(book);
        library.getBooks().add(book);

        tx.commit();
        session.close();

        return library.getId();
    }
}
```

What this does is not complicated: it builds a library with three books associated with it. Then it loads the library from the database, validates that it looks like it's supposed to ("a library with three books"), and removes one from the library. It does *not* delete the Book entity being removed; it only removes it from the Library's set of books, which makes it an orphan.

After committing the Library object's new state–via tx.commit()–we reload the Library from the database and validate that it now has only two books. The book we removed is gone from the library.

That doesn't mean it's *actually* been removed, though, so we then query the database for *all* Book entities to see if we have two or three. We should have only two, and so it is. We removed the orphan object when updating the library.

Lazy Loading, Proxies, and Collection Wrappers

Consider the quintessential Internet web application: the online store. The store maintains a catalog of products. At the crudest level, this can be modeled as a catalog entity managing a series of product entities. In a large store, there may be tens of thousands of products grouped into various overlapping categories.

When a customer visits the store, the catalog must be loaded from the database. We probably don't want the implementation to load every single one of the entities representing the tens of thousands of products to be loaded into memory. For a sufficiently large retailer, this might not even be possible, given the amount of physical memory available on the machine. Even if this were possible, it would probably cripple the performance of the site.

Instead, we want only the catalog to load, possibly with the categories as well. Only when the user drills down into the categories should a subset of the products in that category be loaded from the database.

To manage this problem, Hibernate provides a facility called *lazy loading*. When enabled (this is the default using XML mappings, but not when using annotations), an entity's associated entities will be loaded only when they are directly requested. For example, the following code loads only a single entity from the database:

```
Email email = (Email)session.get(Email.class,new Integer(42));
```

However, if an association of the class is accessed, and lazy loading is in effect, the association is pulled from the database as needed. For instance, in the following snippet, the associated Message object will be loaded since it is explicitly referenced.

```
// surely this email is about the meaning of life, the universe, and everything
Email email = (Email)session.get(Email.class,new Integer(42));
String text = email.getMessage().getContent();
```

The simplest way that Hibernate can force this behavior upon your entities is by providing a proxy implementation of them.[8] Hibernate intercepts calls to the entity by substituting a proxy for it derived from the entity's class. Where the requested information is missing, it will be loaded from the database before control is ceded to the parent entity's implementation. Where the association is represented as a collection class, a wrapper (essentially a proxy for the collection, rather than for the entities that it contains) is created and substituted for the original collection.

Hibernate can only access the database via a session. If an entity is detached from the session when we try to access an association (via a proxy or collection wrapper) that has not yet been loaded, Hibernate throws a LazyInitializationException. The cure is to ensure either that the entity is made persistent again by attaching it to a session or that all of the fields that will be required are accessed *before* the entity is detached from the session.

If you need to determine whether a proxy, a persistence collection, or an attribute has been lazy loaded, you can call the isInitialized(Object proxy) and isPropertyInitialized(Object proxy, String propertyName) methods on the org.hibernate.Hibernate class. You can also force a proxy or collection to become fully populated by calling the initialize(Obect proxy) method on the org.hibernate.Hibernate class. If you initialize a collection using this method, you will also need to initialize each object contained in the collection, as only the collection is guaranteed to be initialized.

---

[8]This is a deeper explanation of some behavior we saw in our sample code for equals() and hashCode().

Querying Objects

Hibernate provides several different ways to query for objects stored in the database. The Criteria Query API is a Java API for constructing a query as an object. HQL is an object-oriented query language, similar to SQL, that you may use to retrieve objects that match the query. We discuss these further in Chapters 9 and 10. Hibernate provides a way to execute SQL directly against the database to retrieve objects, should you have legacy applications that use SQL or if you need to use SQL features that are not supported through HQL and the Criteria Query API (discussed in Chapter 11).

Summary

Hibernate provides a simple API for creating, retrieving, updating, and deleting objects from a relational database through the Session interface. Understanding the differences between transient, persistent, and detached objects in Hibernate will allow you to understand how changes to the objects update the database tables.

We have touched upon the need to create mappings to correlate the database tables with the fields and properties of the Java objects that you want to persist. The next chapter covers these in detail, and it discusses why they are required and what they can contain.

CHAPTER 5

An Overview of Mapping

The purpose of Hibernate is to allow you to treat your database as if it stores Java objects. However, in practice, relational databases do not store objects—they store data in tables and columns. Unfortunately, there is no simple way to correlate the data stored in a relational database with the data represented by Java objects.[1]

The difference between an object-oriented association and a relational one is fundamental. Consider a simple class to represent a user, and another to represent an email address, as shown in Figure 5-1.

Figure 5-1. *An object-oriented association*

User objects contain fields referring to Email objects. The association has a direction; given a User object, you can determine its associated Email object. For example, consider Listing 5-1.

Listing 5-1. Acquiring the Email Object from the User Object

```
User user = ...
Email email = user.email;
```

The reverse, however, is not true. The natural way to represent this relationship in the database, as illustrated in Figure 5-2, is superficially similar.

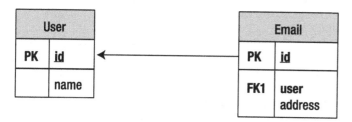

Figure 5-2. *A relational association*

---

[1]If there were, books like this one probably wouldn't exist.

Despite that similarity, the direction of the association is effectively reversed. Given an Email row, you can immediately determine which user row it belongs to in the database; this relationship is mandated by a foreign key constraint. It is possible to reverse the relationship in the database world through suitable use of SQL—another difference.

Given the differences between the two worlds, it is necessary to manually intervene to determine how your Java classes should be represented in database tables.

Why Mapping Cannot Easily Be Automated

It is not immediately obvious why you cannot create simple rules for storing your Java objects in the database so that they can be easily retrieved. For example, the most immediately obvious rule would be that a Java class must correlate to a single table. For example, instances of the User class defined in Listing 5-2 could surely be represented by a simple table like the one for a user, shown in Figure 5-1.

Listing 5-2. A Simple User Class with a Password Field

```java
public class User {
    String name;
    String password;
}
```

And indeed it could, but some questions present themselves:

- How many rows should you end up with if you save a user twice?

- Are you allowed to save a user without a name?

- Are you allowed to save a user without a password?

When you start to think about classes that refer to other classes, there are additional questions to consider. Have a look at the Customer and Email classes defined in Listing 5-3.

Listing 5-3. Customer and Email Classes

```java
public class Customer {
    int customerId;
    int customerReference;
    String name;
    Email email;
}

public class Email {
    String address;
}
```

Based on this, the following questions arise:

- Is a unique customer identified by its customer ID, or its customer reference?

- Can an email address be used by more than one customer?

- Can a customer have more than one email ID?

- Should the relationship be represented in the Customer table?

- Should the relationship be represented in the `Email` table?

- Should the relationship be represented in some third (link) table?

Depending upon the answers to these questions, your database tables could vary considerably. You could take a stab at a reasonable design, such as that given in Figure 5-3, based upon your intuition about likely scenarios in the real world.

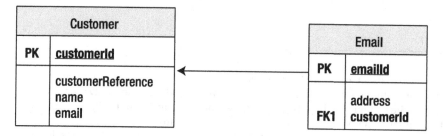

Figure 5-3. *Tables in which the customer is identified by customerId. Here, email address entities can be used only by a single customer, and the relationship is maintained by the Email table*

The field names and foreign keys are important; without them, there's no way to form any useful decision about these entities (see Listing 5-4). It would be a nearly impossible task to design an automated tool that could picture this structure wisely or appropriately.

Listing 5-4. *A Class Identical in Structure to Listing 5-3, but with All Contextual Information Removed*

```
public class Foo {
    int x;
    int y;
    String s;
    Bar bar;
}

public class Bar {
    String a;
}
```

Primary Keys

Most "relational" databases that provide SQL access are prepared to accept tables that have no predefined primary key. Hibernate is not so tolerant; even if your table has been created without a primary key, Hibernate will require you to specify one. This often seems perverse to users who are familiar with SQL and databases but not familiar with ORM tools. As such, let's examine in more depth the problems that arise when there's no primary key.

To begin, without a primary key it is impossible to uniquely identify a row in a table. For example, consider Table 5-1.

Table 5-1. *A Table in Which the Rows Cannot Be Uniquely Identified*

User	Age
dminter	35
dminter	40
dminter	55
dminter	40
jlinwood	57

This table clearly contains information about users and their respective ages. However, there are four users with the same name (Dave Minter, Denise Minter, Daniel Minter, and Dashiel Minter). There is probably a way of distinguishing them somewhere else in the system—perhaps by email address or user number. But if, for example, you want to know the age of Dashiel Minter with user ID 32, there is no way to obtain it from Table 5-1.

While Hibernate will not let you omit the primary key, it will permit you to form the primary key from a collection of columns. For example, Table 5-2 could be keyed by Usernumber and User.

Table 5-2. *A Table in Which the Rows Can Be Uniquely Identified*

User	Usernumber	Age
dminter	1	35
dminter	2	40
dminter	3	55
dminter	32	42
jlinwood	1	57

Neither User nor Usernumber contains unique entries, but in combination they uniquely identify the age of a particular user, and so they are acceptable to Hibernate as a primary key.

Why does Hibernate need to uniquely identify entries when SQL doesn't? Because Hibernate is representing Java objects, which are *always* uniquely identifiable. The classic mistake made by new Java developers is to compare strings using the == operator instead of the equals() method. You can distinguish between references to two String objects that represent the same text and two references to the same String object.[2] SQL has no such obligation, and there are arguably cases in which it is desirable to give up the ability to make the distinction.

For example, if Hibernate could not uniquely identify an object with a primary key, then the following code could have several possible outcomes in the underlying table.

```
String customer = getCustomerFromHibernate("dcminter");
customer.setAge(10);
saveCustomerToHibernate(customer);
```

---

[2]When comparing objects for equivalence, use equals(). It's like comparing two doorknobs: are the two *like* each other, or are they the same doorknob? The equals() method checks to see if they're alike. The == operator checks to see if they're the same.

Let's say the table originally contained the data shown in Table 5-3.

Table 5-3. *Updating an Ambiguous Table*

User	Age
dcminter	30
dcminter	42

Which of the following should be contained in the resulting table?

- A single row for the user dcminter, with the age set to 10

- Two rows for the user, with both ages set to 10

- Two rows for the user, with one age set to 10 and the other to 42

- Two rows for the user, with one age set to 10 and the other to 30

- Three rows for the user, with one age set to 10 and the others to 30 and 42

In short, the Hibernate developers made a decision to enforce the use of primary keys when creating mappings so that this problem does not arise. Hibernate does provide facilities that will allow you to work around this if it is absolutely necessary (you can create views or stored procedures to "fake" the appropriate key, or you can use conventional JDBC to access the table data), but when using Hibernate, it is always more desirable to work with tables that have correctly specified primary keys, if at all possible.

Lazy Loading

When you load classes into memory from the database, you don't necessarily want *all* the information to actually be loaded. To take an extreme example, loading a list of emails should not cause the full body text and attachments of every email to be loaded into memory. First, they might demand more memory than is actually available. Second, even if they fit, it would probably take a long time for all of this information to be obtained. (Remember, data normally goes from a database process to an application over the network, even if the database and application are on the same physical machine.)

If you were to tackle this problem in SQL, you would probably select a subset of the appropriate fields for the query to obtain the list, or limit the range of the data. Here's an example of selecting a subset of data:

```
SELECT from, to, date, subject FROM email WHERE username = 'dcminter';
```

Hibernate will allow you to fashion queries that are rather similar to this, but it also offers a more flexible approach, known as *lazy loading*. Certain relationships can be marked as being "lazy," and they will not be loaded from the database until they are actually required.

The default in Hibernate is that classes (including collections like Set and Map) should be lazily loaded. For example, when an instance of the User class given in the next listing is loaded from the database, the only fields initialized will be userId and username.[3]

---

[3]There are conditions for this. In most of the examples we've seen, where the majority of columns are accessed directly via their attribute references, lazy loading is very much the norm regardless of type. When in doubt, specify and test.

```
public class User {
    int userId;
    String username;
    EmailAddress emailAddress;
    Set<Role> roles;
}
```

With this definition, the appropriate objects for emailAddress and roles will be loaded from the database if and when they are accessed, provided the session is still active.

This is the default behavior only; mappings can be used to specify which classes and fields should behave in this way.

Associations

When we looked at why the mapping process could not be automated, we discussed the following example classes:

```
public class Customer {
    int customerId;
    int customerReference;
    String name;
    Email email;
}

public class Email {
    String address;
}
```

We also gave the following five questions that it raised:

- Is a unique customer identified by its customer ID, or its customer reference?

- Can a given email address be used by more than one customer?

- Should the relationship be represented in the Customer table?

- Should the relationship be represented in the Email table?

- Should the relationship be represented in some third (link) table?

The first question can be answered simply; it depends on what column you specify as the primary key. The remaining four questions are related, and their answers depend on the object relationships. Furthermore, if your Customer class represents the relationship with the EmailAddress using a Collection class or an array, it would be possible for a user to have multiple email addresses.

```
public class Customer {
    int customerId;
    int customerReference;
    String name;
    Set<Email> email;
}
```

So, you should add another question: Can a customer have more than one email address? The set could contain a single entry, so you can't automatically infer that this is the case.

The key questions from the previous options are as follows:

- *Q1*: Can an email address belong to more than one user?

- *Q2*: Can a customer have more than one email address?

The answers to these questions can be formed into a truth table, as shown in Table 5-4.

Table 5-4. *Deciding the Cardinality of an Entity Relationship*

Q1 Answer	Q2 Answer	Relationship Between Customer and Email
No	No	One-to-one
Yes	No	Many-to-one
No	Yes	One-to-many
Yes	Yes	Many-to-many

These are the four ways in which the cardinality[4] of the relationship between the objects can be expressed. Each relationship can then be represented within the mapping table(s) in various ways.

The One-to-One Association

A one-to-one association between classes can be represented in a variety of ways. At its simplest, the properties of both classes are maintained in the same table. For example, a one-to-one association between a User and an Email class might be represented as a single table, as in Table 5-5.

Table 5-5. *A Combined User/Email Table*

ID	Username	Email
1	dcminter	dcminter@example.com
2	jlinwood	jlinwood@example.com
3	tjkitchen	tjkitchen@example.com

The single database entity representing this combination of a User and an Email class is shown in Figure 5-4.

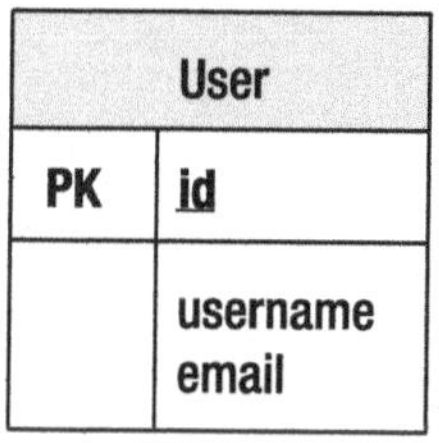

User	
PK	**id**
	username **email**

Figure 5-4. *A single entity representing a one-to-one relationship*

---

[4]*Cardinality* refers to numbering, so cardinality in relationships indicates how many of each participant is being referred to by either side of the relationship.

Alternatively, the entities can be maintained in distinct tables with identical primary keys, or with a key maintained from one of the entities into the other, as in Tables 5-6 and 5-7.

Table 5-6. The User Table

ID	Username
1	Dcminter
2	Jlinwood
3	Tjkitchen

Table 5-7. The Email Table

ID	Username
1	dcminter@example.com
2	jlinwood@example.com
3	tjkitchen@example.com

It is possible to create a mandatory foreign key relationship from one of the entities to the other, but this should not be applied in both directions because a circular dependency would then be created. It is also possible to omit the foreign key relationships entirely (as shown in Figure 5-5) and rely on Hibernate to manage the key selection and assignment.

Figure 5-5. Entities related by primary keys

If it is not appropriate for the tables to share primary keys, then a foreign key relationship between the two tables can be maintained, with a "unique" constraint applied to the foreign key column. For example, reusing the User table from Table 5-6, the Email table can be suitably populated, as shown in Table 5-8.

Table 5-8. An Email Table with a Foreign Key to the User Table

ID	Email	UserID (Unique)
34	dcminter@example.com	1
35	jlinwood@example.com	2
36	tjkitchen@example.com	3

This has the advantage that the association can easily be changed from one-to-one to many-to-one by removing the unique constraint. Figure 5-6 shows this type of relationship.

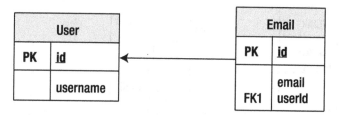

Figure 5-6. *Entities related by a foreign key relationship*

The One-to-Many and Many-to-One Association

A one-to-many association (or from the perspective of the other class, a many-to-one association) can most simply be represented by the use of a foreign key, with no additional constraints.

The relationship can also be maintained by the use of a link table. This will maintain a foreign key into each of the associated tables, which will itself form the primary key of the link table. An example of this is shown in Tables 5-9, 5-10, and 5-11.

Table 5-9. *A Simple User Table*

ID	Username
1	dcminter
2	jlinwood

Table 5-10. *A Simple Email Table*

ID	Email
1	dcminter@example.com
2	dave@example.com
3	jlinwood@example.com
4	jeff@example.com

Table 5-11. *A Link Table Joining User and Email in a One-to-Many Relationship*

UserID	EmailID
1	1
1	2
2	3
2	4

Additional columns can be added to the link table to maintain information on the ordering of the entities in the association.

A unique constraint must be applied to the "one" side of the relationship (the userId column of the UserEmailLink table in Figure 5-7); otherwise, the link table can represent the set of all possible relationships between User and Email entities, which is a many-to-many set association.

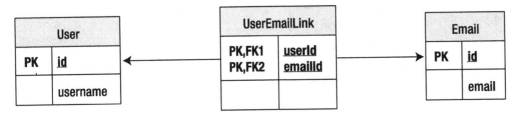

Figure 5-7. *A relationship represented by a link table (duplicates are not permitted because of the use of a compound primary key)*

The Many-to-Many Association

As noted at the end of the previous section, if a unique constraint is not applied to the "one" end of the relationship when using a link table, it becomes a limited sort of many-to-many relationship. All of the possible combinations of User and Email can be represented, but it is not possible for the same user to have the same e-mail address entity associated twice, because that would require the compound primary key to be duplicated.

If instead of using the foreign keys together as a compound primary key, we give the link table its own primary key (usually a surrogate key), the association between the two entities can be transformed into a full many-to-many relationship, as shown in Table 5-12.

Table 5-12. *A Many-to-Many User/Email Link Table*

ID	UserID	EmailID
1	1	1
2	1	2
3	1	3
4	1	4
5	2	1
6	2	2

Table 5-12 might describe a situation in which the user dcminter receives all email sent to any of the four addresses, whereas jlinwood receives only email sent to his own accounts.

When the link table has its own independent primary key, as with the association shown in Figure 5-8, thought should be given to the possibility that a new class needs to be created to represent the contents of the link table as an entity in its own right.

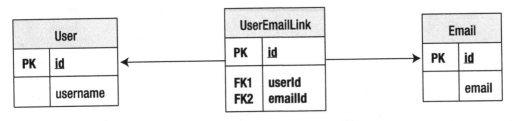

Figure 5-8. *A many-to-many relationship represented by a link table (duplicates are permitted because of the use of a surrogate key)*

Applying Mappings to Associations

The mappings are applied to express the various different ways of forming associations in the underlying tables; there is no absolutely correct way to represent them.[5]

In addition to the basic choice of approach to take, the mappings are used to specify the minutiae of the tables' representations. While Hibernate tends to use sensible default values when possible, it is often desirable to override these. For example, the foreign key names generated automatically by Hibernate will be effectively random, whereas an informed developer can apply a name (e.g., FK_USER_EMAIL_LINK) to aid in the debugging of constraint violations at run time.

Other Supported Features

While Hibernate can determine a lot of sensible default values for the mappings, most of these can be overridden by one or both of the annotation- and XML-based[6] approaches. Some apply directly to mapping; others, such as the foreign key names, are really only pertinent when the mapping is used to create the database schema. Lastly, some mappings can also provide a place to configure some features that are perhaps not "mappings" in the purest sense.

The final sections of this chapter discuss the features that Hibernate supports in addition to those already mentioned.

Specification of (Database) Column Types and Sizes

Java provides the primitive types and allows user declaration of interfaces and classes to extend these. Relational databases generally provide a small subset of "standard" types and then offer additional proprietary types.

Restricting yourself to the proprietary types will still cause problems, as there are only approximate correspondences between these and the Java primitive types.

A typical example of a problematic type is java.lang.String (treated by Hibernate as if it were a primitive type since it is used so frequently), which by default will be mapped to a fixed-size character data database type. Typically, the database would perform poorly if a character field of unlimited size were chosen, but lengthy String fields will be truncated as they are persisted into the database. In most databases, you would choose to represent a lengthy String field as a TEXT, CLOB, or long VARCHAR type (assuming the database supports the specific type). This is one of the reasons why Hibernate can't do all of the mapping for you and why you still need to understand some database fundamentals when you create an application that uses ORM.

By specifying mapping details, the developer can make appropriate trade-offs among storage space, performance, and fidelity to the original Java representation.

The Mapping of Inheritance Relationships to the Database

There is no SQL standard for representing inheritance relationships for the data in tables; and while some database implementations provide a proprietary syntax for this, not all do. Hibernate offers several configurable ways in which to represent inheritance relationships, and the mapping permits users to select a suitable approach for their model.

---

[5]This is why otherwise fantastic tools like Hibernate haven't replaced good database analysts.
[6]We haven't actually spent much time in XML configuration for a very good reason: most people don't use it in the real world unless they absolutely have to. It's also excessively verbose, especially compared to the annotations.

Primary Key

As stated earlier in this chapter (in the section entitled "Primary Keys," of all things), Hibernate demands that a primary key be used to identify entities. The choice of a surrogate key, a key chosen from the business data, and/or a compound primary key can be made via configuration.

When a surrogate key is used, Hibernate also permits the key-generation technique to be selected from a range of techniques that vary in portability and efficiency. (This was shown in Chapter 4, in "Identifiers.")

The Use of SQL Formula–Based Properties

It is sometimes desirable that a property of an entity be maintained not as data directly stored in the database but, rather, as a function performed on that data—for example, a subtotal field should not be managed directly by the Java logic, but instead be maintained as an aggregate function of some other property.

Mandatory and Unique Constraints

As well as the implicit constraints of a primary or foreign key relationship, you can specify that a field must not be duplicated—for example, a username field should often be unique.

Fields can also be made mandatory—for example, requiring a message entity to have both a subject and message text.

The generated database schema will contain corresponding NOT NULL and UNIQUE constraints so that it is very, very difficult to corrupt the table with invalid data (rather, the application logic will throw an exception if any attempt to do so is made).

Note that primary keys are implicitly both mandatory and unique.

Summary

This chapter has given you an overview of the reason why mappings are needed, and what features they support beyond these absolute requirements. It has discussed the various types of associations and the circumstances under which you would choose to use them.

The next chapter looks at how mappings are specified.

CHAPTER 6

■ ■ ■

Mapping with Annotations

In Chapter 5, we discussed the need to create mappings between the database model and the object model. Mappings can be created in two different ways: via inline annotations (as we've done through the book so far), or as separate XML files in one of two primary formats.

The XML-based mapping is rarely used outside of situations where mapping an object model to a preexisting schema is required; even then, adept use of the annotations can match the XML configuration's features.

Creating Hibernate Mappings with Annotations

Prior to the inline annotations, the only way to create mappings was through XML files—although tools from Hibernate and third-party projects allowed part or all of these to be generated from Java source code. Although using annotations is the newest way to define mappings, it is not automatically the best way to do so. We will briefly discuss the drawbacks and benefits of annotations before discussing when and how to apply them.

The Cons of Annotations

If you are upgrading from a Hibernate 2 environment or working with an existing Hibernate 3 environment, you will already have XML-based mapping files to support your code base. All else being equal, you will not want to re-express these mappings using annotations just for the sake of it.

If you are migrating from a legacy environment, you may not want to alter the preexisting POJO source code, lest you contaminate known good code with possible bugs.[1]

If you do not have the source code to your POJOs (because it was generated by an automated tool or something similar), you may prefer the use of external XML-based mappings to the decompilation of class files to obtain Java source code for alteration.

Maintaining the mapping information as external XML files allows that mapping information to be modified to reflect business changes or schema alterations without forcing you to rebuild the application as a whole.

The Pros of Annotations

Having considered the drawbacks, there are some powerful benefits to using annotations.

First, and perhaps most persuasively, we find annotations-based mappings to be far more intuitive than their XML-based alternatives, as they are immediately in the source code along with the properties with which they are associated. Most coders tend to prefer the annotations because fewer files have to be kept synchronized with each other.

---

[1]There's probably value in creating tests for your object model, which would, you hope, eliminate this as a concern, but there's no point in creating extra work for its own sake.

Partly as a result of this, annotations are less verbose than their XML equivalents, as evidenced by the contrast between Listings 6-1 and 6-2.

Listing 6-1. A Minimal Class Mapped Using Annotations

```
import javax.persistence.* ;

@Entity
public class Sample {
    @Id
    @GeneratedValue(strategy = GenerationType.IDENTITY)
    public Integer id;
    public String name;
}
```

Listing 6-2. A Minimal Class Mapped Using XML

```
<?xml version='1.0' encoding='utf-8'?>
<!DOCTYPE
    hibernate-mapping
    PUBLIC
    "-//Hibernate/Hibernate Mapping DTD//EN"
    "http://hibernate.sourceforge.net/hibernate-mapping-3.0.dtd">

<hibernate-mapping default-access="field">
    <class name="Sample">
        <id type="int" column="id">
            <generator class="native"/>
        </id>
        <property name="name" type="string"/>
    </class>
</hibernate-mapping>
```

Some of the latter's verbosity is in the nature of XML itself (the tag names and the boilerplate document-type declaration), and some of it is due to the closer integration of annotations with the source code. Here, for example, the XML file must explicitly declare that field access is used in place of property access (i.e., the fields are accessed directly rather than through their get/set methods); but the annotation infers this from the fact that it has been applied to the id field rather than the getId() method.

Hibernate uses and supports the JPA 2 persistence annotations. If you elect not to use Hibernate-specific features in your code and annotations, you will have the freedom to deploy your entities to environments using other ORM tools that support JPA 2.

Finally—and perhaps a minor point—because the annotations are compiled directly into the appropriate class files, there is less risk that a missing or stale mapping file will cause problems at deployment (this point will perhaps prove most persuasive to those who already have some experience with this hazard of the XML technique).

Choosing Which to Use

In general, prefer annotations; the annotations themselves are portable across JPA implementations, and they're well known. Tools can create the annotated source code directly from a database, so synchronization is less of an issue than it could be, even with a preexisting schema.

The XML mapping can be done either in Hibernate's proprietary format or JPA's standard XML configuration, which is similar but not identical; if you somehow find XML to be a preferable configuration format, you're probably better off using the XML format from the industry-standard JPA configuration.[2]

JPA 2 Persistence Annotations

When you develop using annotations, you start with a Java class and then annotate the source code listing with metadata notations. The Java Runtime Environment (JRE) parses these annotations. Hibernate uses Java reflection to read the annotations and apply the mapping information. If you want to use the Hibernate tools to generate your database schema, you must first compile your entity classes containing their annotations.In this section, we are going to introduce the significant core of the JPA 2 annotations alongside a simple set of classes to illustrate how they are applied.

The set of example classes represents a publisher's catalog of books. You start with a single class, Book, which has no annotations or mapping information. For purposes of this example, you do not have an existing database schema to work with, so you need to define your relational database schema as you go.

At the beginning of the example, the Book class is very simple. It has two fields, title and pages; and an identifier, id, which is an integer. The title is a String object, and pages is an integer. As we go through this example, we will add annotations, fields, and methods to the Book class. The complete source code listing for the Book and Author classes is given at the end of this chapter; the source files for the rest are available in the source code download for this chapter on the Apress web site (www.apress.com).

Listing 6-3 gives the source code of the Book class, in its unannotated form, as a starting point for the example.

Listing 6-3. The Book Class, Unannotated

```
ppackage chapter06.primarykey.before;

public class Book {
    String title;
    int pages;
    int id;

    public String getTitle() {
        return title;
    }

    public void setTitle(String title) {
        this.title = title;
    }

    public int getPages() {
        return pages;
    }

    public void setPages(int pages) {
        this.pages = pages;
    }
```

---

[2]The JPA configuration was largely derived from Hibernate's configuration specification, which preceded JPA.

```
    public int getId() {
        return id;
    }

    public void setId(int id) {
        this.id = id;
    }
}
```

As you can see, this is a POJO. We are going to annotate this class as we go along, explaining the concepts behind annotation. In the end, we'll move it to a different package so that we'll have a good before-and-after picture of what the entity should be.

Entity Beans with @Entity

The first step is to annotate the Book class as a JPA 2 entity bean. We add the @Entity annotation to the Book class, as follows:

```
package chapter06.primarykey.after;

import javax.persistence.*;

@Entity
public class Book
    public Book() {
    }
```

The JPA 2 standard annotations are contained in the javax.persistence package, so we import the appropriate annotations. Some IDEs will use specific imports, as opposed to "star imports," in situations where few classes in a given package are imported; typically, an entity will use quite a few annotations from *this* package so chances are it'll end up with star imports in any event.

The @Entity annotation marks this class as an entity bean, so it must have a no-argument constructor that is visible with at least protected scope.[3] Hibernate supports package scope as the minimum, but you lose portability to other JPA implementations if you take advantage of this. Other JPA 2 rules for an entity bean class are (1) that the class must not be final, and (2) that the entity bean class must be concrete. Many of the rules for JPA 2 entity bean classes and Hibernate's persistent objects are the same—partly because the Hibernate team had much input into the JPA 2 design process, and partly because there are only so many ways to design a relatively unobtrusive object-relational persistence solution.

So far, we've added the Entity annotation, a constructor, and an import statement. The rest of the POJO has been left alone.

Primary Keys with @Id and @GeneratedValue

Each entity bean has to have a primary key, which you annotate on the class with the @Id annotation. Typically, the primary key will be a single field, though it can also be a composite of multiple fields.

The placement of the @Id annotation determines the default access strategy that Hibernate will use for the mapping. If the annotation is applied to a field as shown in Listing 6-4, then field access will be used.

---

[3]Naturally, there's a way around this. The normal requirement is to have a no-argument constructor; interceptors allow you to not have to do this.

Listing 6-4. A Class with Field Access

```java
import javax.persistence.*;

@Entity
public class Sample {
    @Id
    int id;

    public int getId() {
        return this.id;
    }

    public void setId(int id) {
        this.id = id;
    }
}
```

If, instead, the annotation is applied to the accessor for the field, as shown in Listing 6-5, then property access will be used. *Property access* means that Hibernate will call the mutator instead of actually setting the field directly; this also means the mutator can alter the value as it's being set, or change other state available in the object. Which one you choose depends on your preference and need; usually field access is enough.[4]

Listing 6-5. The Same Class with Property Access

```java
import javax.persistence.*;

@Entity
public class Sample {
    int id;

    @Id
    public int getId() {
        return this.id;
    }

    public void setId(int id) {
        this.id = id;
    }
}
```

Here you can see one of the strengths of the annotations approach. Because the annotations are placed inline with the source code, information can be extracted from the context of the mapping in the code, allowing many mapping decisions to be inferred rather than stated explicitly—which helps to further reduce the verbosity of the annotations.

By default, the @Id annotation will not create a primary key generation strategy,[5] which means that you, as the code's author, need to determine what valid primary keys are. You can have Hibernate determine primary keys for you through the use of the @GeneratedValue annotation. This takes a pair of attributes: strategy and generator.

---

[4] The reasoning here is that if you needed something to be part of the object's state, you'd include it in the database, which would mean you wouldn't *need* to set it when the object was instantiated. With that said, your mileage may vary; do what works for you.
[5] Actually, the default generator is the "assigned" generator, which means the application is responsible for assigning the primary key before save() is called. This ends up having the same effect as if no key generation is specified.

The strategy attribute must be a value from the javax.persistence.GeneratorType enumeration. If you do not specify a generator type, the default is AUTO. There are four different types of primary key generators on GeneratorType, as follows:

- AUTO: Hibernate decides which generator type to use, based on the database's support for primary key generation.

- IDENTITY: The database is responsible for determining and assigning the next primary key.

- SEQUENCE: Some databases support a SEQUENCE column type. See the "Generating Primary Key Values with @SequenceGenerator" section later in the chapter.

- TABLE: This type keeps a separate table with the primary key values. See the "Generating Primary Key Values with @TableGenerator" section later in the chapter.

The generator attribute allows the use of a custom generation mechanism. Hibernate provides named generators for each of the four strategies in addition to others, such as "hilo," "uuid," and "guid." If you need to use Hibernate-specific primary key generators, you risk forfeiting portability of your application to other JPA 2 environments; that said, the Hibernate generators provide more flexibility and control.

For the Book class, we are going to use the AUTO key generation strategy. Letting Hibernate determine which generator type to use makes your code portable between different databases.

```
@Id
@GeneratedValue(strategy=GenerationType.AUTO)
int id;
```

Generating Primary Key Values with @SequenceGenerator

As noted in the section on the @Id tag, we can declare the primary key property as being generated by a database sequence. A *sequence* is a database object that can be used as a source of primary key values. It is similar to the use of an identity column type, except that a sequence is independent of any particular table and can therefore be used by multiple tables.

To declare the specific sequence object to use and its properties, you must include the @SequenceGenerator annotation on the annotated field. Here's an example:

```
@Id
@SequenceGenerator(name="seq1",sequenceName="HIB_SEQ")
@GeneratedValue(strategy=SEQUENCE,generator="seq1")
int id;
```

Here, a sequence-generation annotation named seq1 has been declared. This refers to the database sequence object called HIB_SEQ. The name seq1 is then referenced as the generator attribute of the @GeneratedValue annotation.

Only the sequence generator name is mandatory; the other attributes will take sensible default values, but you should provide an explicit value for the sequenceName attribute as a matter of good practice anyway. If not specified, the sequenceName value to be used is selected by the persistence provider (in this case, Hibernate). The other (optional) attributes are initialValue (the generator starts with this number) and allocationSize (the number of ids in the sequence reserved at a time); these default to values of 1 and 50, respectively.

Generating Primary Key Values with @TableGenerator

The @TableGenerator annotation is used in a very similar way to the @SequenceGenerator annotation, but because @TableGenerator manipulates a standard database table to obtain its primary key values, instead of using a vendor-specific sequence object, it is guaranteed to be portable between database platforms.

Note For optimal portability *and* optimal performance, you should not specify the use of a table generator, but instead use the @GeneratorValue(strategy=GeneratorType.AUTO) configuration, which allows the persistence provider to select the most appropriate strategy for the database in use.

As with the sequence generator, the name attributes of @TableGenerator are mandatory and the other attributes are optional, with the table details being selected by the persistence provider:

```
@Id
@TableGenerator(name="tablegen",
                table="ID_TABLE",
                pkColumnName="ID",
                valueColumnName="NEXT_ID")
@GeneratedValue(strategy=TABLE,generator="tablegen")
int id;
```

The optional attributes are as follows:

- allocationSize: Allows the number of primary keys set aside at one time to be tuned for performance.

- catalog: Allows the catalog that the table resides within to be specified.

- initialValue: Allows the starting primary key value to be specified.

- pkColumnName: Allows the primary key column of the table to be identified. The table can contain the details necessary for generating primary key values for multiple entities.

- pkColumnValue: Allows the primary key for the row containing the primary key generation information to be identified.

- schema: Allows the schema that the table resides within to be specified.

- table: The name of the table containing the primary key values.

- uniqueConstraints: Allows additional constraints to be applied to the table for schema generation.

- valueColumnName: Allows the column containing the primary key generation information for the current entity to be identified.

Because the table can be used to contain the primary key values for a variety of entries, it is likely to have a single row for each of the entities using it. It therefore needs its own primary key (pkColumnName), as well as a column containing the next primary key value to be used (pkColumnValue) for any of the entities obtaining their primary keys from it.

Compound Primary Keys with @Id, @IdClass, or @EmbeddedId

While the use of single-column surrogate keys is advantageous for various reasons, you may sometimes be forced to work with business keys. When these are contained in a single column, you can use @Id without specifying a generation strategy (forcing the user to assign a primary key value before the entity can be persisted). However, when the primary key consists of multiple columns, you need to take a different strategy to group these together in a way that allows the persistence engine to manipulate the key values as a single object.

You must create a class to represent this primary key. It will not require a primary key of its own, of course, but it must be a public class, must have a default constructor, must be serializable, and must implement hashCode() and equals() methods to allow the Hibernate code to test for primary key collisions (i.e., they must be implemented with the appropriate database semantics for the primary key values).

Your three strategies for using this primary key class once it has been created are as follows:

1. Mark it as @Embeddable and add to your entity class a normal property for it, marked with @Id.

2. Add to your entity class a normal property for it, marked with @EmbeddableId.

3. Add properties to your entity class for all of its fields, mark them with @Id, and mark your entity class with @IdClass, supplying the class of your primary key class.

All these techniques require the use of an id class because Hibernate must be supplied with a primary key object when various parts of its persistence API are invoked. For example, you can retrieve an instance of an entity by invoking the Session object's get() method, which takes as its parameter a single serializable object representing the entity's primary key.

The use of @Id with a class marked as @Embeddable, as shown in Listing 6-6, is the most natural approach. The @Embeddable tag can be used for nonprimary key embeddable values anyway (@Embeddable is discussed in more detail later in the chapter). It allows you to treat the compound primary key as a single property, and it permits the reuse of the @Embeddable class in other tables.

One thing worth pointing out: the embedded primary key classes must be serializable (i.e., they must implement java.io.Serializable, although it's possible you could use java.io.Externalizable as well[6]).

Listing 6-6. Using the @Id and @Embeddable Annotations to Map a Compound Primary Key: The CPKBook

```
package chapter06.compoundpk;

import javax.persistence.Column;
import javax.persistence.Entity;
import javax.persistence.Id;

@Entity
public class CPKBook {
    @Id
    ISBN id;
    @Column
    String name;

    public CPKBook() {
    }

    public ISBN getId() {
        return id;
    }

    public void setId(ISBN id) {
        this.id = id;
    }
```

---

[6]Serializable relies on Java's introspection to serialize and deserialize data. Externalizable forces the author to implement explicit serialization mechanisms. Externalizable can be far faster, but this doesn't give you any real benefits in this case.

```
    public String getName() {
        return name;
    }

    public void setName(String title) {
        this.name = title;
    }
}
```

The next most natural approach is the use of the @EmbeddedId tag. Here, the primary key class cannot be used in other tables since it is not an @Embeddable entity, but it does allow us to treat the key as a single attribute of the Account class (in Listings 6-7 and 6-8, the implementation of AccountPk is identical to that in Listing 6-6, and is thus omitted for brevity). Note that in Listings 6-7 and 6-8, the AccountPk class is *not* marked as @Embeddable.

Listing 6- 7. Using the @Id and @Embeddable Annotations to Map a Compound Primary Key: The ISBN

```
package chapter06.compoundpk;

import javax.persistence.Embeddable;
import java.io.Serializable;

@Embeddable
public class ISBN implements Serializable {
    @Column(name="group_number") // because "group" is an invalid column name for SQL
    int group;
    int publisher;
    int title;
    int checkdigit;

    public ISBN() {
    }

    public int getGroup() {
        return group;
    }

    public void setGroup(int group) {
        this.group = group;
    }

    public int getPublisher() {
        return publisher;
    }

    public void setPublisher(int publisher) {
        this.publisher = publisher;
    }
```

```java
    public int getTitle() {
        return title;
    }

    public void setTitle(int title) {
        this.title = title;
    }

    public int getCheckdigit() {
        return checkdigit;
    }

    public void setCheckdigit(int checkdigit) {
        this.checkdigit = checkdigit;
    }

    @Override
    public boolean equals(Object o) {
        if (this == o) return true;
        if (!(o instanceof ISBN)) return false;

        ISBN isbn = (ISBN) o;

        if (checkdigit != isbn.checkdigit) return false;
        if (group != isbn.group) return false;
        if (publisher != isbn.publisher) return false;
        if (title != isbn.title) return false;

        return true;
    }

    @Override
    public int hashCode() {
        int result = group;
        result = 31 * result + publisher;
        result = 31 * result + title;
        result = 31 * result + checkdigit;
        return result;
    }
}
```

■ **Note** The use of `@Column(name="group_number")` in the ISBN class will be discussed further, in "Mapping Properties and Fields with `@Column`" later in this chapter; this is required here because "group"—the natural column name for this field—is an invalid column name for SQL. We're going to be seeing more embedded primary keys with the same format, and this annotation will be used in them, as well.

Listing 6-8. Using the @EmbeddedId Annotation to Map a Compound Primary Key

```
package chapter06.compoundpk;

import javax.persistence.Column;
import javax.persistence.EmbeddedId;
import javax.persistence.Entity;
import java.io.Serializable;

@Entity
public class EmbeddedPKBook {
    @EmbeddedId
    EmbeddedISBN id;
    @Column
    String name;

    static class EmbeddedISBN implements Serializable {
    // looks fundamentally the same as the ISBN class from Listing 6-7
    }
}
```

Finally, the use of the @IdClass and @Id annotations allows us to map the compound primary key class using properties of the entity itself corresponding to the names of the properties in the primary key class. The names must correspond (there is no mechanism for overriding this), and the primary key class must honor the same obligations as with the other two techniques. The only advantage to this approach is its ability to "hide" the use of the primary key class from the interface of the enclosing entity.

The @IdClass annotation takes a value parameter of Class type, which must be the class to be used as the compound primary key. The fields that correspond to the properties of the primary key class to be used must all be annotated with @Id—note in Listing 6-9 that the getCode() and getNumber() methods of the Account class are so annotated, and the AccountPk class is not mapped as @Embeddable, but it is supplied as the value of the @IdClass annotation.

Listing 6-9. Using the @IdClass and @Id Annotations to Map a Compound Primary Key

```
package chapter06.compoundpk;

import javax.persistence.Entity;
import javax.persistence.Id;
import javax.persistence.IdClass;
import java.io.Serializable;

@Entity
@IdClass(IdClassBook.EmbeddedISBN.class)
public class IdClassBook {
    @Id
    int group;
    @Id
    int publisher;
    @Id
    int title;
    @Id
    int checkdigit;
    String name;
```

```
    public IdClassBook() {
    }

    public int getGroup() {
        return group;
    }

    public void setGroup(int group) {
        this.group = group;
    }

    public int getPublisher() {
        return publisher;
    }

    public void setPublisher(int publisher) {
        this.publisher = publisher;
    }

    public int getTitle() {
        return title;
    }

    public void setTitle(int title) {
        this.title = title;
    }

    public int getCheckdigit() {
        return checkdigit;
    }

    public void setCheckdigit(int checkdigit) {
        this.checkdigit = checkdigit;
    }

    public String getName() {
        return name;
    }

    public void setName(String name) {
        this.name = name;
    }

    static class Emb eddedISBN implements Serializable {
    // identical to EmbeddedISBN from Listing 6-8
    }
}
```

Regardless of which of these approaches we take to declare our compound primary key, the table that will be used to represent it will require the same set of columns. Listing 6-10 shows the DDL that will be generated from Listings 6-7, 6-8, and 6-9; the other table names would differ, but the DDL for each table would be the same.

Listing 6-10. The DDL Generated from the CPKBook Class

```
create table CPKBook (
    checkdigit integer not null,
    group integer not null,
    publisher integer not null,
    title integer not null,
    name varchar(255),
    primary key (checkdigit, group, publisher, title)
)
```

Database Table Mapping with @Table and @SecondaryTable

By default, table names are derived from the entity names. Therefore, given a class Book with a simple @Entity annotation, the table name would be "book," adjusted for the database's configuration.

If the entity name is changed (by providing a different name in the @Entity annotation, such as @Entity("BookThing")), the new name will be used for the table name. (Queries would need to use the entity name; from the user's perspective, the table name would be irrelevant.)

The table name can be customized further, and other database-related attributes can be configured via the @Table annotation. This annotation allows you to specify many of the details of the table that will be used to persist the entity in the database. As already pointed out, if you omit the annotation, Hibernate will default to using the class name for the table name, so you need only provide this annotation if you want to override that behavior.

The @Table annotation provides four attributes, allowing you to override the name of the table, its catalog, and its schema, and to enforce unique constraints on columns in the table. Typically, you would only provide a substitute table name thus: @Table(name="ORDER_HISTORY"). The unique constraints will be applied if the database schema is generated from the annotated classes, and will supplement any column-specific constraints (see discussions of @Column and @JoinColumn later in this chapter). They are not otherwise enforced.

The @SecondaryTable annotation provides a way to model an entity bean that is persisted across several different database tables. Here, in addition to providing an @Table annotation for the primary database table, your entity bean can have an @SecondaryTable annotation, or an @SecondaryTables annotation in turn containing zero or more @SecondaryTable annotations. The @SecondaryTable annotation takes the same basic attributes as the @Table annotation, with the addition of the join attribute. The join attribute defines the join column for the primary database table. It accepts an array of javax.persistence.PrimaryKeyJoinColumn objects. If you omit the join attribute, then it will be assumed that the tables are joined on identically named primary key columns.

When an attribute in the entity is drawn from the secondary table, it must be marked with the @Column annotation, with a table attribute identifying the appropriate table. Listing 6-11 shows how a property of the Customer entity could be drawn from a second table mapped in this way.

Listing 6-11. An Example of a Field Access Entity Mapped Across Two Tables

```
package chapter06.twotables;

import javax.persistence.*;

@Entity
@Table(name = "customer")
@SecondaryTable(name = "customer_details")
public class Customer {
    @Id
    public int id;
```

```
    public String name;
    @Column(table = "customer_details")
    public String address;

    public Customer() {
    }
}
```

Columns in the primary or secondary tables can be marked as having unique values within their tables by adding one or more appropriate @UniqueConstraint annotations to @Table or @SecondaryTable's uniqueConstraints attribute. You may also set uniqueness at the field level with the unique attribute on the @Column attribute. For example, to mark the name field in the preceding declaration as being unique, use the following:

```
@Entity
@Table(
    name="customer",
    uniqueConstraints={@UniqueConstraint(columnNames="name")}
)
@SecondaryTable(name="customer_details")
public class Customer {
    ...
}
```

Persisting Basic Types with @Basic

By default, properties and instance variables in your POJO are persistent; Hibernate will store their values for you. The simplest mappings are therefore for the "basic" types. These include primitives, primitive wrappers, arrays of primitives or wrappers, enumerations, and any types that implement Serializable but are not themselves mapped entities. These are all mapped implicitly—no annotation is needed. By default, such fields are mapped to a single column, and eager fetching is used to retrieve them (i.e., when the entity is retrieved from the database, all the basic fields and properties are retrieved[7]). Also, when the field or property is not a primitive, it can be stored and retrieved as a null value.

This default behavior can be overridden by applying the @Basic annotation to the appropriate class member. The annotation takes two optional attributes, and is itself entirely optional. The first attribute is named optional and takes a boolean. Defaulting to true, this can be set to false to provide a hint to schema generation that the associated column should be created NOT NULL. The second is named fetch and takes a member of the enumeration FetchType. This is EAGER by default, but can be set to LAZY to permit loading on access of the value.

The use of lazy loading is unlikely to be valuable, except when large serializable objects have been mapped as basic types (rather than given entity mappings of their own) and retrieval time may become significant. While the (default) EAGER value must be honored, the LAZY flag is considered to be a hint, and can be ignored by the persistence engine.

The @Basic attribute is usually omitted, with the @Column attribute being used where the @Basic annotation's optional attribute might otherwise be used to provide the NOT NULL behavior.

---

[7]However, the data for the class might not be initialized yet. When an instance is loaded from the session, the data might have been retrieved eagerly, but the object won't be initialized until something in it has been requested. This can yield some "interesting" behaviors, some of which were exposed in the previous chapters.

Omitting Persistence with @Transient

Some fields, such as calculated values, may be used at run time only, and they should be discarded from objects as they are persisted into the database. The JPA specification provides the @Transient annotation for these transient fields. The @Transient annotation does not have any attributes—you just add it to the instance variable or the getter method as appropriate for the entity bean's property access strategy.

The @Transient annotation highlights one of the more important differences between using annotations with Hibernate and using XML mapping documents. With annotations, Hibernate will default to persisting all of the fields on a mapped object. When using XML mapping documents, Hibernate requires you to tell it explicitly which fields will be persisted.[8]

For our example, if we wanted to add a Date field named publicationDate, not be stored in the database to our Book class, we could mark this field transient thus:

```
@Transient
Date publicationDate;
```

If we are using a property access strategy for our Book class, we would need to put the @Transient annotation on the accessor instead.

Mapping Properties and Fields with @Column

The @Column annotation is used to specify the details of the column to which a field or property will be mapped. Some of the details are schema related, and therefore apply only if the schema is generated from the annotated files. Others apply and are enforced at run time by Hibernate (or the JPA 2 persistence engine). It is optional, with an appropriate set of default behaviors, but is often useful when overriding default behavior, or when you need to fit your object model into a preexisting schema. It is more commonly used than the similar @Basic annotation, with the following attributes commonly being overridden:

- name permits the name of the column to be explicitly specified—by default, this would be the name of the property. However, it is often necessary to override the default behavior when it would otherwise result in an SQL keyword being used as the column name (e.g., user).

- length permits the size of the column used to map a value (particularly a String value) to be explicitly defined. The column size defaults to 255, which might otherwise result in truncated String data, for example.

- nullable permits the column to be marked NOT NULL when the schema is generated. The default is that fields should be permitted to be null; however, it is common to override this when a field is, or ought to be, mandatory.

- unique permits the column to be marked as containing only unique values. This defaults to false, but commonly would be set for a value that might not be a primary key but would still cause problems if duplicated (such as username).

We have marked up the title field of our Book entity using the @Column entity to show how three of these attributes would be applied:

```
@Column(name="working_title",length=200,nullable=false)
String title;
```

---

[8]This is not an endorsement of XML configuration. Use @Transient instead.

The remaining attributes, less commonly used, are as follows:

- `table` is used when the owning entity has been mapped across one or more secondary tables. By default, the value is assumed to be drawn from the primary table, but the name of one of the secondary tables can be substituted here (see the `@SecondaryTable` annotation example earlier in this chapter).

- `insertable` defaults to `true`, but if set to `false`, the annotated field will be omitted from insert statements generated by Hibernate (i.e., it won't be persisted).

- `updatable` defaults to `true`, but if set to `false`, the annotated field will be omitted from update statements generated by Hibernate (i.e., it won't be altered once it has been persisted).

- `columnDefinition` can be set to an appropriate DDL fragment to be used when generating the column in the database. This can only be used during schema generation from the annotated entity, and should be avoided if possible, since it is likely to reduce the portability of your application between database dialects.

- `precision` permits the precision of decimal numeric columns to be specified for schema generation, and will be ignored when a nondecimal value is persisted. The value given represents the number of digits in the number (usually requiring a minimum length of $n+1$, where n is the scale).

- `scale` permits the scale of decimal numeric columns to be specified for schema generation and will be ignored where a nondecimal value is persisted. The value given represents the number of places after the decimal point.

Modeling Entity Relationships

Naturally, annotations also allow you to model associations between entities. JPA 2 supports one-to-one, one-to-many, many-to-one, and many-to-many associations. Each of these has its corresponding annotation.

We discussed the various ways in which these mappings can be established in the tables in Chapter 5. In this section, we will show how the various mappings are requested using the annotations.

Mapping an Embedded (Component) One-to-One Association

When all the fields of one entity are maintained within the same table as another, the enclosed entity is referred to in Hibernate as a *component*. The JPA standard refers to such an entity as being *embedded*.

The `@Embedded` and `@Embeddable` attributes are used to manage this relationship. In this chapter's example of primary keys, we associate an `ISBN` class with a `Book` class in this way.

The `ISBN` class is marked with the `@Embeddable` annotation. An embeddable entity must be composed entirely of basic fields and attributes. An embeddable entity can only use the `@Basic`, `@Column`, `@Lob`, `@Temporal`, and `@Enumerated` annotations. It cannot maintain its own primary key with the `@Id` tag because its primary key is the primary key of the enclosing entity.

The `@Embeddable` annotation itself is purely a marker annotation, and it takes no additional attributes, as demonstrated in Listing 6-12. Typically, the fields and properties of the embeddable entity need no further markup.[9]

Listing 6-12. Marking an Entity for Embedding Within Other Entities

```
@Embeddable
public class AuthorAddress {
    ...
}
```

---

[9]The ISBN example required an additional annotation for "group" because *group* is a reserved word in SQL.

The enclosing entity then marks appropriate fields or getters in entities, making use of the embeddable class with the @Embedded annotation, as shown in Listing 6-13.

Listing 6-13. Marking an Embedded Property

```
@Embedded
AuthorAddress address;
```

The @Embedded annotation draws its column information from the embedded type, but permits the overriding of a specific column or columns with the @AttributeOverride and @AttributeOverrides tags (the latter to enclose an array of the former if multiple columns are being overridden). For example, Listing 6-14 shows how to override the default column names of the address and country attributes of AuthorAddress with columns named ADDR and NATION.

Listing 6-14. Overriding Default Attributes of an Embedded Property

```
@Embedded
@AttributeOverrides({
    @AttributeOverride(name="address",column=@Column(name="ADDR")),
    @AttributeOverride(name="country",column=@Column(name="NATION"))
})
AuthorAddress address;
```

Neither Hibernate nor the JPA standard supports mapping an embedded object across more than one table. In practice, if you want this sort of persistence for your embedded entity, you will usually be better off making it a first-class entity (i.e., *not* embedded) with its own @Entity marker and @Id annotations, and then mapping it via a conventional one-to-one association, as explained in the next section.

Mapping a Conventional One-to-One Association

There is nothing intrinsically wrong with mapping a one-to-one association between two entities where one is not a component of (i.e., embedded into) the other. The relationship is often somewhat suspect, however. You should give some thought to using the embedded technique described previously before using the @OneToOne annotation.

You can have a bidirectional relationship with a one-to-one association. One side will need to own the relationship and be responsible for updating a join column with a foreign key to the other side. The nonowning side will need to use the mappedBy attribute to indicate the entity that owns the relationship.

Assuming that you are resolute on declaring the association in this way (perhaps because you anticipate converting it to a one-to-many or many-to-one relationship in the foreseeable future), applying the annotation is quite simple—all of the attributes are optional. Listing 6-15 shows how simply a relationship like this might be declared.

Listing 6-15. Declaring a Simple One-to-One Relationship

```
@OneToOne
Address address;
```

The @OneToOne annotation permits the following optional attributes to be specified:

- targetEntity can be set to the class of an entity storing the association. If left unset, the appropriate type will be inferred from the field type, or the return type of the property's getter.

- cascade can be set to any of the members of the javax.persistence.CascadeType enumeration. It defaults to none being set. See the "Cascading Operations" sidebar for a discussion of these values.

- `fetch` can be set to the EAGER or LAZY members of `FetchType`.

- `optional` indicates whether the value being mapped can be null.

- `orphanRemoval` indicates that if the value being mapped is deleted, this entity will also be deleted.

- `mappedBy` indicates that a bidirectional one-to-one relationship is owned by the named entity.[10] The owning entity contains the primary key of the subordinate entity.

Mapping a Many-to-One or One-to-Many Association

A many-to-one association and a one-to-many association are the same association seen from the perspective of the owning and subordinate entities, respectively.

CASCADING OPERATIONS

When an association between two entities is established (such as a one-to-one association between Human and Pet or a one-to-many association between Customer and Orders), it is common to want certain persistence operations on one entity to also be applied to the entity that it is linked to. Take, for example, the following code:

```
Human dave = new Human("dave");
Pet cat = new PetCat("Tibbles");
dave.setPet(cat);
session.save(dave);
```

In the last line, we are likely to want to save the Pet object associated with the Human object. In a one-to-one relationship, we usually expect all operations on the owning entity to be propagated through—that is, to be *cascaded to*—the dependent entity. In other associations this is not true, and even in a one-to-one relationship we may have special reasons for wanting to spare the dependent entity from delete operations (perhaps for auditing reasons).

We are therefore able to specify the types of operations that should be cascaded through an association to another entity using the cascade annotation, which takes an array of members of the `CascadeType` enumeration. The members correspond with the names of the key methods of the `EntityManager` class used for EJB 3 persistence, and have the following rough correspondence with operations on entities:

- ALL requires all operations to be cascaded to dependent entities. This is the same as including `MERGE`, `PERSIST`, `REFRESH`, `DETACH`, and `REMOVE`.

- MERGE cascades updates to the entity's state in the database (i.e., `UPDATE...`).

- PERSIST cascades the initial storing of the entity's state in the database (i.e., `INSERT...`).

- REFRESH cascades the updating of the entity's state from the database (i.e., `SELECT...`).

---

[10]An association is bidirectional if each entity maintains a property or field representing its end of the same relationship. For example, if our Address**<au: code here?>** class maintained a reference to the Publisher located there, and the Publisher**<au: code?>** class maintained a reference to its Address, then the association would be bidirectional.

- DETACH cascades the removal of the entity from the managed persistence context.

- REMOVE cascades deletion of the entity from the database (i.e., DELETE...).

- If no cascade type is specified, no operations will be cascaded through the association.

In the light of these options, the appropriate annotation for the relationship between a publisher and its address would be as follows:

```
@OneToOne(cascade=CascadeType.ALL)
Address address;
```

The simplest way to maintain a many-to-one relationship between two entities is by managing the foreign key of the entity at the "one" end of the one-to-many relationship as a column in the "many" entity's table.

The @OneToMany annotation can be applied to a field or property value for a collection or an array representing the mapped "many" end of the association.

COLLECTION ORDERING

An ordered collection can be persisted in Hibernate or JPA 2 using the @OrderColumn annotation to maintain the order of the collection. You can also order the collection at retrieval time by means of the @OrderBy annotation. For example, if you were to retrieve a list ordered by the books' names in ascending order, you could annotate a suitable method.

The following code snippet specifies a retrieval order for an ordered collection:

```
@OneToMany(cascade = ALL, mappedBy = "publisher"
@OrderBy("name ASC")
List<Book> books;
```

The value of the @OrderBy annotation is an ordered list of the field names to sort by, each one optionally appended with ASC (for ascending order, as in the preceding code) or DESC (for descending order). If neither ASC nor DESC is appended to one of the field names, the order will default to ascending. @OrderBy can be applied to any collection-valued association.

- The mappedBy attribute is mandatory on a bidirectional association and optional (being implicit) on a unidirectional association.

- cascade is optional, taking a member of the javax.persistence.CascadeType enumeration and dictating the cascade behavior of the mapped entity.

- targetEntity is optional, as it can usually be deduced from the type of the field or property, as in Listing 6-15, where the property represents a Set of Book entities, making the target entity implicitly Book. However, if necessary (if generics are not being used, for example), the class of the target entity can be provided here.

fetch is optional, allowing lazy or eager fetching to be specified as a member of the javax.persistence. FetchType enumeration.

Listing 6-16. Mapping a One-to-Many Relationship from the Book Entity to the Publisher Entity

```
@OneToMany(cascade = ALL,mappedBy = "publisher")
Set<Book> books;
```

The many-to-one end of this relationship is expressed in similar terms to the one-to-many end, as shown in Listing 6-17.

Listing 6-17. Mapping a Many-to-One Relationship from the Publisher Entity to the Book Entity

```
@ManyToOne
@JoinColumn(name = "publisher_id")
Publisher publisher;
```

The @ManyToOne annotation takes a similar set of attributes to @OneToMany. The following list describes the attributes, all of which are optional.

- cascade indicates the appropriate cascade policy for operations on the association; it defaults to none.

- fetch indicates the fetch strategy to use; it defaults to LAZY.

- optional indicates whether the value can be null; it defaults to true.

- targetEntity indicates the entity that stores the primary key—this is normally inferred from the type of the field or property (Publisher, in the preceding example).

We have also supplied the optional @JoinColumn attribute to name the foreign key column required by the association something other than the default (publisher)—this is not necessary, but it illustrates the use of the annotation.

When a unidirectional one-to-many association is to be formed, it is possible to express the relationship using a link table. This is achieved by adding the @JoinTable annotation, as shown in Listing 6-18.[11]

Listing 6-18. A Simple Unidirectional One-to-Many Association with a Join Table

```
@OneToMany(cascade = ALL)
@JoinTable
Set<Book> books;
```

The @JoinTable annotation provides attributes that allow various aspects of the link table to be controlled. These attributes are as follows:

- name is the name of the join table to be used to represent the association.

- catalog is the name of the catalog containing the join table.

- schema is the name of the schema containing the join table.

- joinColumns is an array of @JoinColumn attributes representing the primary key of the entity at the "one" end of the association.

- inverseJoinColumns is an array of @JoinColumn attributes representing the primary key of the entity at the "many" end of the association.

---

[11]When a join table is being used, the foreign key relationship is maintained within the join table itself—it is therefore not appropriate to combine the mappedBy attribute of the @OneToMany annotation with the use of an @JoinTable annotation.

Listing 6-19 shows a fairly typical application of the @JoinTable annotation to specify the name of the join table and its foreign keys into the associated entities.

Listing 6-19. A Unidirectional One-to-Many Association with a More Fully Specified Join Table

```
@OneToMany(cascade = ALL)
@JoinTable(
        name="PublishedBooks",
        joinColumns = { @JoinColumn( name = "publisher_id") },
        inverseJoinColumns = @JoinColumn( name = "book_id")
)
Set<Book> books;
```

Mapping a Many-to-Many Association

When a many-to-many association does not involve a first-class entity joining the two sides of the relationship, a link table must be used to maintain the relationship. This can be generated automatically, or the details can be established in much the same way as with the link table described in the earlier "Mapping a Many-to-One or One-to-Many Association" section of the chapter.

The appropriate annotation is naturally @ManyToMany, and takes the following attributes:

- mappedBy is the field that owns the relationship—this is only required if the association is bidirectional. If an entity provides this attribute, then the other end of the association is the owner of the association, and the attribute must name a field or property of that entity.

- targetEntity is the entity class that is the target of the association. Again, this may be inferred from the generic or array declaration, and only needs to be specified if this is not possible.

- cascade indicates the cascade behavior of the association, which defaults to none.

- fetch indicates the fetch behavior of the association, which defaults to LAZY.

The example maintains a many-to-many association between the Book class and the Author class. The Book entity owns the association, so its getAuthors() method must be marked with an appropriate @ManyToMany attribute, as shown in Listing 6-20.

Listing 6-20. The Book Side of the Many-to-Many Association

```
@ManyToMany(cascade = ALL)
Set<Author> authors;
```

The Author entity is managed by the Book entity. The link table is not explicitly managed, so, as shown in Listing 6-21, we mark it with a @ManyToMany annotation and indicate that the foreign key is managed by the authors attribute of the associated Book entity.

Listing 6-21. The Author Side of the Many-to-Many Association

```
@ManyToMany(mappedBy = "authors")
Set<Book> books;
```

Alternatively, we could specify the link table in full, as in Listing 6-22.

Listing 6-22. Specifying the Link Table in Full Using the Book Entity Annotations

```
@ManyToMany(cascade = ALL)
@JoinTable(
        name="Books_to_Author",
        joinColumns={@JoinColumn(name="book_ident")},
        inverseJoinColumns={@JoinColumn(name="author_ident")}
)
Set272103_1_En authors;
```

Inheritance

The JPA 2 standard and Hibernate both support three approaches to mapping inheritance hierarchies into the database. These are as follows:

1. Single table (SINGLE_TABLE): One table for each class hierarchy

2. Joined (JOINED): One table for each subclass (including interfaces and abstract classes)

3. Table-per-class (TABLE_PER_CLASS): One table for each concrete class implementation

Persistent entities that are related by inheritance must be marked up with the @Inheritance annotation. This takes a single strategy attribute, which is set to one of three javax.persistence. InheritanceType enumeration values corresponding to these approaches (shown in brackets in the preceding numbered list).

Single Table

The single-table approach manages one class for the superclass and all its subtypes. There are columns for each mapped field or property of the superclass, and for each distinct field or property of the derived types. When following this strategy, you will need to ensure that columns are appropriately renamed when any field or property names collide in the hierarchy.

To determine the appropriate type to instantiate when retrieving entities from the database, a @DiscriminatorColumn annotation should be provided in the root (and only in the root) of the persistent hierarchy.[12] This defines a column containing a value that distinguishes between the types used. The attributes permitted by the @DiscriminatorColumn annotation are as follows:

- name is the name of the discriminator column.

- discriminatorType is the type of value to be stored in the column as selected from the javax.persistence.DiscriminatorType enumeration of STRING, CHAR, or INTEGER.

- columnDefinition is a fragment of DDL defining the column type. Using this is liable to reduce the portability of your code across databases.

- length is the column length of STRING discriminator types. It is ignored for CHAR and INTEGER types.

All of these (and the annotation itself) are optional, but we recommend supplying at least the name attribute. If no @DiscriminatorColumn is specified in the hierarchy, a default column name of DTYPE and type of STRING will be used.

---

[12]That is to say, the highest class in the hierarchy that is mapped to the database as an entity should be annotated in this way.

Hibernate will supply an appropriate discriminator value for each of your entities. For example, if the STRING discriminator type is used, the value this column contains will be the name of the entity (which defaults to the class name). You can also override this behavior with specific values using the @DiscriminatorValue annotation. If the discriminator type is INTEGER, any value provided via the @DiscriminatorValue annotation must be convertible directly into an integer.

In Listing 6-23, we specify that an INTEGER discriminator type should be stored in the column named DISCRIMINATOR. Rows representing Book entities will have a value of 1 in this column, whereas the following mapping in Listing 6-24 requires that rows representing ComputerBook entities should have a value of 2 in the same column.

Listing 6-23. The Root of the Inheritance Hierarchy Mapped with the SINGLE_TABLE Strategy

```
@Entity
@Inheritance(strategy = SINGLE_TABLE)
@DiscriminatorColumn(
    name="DISCRIMINATOR",
    discriminatorType=INTEGER
)
@DiscriminatorValue("1")
public class Book {
...
}
```

Listing 6-24. A Derived Entity in the Inheritance Hierarchy

```
@Entity
@DiscriminatorValue("2")
public class ComputerBook extends Book {
...
}
```

Joined Table

An alternative to the monolithic single-table approach is the otherwise similar joined-table approach. Here a discriminator column is used, but the fields of the various derived types are stored in distinct tables. Other than the differing strategy, this inheritance type is specified in the same way (as shown in Listing 6-25).

Listing 6-25. The Root of the Inheritance Hierarchy Mapped with the JOINED Strategy

```
@Entity
@Inheritance(strategy = JOINED)
@DiscriminatorColumn(
    name="DISCRIMINATOR"
)
public class Book {
...
}
```

Table per Class

Finally, there is the table-per-class approach, in which all of the fields of each type in the inheritance hierarchy are stored in distinct tables. Because of the close correspondence between the entity and its table, the @DiscriminatorColumn annotation is not applicable to this inheritance strategy. Listing 6-26 shows how our Book class could be mapped in this way.

Listing 6-26. The Root of the Inheritance Hierarchy Mapped with the TABLE_PER_CLASS Strategy

```
@Entity
@Inheritance(strategy = TABLE_PER_CLASS)
public class Book {
...
}
```

Choosing Between Inheritance Types When Modeling Inheritance

Each of these different inheritance types has tradeoffs. When you create a database schema that models a class hierarchy, you have to weigh performance and database maintainability to decide which inheritance type to use.

It is easiest to maintain your database when using the joined-table approach. If fields are added or removed from any class in the class hierarchy, only one database table needs to be altered to reflect the changes. In addition, adding new classes to the class hierarchy only requires that a new table be added, eliminating the performance problems of adding database columns to large data sets. With the table-per-class approach, a change to a column in a parent class requires that the column change be made in all child tables. The single-table approach can be messy, leading to many columns in the table that aren't used in every row, as well as a rapidly horizontally growing table.

Read performance will be best with the single-table approach. A select query for any class in the hierarchy will only read from one table, with no joins necessary. The table-per-class type has great performance if you only work with the leaf nodes in the class hierarchy. Any queries related to the parent classes will require joins on a number of tables to get results. The joined-table approach will also require joins for any select query, so this will affect performance. The number of joins will be related to the size of the class hierarchy—large, deep class hierarchies may not be good candidates for the joined-table approach.

We recommend using the joined-table approach unless performance could be a problem because of the size of the data set and the depth of the class hierarchy.

Other JPA 2 Persistence Annotations

Although we have now covered most of the core JPA 2 persistence annotations, there are a few others that you will encounter fairly frequently. We cover some of these in passing in the following sections.

Temporal Data

Fields or properties of an entity that have java.util.Date or java.util.Calendar types represent temporal data. By default, these will be stored in a column with the TIMESTAMP data type, but this default behavior can be overridden with the @Temporal annotation.

The annotation accepts a single value attribute from the javax.persistence.TemporalType enumeration. This offers three possible values: DATE, TIME, and TIMESTAMP. These correspond, respectively, to java.sql.Date, java.sql.Time, and java.sql.Timestamp. The table column is given the appropriate data type at schema generation time. Listing 6-27 shows an example mapping a java.util.Date property as a TIME type—the java.sql.Date and java.sql.Time classes are both derived from the java.util.Date class, so confusingly, both are capable of representing dates *and* times!

Listing 6-27. A Date Property Mapped as a Time Temporal Field

```
@Temporal(TemporalType.TIME)
java.util.Date startingTime;
```

Element Collections

In addition to mapping collections using one-to-many mappings, JPA 2 introduced an @ElementCollection annotation for mapping collections of basic or embeddable classes. You can use the @ElementCollection annotation to simplify your mappings. Listing 6-28 shows an example where you use the @ElementCollection annotation to map a java.util.List collection of string objects.

Listing 6-28. An Example of ElementCollections

```
@ElementCollection
List<String> passwordHints;
```

There are two attributes on the @ElementCollection annotation: targetClass and fetch. The targetClass attribute tells Hibernate which class is stored in the collection. If you use generics on your collection, you do not need to specify targetClass because Hibernate will infer the correct class. The fetch attribute takes a member of the enumeration, FetchType. This is EAGER by default, but can be set to LAZY to permit loading when the value is accessed.

Large Objects

A persistent property or field can be marked for persistence as a database-supported large object type by applying the @Lob annotation.

The annotation takes no attributes, but the underlying large object type to be used will be inferred from the type of the field or parameter. String- and character-based types will be stored in an appropriate character-based type. All other objects will be stored in a BLOB. Listing 6-29 maps a String–a title of some kind[13]-into a large object column type.

Listing 6-29. An Example of a Large Object Property

```
@Lob
String title; // a very, very long title indeed
```

The @Lob annotation can be used in combination with the @Basic or the @ElementCollection annotation.

Mapped Superclasses

A special case of inheritance occurs when the root of the hierarchy is not itself a persistent entity, but various classes derived from it are. Such a class can be abstract or concrete. The @MappedSuperclass annotation allows you to take advantage of this circumstance.

The class marked with @MappedSuperclass is not an entity, and is not queryable (it cannot be passed to methods that expect an entity in the Session or EntityManager objects). It cannot be the target of an association.

The mapping information for the columns of the superclass will be stored in the same table as the details of the derived class (in this way, the annotation resembles the use of the @Inheritance tag with the SINGLE_TABLE strategy).

---

[13]Before you think this example is *entirely* contrived, some titles can be amazingly long. Check out http://oldbooktitles.tumblr.com/ for some examples that might not fit in traditional-size columns.

In other respects, the superclass can be mapped as a normal entity, but the mappings will apply to the derived classes only (since the superclass itself does not have an associated table in the database). When a derived class needs to deviate from the superclass's behavior, the @AttributeOverride annotation can be used (much as with the use of an embeddable entity).

For example, if in our example, model Book was a superclass of ComputerBook, but Book objects themselves were never persisted directly, then Book could be marked as @MappedSuperclass, as shown in Listing 6-30.

Listing 6-30. Marking the Book Class As a Mapped Superclass

```
@MappedSuperclass
public class BookSuperclass {
...
}
```

The fields of the ComputerBook entity derived from Book would then be stored in the ComputerBook entity class's table. Classes derived directly from Book but not mapped as entities in their own right, such as a hypothetical MarketingBook class, would not be persistable. In this respect alone, the mapped superclass approach behaves differently from the conventional @Inheritance approach with a SINGLE_TABLE strategy.

Ordering Collections with @OrderColumn

While @OrderBy allows data to be ordered once it has been retrieved from the database, JPA 2 also provides an annotation that allows the ordering of appropriate collection types (e.g., List) to be maintained in the database; it does so by maintaining an order column to represent that order. Here's an example:

```
@OneToMany
@OrderColumn(
    name="employeeNumber"
)
List<Employee> employees;
```

Here, we are declaring that an employeeNumber column will maintain a value, starting at 0 and incrementing as each entry is added to the list. The default starting value can be overridden by the base attribute. By default, the column can contain null (unordered) values. The nullability can be overridden by setting the nullable attribute to false. By default, when the schema is generated from the annotations, the column is assumed to be an integer type; however, this can be overridden by supplying a columnDefinition attribute specifying a different column definition string.

Named Queries (HQL or JPQL)

@NamedQuery and @NamedQueries allow one or more Hibernate Query Language or Java Persistence Query Language (JPQL) queries to be associated with an entity. The required attributes are as follows:

- name is the name by which the query is retrieved.

- query is the JPQL (or HQL) query associated with the name.

Listing 6-31 shows an example associating a named query with the Author entity. The query would retrieve Author entities by name, so it is natural to associate it with that entity; however, there is no actual requirement that a named query be associated in this way with the entity that it concerns.

Listing 6-31. A JPQL Named Query Annotation

```
@Entity
@NamedQuery(
        name="findAuthorsByName",
        query="from Author where name = :author"
)
public class Author {
...
}
```

There is also a hints attribute, taking a QueryHint annotation name/value pair, which allows caching mode, timeout value, and a variety of other platform-specific tweaks to be applied (this can also be used to comment the SQL generated by the query).

You do not need to directly associate the query with the entity against which it is declared, but it is normal to do so. If a query has no natural association with any of the entity declarations, it is possible to make the @NamedQuery annotation at the package level.[14]

There is no natural place to put a package-level annotation, so Java annotations allow for a specific file, called package-info.java, to contain them. Listing 6-32 gives an example of this.

Listing 6-32. A package-info.java File

```
@javax.annotations.NamedQuery(
    name="findAuthorsByName",
    query="from Author where name = :author"
)
package chapter06.annotations;
```

Hibernate's session allows named queries to be accessed directly, as shown in Listing 6-33.

Listing 6-33. Invoking a Named Query via the Session

```
Query query = session.getNamedQuery("findAuthorsByName");
query.setParameter("author", "Dave");
List booksByDave = query.list();
System.out.println("There is/are " + booksByDave.size()
        + " author(s) called Dave in the catalog");
```

If you have multiple @NamedQuery annotations to apply to an entity, they can be provided as an array of values of the @NamedQueries annotation.

Named Native Queries (SQL)

Hibernate also allows the database's native query language (usually a dialect of SQL) to be used in place of HQL or JPQL. You risk losing portability here if you use a database-specific feature, but as long as you choose reasonably generic SQL, you should be okay. The @NamedNativeQuery annotation is declared in almost exactly the same manner

---

[14]Note that something being *possible* is very different from something being *preferable*. Your author knows of exactly zero instances of this feature having been used in production; this doesn't mean it's not ever been used, but it's far from common.

as the @NamedQuery annotation. The following block of code shows a simple example of the declaration of a named native query:

```
@NamedNativeQuery(
    name="nativeFindAuthorNames",
    query="select name from author"
)
```

All queries are used in the same way; the only difference is how they're accessed, whether by Session. getNamedQuery(), Session.createQuery(), or Session.createSQLQuery(); the results can be retrieved as a List through Query.list(), or a scrollable result set can be accessed via Query.scroll(), Query.iterate() provides an Iterator (surprise!), and if the Query has only one object returned, Query.uniqueResult() can be used.

Multiple @NamedNativeQuery annotations can be grouped with the @NamedNativeQueries annotation.

Configuring the Annotated Classes

Once you have an annotated class, you will need to provide the class to your application's Hibernate configuration, just as if it were an XML mapping. With annotations, you can either use the declarative configuration in the hibernate.cfg.xml XML configuration document, or programmatically add annotated classes to Hibernate's org.hibernate.cfg.AnnotationConfiguration object. Your application may use both annotated entities and XML mapped entities in the same configuration.

To provide declarative mapping, we use a normal hibernate.cfg.xml XML configuration file and add the annotated classes to the mapping using the mapping element (see Listing 6-34). Notice that we have specified the name of the annotated classes as mappings.

Listing 6-34. A Hibernate XML Configuration File with Annotated Classes

```xml
<?xml version="1.0"?>
<!DOCTYPE hibernate-configuration PUBLIC
        "-//Hibernate/Hibernate Configuration DTD 3.0//EN"
        "http://www.hibernate.org/dtd/hibernate-configuration-3.0.dtd">
<hibernate-configuration>
    <session-factory>
        <!-- Database connection settings  -->
        <property name="connection.driver_class">org.hsqldb.jdbc.JDBCDriver</property>
        <property name="connection.url">jdbc:hsqldb:db7;shutdown=true</property>
        <property name="connection.username">sa</property>
        <property name="connection.password"/>
        <property name="dialect">org.hibernate.dialect.HSQLDialect</property>
        <!-- set up c3p0 for use -->
        <property name="ac3p0.max_size">10</property>
        <!-- Echo all executed SQL to stdout  -->
        <property name="show_sql">true</property>
        <!-- Drop and re-create the database schema on startup  -->
        <property name="hbm2ddl.auto">create</property>

        <mapping class="chapter06.primarykey.after.Book"/>
        <mapping class="chapter06.compoundpk.CPKBook"/>
        <mapping class="chapter06.compoundpk.EmbeddedPKBook"/>
        <mapping class="chapter06.compoundpk.IdClassBook"/>
```

```
            <mapping class="chapter06.twotables.Customer"/>
            <mapping class="chapter06.mappedsuperclass.BookSuper"/>
            <mapping class="chapter06.mappedsuperclass.ComputerBook"/>
        </session-factory>
</hibernate-configuration>
```

You can also add an annotated class to your Hibernate configuration programmatically. The annotations toolset comes with an org.hibernate.cfg.AnnotationConfiguration object that extends the base Hibernate Configuration object for adding mappings. The methods on AnnotationConfiguration for adding annotated classes to the configuration are as follows:

```
addAnnotatedClass(Class persistentClass) throws MappingException
addAnnotatedClasses(List<Class> classes)
addPackage(String packageName) throws MappingException
```

Using these methods, you can add one annotated class, a list of annotated classes, or an entire package (by name) of annotated classes. As with the Hibernate XML configuration file, the annotated entities are interoperable with XML mapped entities.[15]

Hibernate-Specific Persistence Annotations

Hibernate has various annotations that extend the standard persistence annotations. They can be very useful, but you should keep in mind that their use will constrict your application to Hibernate; this won't affect any of the code we've written so far, since most of it uses Hibernate-specific classes already.

■ **Tip** It is possible to overstate the importance of portability—most bespoke applications are never deployed to an environment other than the one for which they were originally developed. As a mature product, Hibernate has numerous features to offer above and beyond the base JPA 2 specification. You should not waste too much time trying to achieve a portable solution in preference to these proprietary features unless you have a definite requirement for portability.

@Immutable

The @Immutable annotation marks an entity as being, well, immutable. This is useful for situations in which your entity represents reference data–things like lists of states, genders, or other rarely mutated data.

Since things like states tend to be rarely changed, someone usually updates the data manually, via SQL or an administration application. Hibernate can cache this data aggressively, which needs to be taken into consideration; if the reference data changes, you'd want to make sure that the applications using it are notified or restarted somehow.

What the annotation tells Hibernate is that any updates to an immutable entity should not be passed on to the database. It's a "safe" object; one probably shouldn't update it very often, if only to avoid confusion.

@Immutable can be placed on a collection; in this case, changes to the collection (additions, or removals) will cause a HibernateException to be thrown.

---

[15]Again, this is *not* an endorsement of the Hibernate XML configuration. It's also not a condemnation, but...

Natural IDs

The first part of this chapter spent a lot of pages discussing primary keys, including generated values. Generated values are referred to as "artificial primary keys," and are very much recommended[16] as a sort of shorthand reference for a given row.

However, there's also the concept of a "natural ID," which provides another convenient way to refer to an entity, apart from an artificial or composite primary key.

An example might be a Social Security number or a Tax Identification Number in the United States. An entity (being a person or a corporation) might have an artificial primary key generated by Hibernate, but it also might have a unique tax identifier. This might be annotated with @Column(unique=true, nullable=false, updatable=false), which would create a unique, immutable index,[17] but a natural ID also provides a loadable mechanism that we've not seen yet in any of our previous code, plus an actual optimization.

The Session provides the concept of a loader mechanism, known as a "load access." There are three loaders contained in Hibernate 4.2, able to load by ID, natural ID, and simple natural ID.

Loading by ID refers to an internal reference for a given instance. For example, if an object with an ID of 1 is already referred to by Hibernate, Hibernate doesn't need to go to the database to load that object–it can look the object up through its ID, and return that reference.

A natural ID is another form of that ID; in the case of a tax identifier, the system could look it up by the actual object ID (which would be an artificial key in most cases) or by the tax ID number itself–and if the tax ID is a "natural ID," then the library is able to look that object up internally instead of building a query for the database.

Just as there are simple identifiers and composite identifiers comprising single fields and multiple fields, respectively–there are two forms of natural ID, similarly being made up of single fields or multiple fields.

In the case of the simple IDs, the load process provides a simple load() method, with the ID in question being the parameter. If no instance with the ID exists, load() returns null. The loader also provides an alternative, a getReference() method, which will throw an exception if no object with that natural ID is in the database.

For natural IDs, there are two forms of load mechanisms; one uses the simple natural ID (where the natural ID is one and only one field), and the other uses named attributes as part of a composite natural ID.

Now let's look at some actual code. First, let's create a class representing an employee in Listing 6-35; our employee will have a name (everyone has a name), an artificial ID (an employee number) assigned by the database, and a natural ID, representing a manually assigned badge number.

Listing 6-35. `SimpleNaturalIdEmployee.java`, Without Accessors, Mutators, or Ancillary Methods

```
package chapter06.naturalid;

import org.hibernate.annotations.NaturalId;

import javax.persistence.Entity;
import javax.persistence.GeneratedValue;
import javax.persistence.GenerationType;
import javax.persistence.Id;

@Entity
public class SimpleNaturalIdEmployee {
```

---

[16]Note that there are different views of this. Most anecdotal data would suggest artificial keys as primary keys, because they're short and immutable by nature; however, you can find many who advocate natural keys, because they naturally map to the data model instead of adding to it. With that said, there are some data-oriented applications (data warehousing, for example) in which artificial keys are advocated without opposition. With this in mind, the recommendation stands: use artificial keys. Your data is likely to be warehoused at some point.

[17]The @UniqueConstraints annotation, mentioned earlier in this chapter, can do the same for a compound index. With that said, we're trying to look at a better way to do at least *some* ordering and indexing.

```
    @Id
    @GeneratedValue(strategy = GenerationType.AUTO)
    Integer id;
    @NaturalId
    Integer badge;
    String name;

    public SimpleNaturalIdEmployee() {
    }
}
```

The simple natural ID is declared by annotating a single field, badge, with @NaturalId.

To use the loader mechanism, you would get a reference through the use of Session.byId(), Session.byNaturalId(), or Session.bySimpleNaturalId(), with the type of the entity being passed in. The simple loaders (for the ID and for the simple natural ID) follow the same form: you acquire the loader, then either load or get the reference, using the key value as a parameter. Let's see how that would look, shown in Listing 6-36.

Listing 6-36: A Simple Test Showing the Use of Both ID and Natural ID Loaders

```
@Test
public void testSimpleNaturalId() {
        Integer id = createSimpleEmployee("Sorhed", 5401).getId();

        Session session = SessionUtil.getSession();
        Transaction tx = session.beginTransaction();

        SimpleNaturalIdEmployee employee =
                    (SimpleNaturalIdEmployee) session
                                .byId(SimpleNaturalIdEmployee.class)
                                .load(id);
        assertNotNull(employee);
        SimpleNaturalIdEmployee badgedEmployee =
                    (SimpleNaturalIdEmployee) session
                                .bySimpleNaturalId(SimpleNaturalIdEmployee.class)
                                .load(5401);
        assertEquals(badgedEmployee, employee);

        tx.commit();
        session.close();
}

private SimpleNaturalIdEmployee createSimpleEmployee(String name, int badge) {
        SimpleNaturalIdEmployee employee = new SimpleNaturalIdEmployee();
        employee.setName(name);
        employee.setBadge(badge);

        Session session = SessionUtil.getSession();
        Transaction tx = session.beginTransaction();
        session.save(employee);
        tx.commit();
        session.close();
        return employee;
}
```

This code creates a new employee, with a specific badge number (5401). It then uses Session.byId(SimpleNaturalIdEmployee.class) to acquire a loader for the entity, and calls load(id), with the ID returned by the createSimpleEmployee() method.

There's an interesting thing happening here, though, that the code demonstrates without it necessarily being obvious from the code level.

When we run this method, we actually load *two* references–or else the test for equivalency wouldn't make any sense.[18] However, if we look at the actual SQL executed in the Session, we see only *one* call being issued.

This is because Hibernate will cache the natural IDs in objects that it loads in a session. When we use the natural ID in the load accessor, Hibernate looks in the session cache and finds that natural ID–and knows that this is the reference for which we're asking. It doesn't need to go to the database because it already has it in memory.

This helps make the class more self-documenting, as well as slightly more efficient; it means that if we have a data about a person from the real world, the API is more efficient. We can find a given employee by using a naturally indexed badge number instead of relying on other indexes, even if at the database level the other indexes do come into play.

An entity with a compound natural ID merely has more fields annotated with @NaturalId. Let's create an employee for whom a section and department are a natural ID,[19] as shown in Listing 6-37.

Listing 6-37. An Entity with a Compound Natural ID

```
package chapter06.naturalid;

import org.hibernate.annotations.NaturalId;

import javax.persistence.Entity;
import javax.persistence.GeneratedValue;
import javax.persistence.GenerationType;
import javax.persistence.Id;

@Entity
public class Employee {
    @Id
    @GeneratedValue(strategy = GenerationType.AUTO)
    Integer id;
    @NaturalId
    Integer section;
    @NaturalId
    Integer department;
    String name;

    public Employee() {
    }

    // accessors and mutators removed for brevity
}
```

---

[18]Let's assume that we usually make sense.

[19]In the previous footnote, we said that we *usually* make sense. This is a good example of when we really don't; this is horribly contrived and would earn a solid scolding in an actual project. With that said, the code works and is fairly demonstrative of the concept.

Next, let's look at a test that demonstrates the use of the natural ID loader, shown in Listing 6-38.

Listing 6-38. The Natural ID Loader in Action

```
@Test
public void testLoadByNaturalId() {
        Employee initial=createEmployee("Arrowroot", 11, 291);
        Session session = SessionUtil.getSession();
        Transaction tx = session.beginTransaction();

        Employee arrowroot = (Employee) session
                        .byNaturalId(Employee.class)
                        .using("section", 11)
                        .using("department", 291)
                        .load();
        assertNotNull(arrowroot);
        assertEquals(initial, arrowroot);

        tx.commit();
        session.close();
}

private Employee createEmployee(String name, int section, int department) {
        Employee employee = new Employee();
        employee.setName(name);
        employee.setDepartment(department);
        employee.setSection(section);
        Session session = SessionUtil.getSession();
        Transaction tx = session.beginTransaction();
        session.save(employee);
        tx.commit();
        session.close();
        return employee;
}
```

This is very similar to our previous test for natural ID usage: we create an employee, and then search for the ID. The object returned by Session.byNaturalId() has a using() method that takes a field name and the field value, as opposed to using a single reference for the identifier. If we don't include *every* field making up the natural ID, we'll get an exception.

Note that we're using the load() method; if the natural ID is not present in the database, load() will return a signal value of null.

Now let's look at another test in Listing 6-39. This one, which uses getReference(), will throw an exception if the ID isn't present, so we don't need the check for null.

Listing 6-39. A Test that Uses getReference() Instead of load()

```
@Test
public void testGetByNaturalId() {
        Employee initial = createEmployee("Eorwax", 11, 292);
        Session session = SessionUtil.getSession();
        Transaction tx = session.beginTransaction();
```

```
Employee eorwax = (Employee) session
                    .byNaturalId(Employee.class)
                    .using("section", 11)
                    .using("department", 292)
                    .getReference();
assertEquals(initial, eorwax);

tx.commit();
session.close();
}
```

Summary

In this chapter, we used JPA 2 annotations to add metadata to our POJOs for Hibernate, and we looked at some Hibernate-specific annotations that can enhance these at the cost of reduced portability.

In the next chapter, we're going to discuss JPA configuration for Hibernate, more of the object lifecycle, and data validation.

CHAPTER 7

JPA Integration and Lifecycle Events

Hibernate provides a number of capabilities beyond the simple "native Hibernate API." In this chapter, we are going to discuss using the standard JPA configuration resource, Hibernate's object validation facilities, and object lifecycle events—along with a few other tricks.

The Java Persistence Architecture

The Java Persistence Architecture, or JPA, is a standard approved by the Java Community Process, with input from representatives of a number of projects and vendors. It was created as part of a new Enterprise Java specification, largely because Entity Beans—the prior standard for enterprise persistence—were difficult to write and use, and even more difficult to use well.

Hibernate was represented in the community team that created JPA, and it's fair to say that the JPA specification bears a strong resemblance to Hibernate's API; and Hibernate has integrated many JPA practices itself, as the previous chapter on mapping shows. (Most of the mapping features and annotations are part of the JPA specification; now, the native Hibernate versions of those annotations are available but rarely used in practice.[1])

Hibernate provides an implementation of the JPA specification. Therefore, you can use JPA directly, with a JPA-specific configuration file, and acquire an `EntityManager` instead of a `Session`.

There are a few reasons you might want to do this. For one thing, JPA is a standard, which means that code that conforms to the standard is generally portable, allowing for differences among varying implementations. You can use Hibernate for development, for example, and for production you could deploy into an application server that provides EclipseLink instead. (The opposite applies as well: you could develop with EclipseLink and deploy into an architecture that uses Hibernate.)

Another reason is the Java EE specification itself. Java EE containers are required to provide JPA, which means the container can manage and profile resources; leveraging a non-JPA configuration puts a larger burden on the application developer. However, it's worth pointing out that one can use Hibernate as the JPA implementation even in a container that defaults to a different JPA implementation, providing you the best of both worlds: a JPA standard for configuration (which has its own benefits, in some slight ways), and Hibernate's excellent performance and expanded featureset.[2]

---

[1]Statements like this ("*X* is rarely used in practice") are almost always anecdotal. This one certainly is; you can probably find projects that fanatically rely on the Hibernate-specific annotations. The anecdote stands.

[2]The mechanism for using Hibernate in an environment where it's not the default provider is fairly simple: in the persistence.xml, add `<provider>org.hibernate.ejb.HibernatePersistence</provider>`. You'll still want to look up how to install Hibernate into your application server, however.

So let's look at what we would need to do to support the JPA configuration file, as opposed to the Hibernate configuration process. We're going to walk through a series of simple steps to give us a working toolkit. They are:

1. Add Hibernate's JPA support to the util project, as a nontransitive dependency.[3]

2. Add a JPASessionUtil class, as a close analog to the SessionUtil utility. Much as SessionUtil provides a Session instance, JPASessionUtil will provide an EntityManager instance, and we will also add a mechanism by which it will provide a Hibernate Session; this way, we can use the JPA configuration with the Hibernate API.

3. Write a JPA configuration and a test to show functional operation; this will give us an idea of some of the differences between JPA and Hibernate.

The Project Object Model

Let's look at the project object model for the util project, which will tell Maven what dependencies to include; see Listing 7-1.

Listing 7-1. The Util Module's pom.xml

```xml
<?xml version="1.0" encoding="UTF-8"?>
<project xmlns="http://maven.apache.org/POM/4.0.0"
        xmlns:xsi="http://www.w3.org/2001/XMLSchema-instance"
        xsi:schemaLocation="http://maven.apache.org/POM/4.0.0
            http://maven.apache.org/xsd/maven-4.0.0.xsd">
    <parent>
        <artifactId>hibernate-parent</artifactId>
        <groupId>com.redhat.osas.books.hibernate</groupId>
        <version>1.0-SNAPSHOT</version>
    </parent>
    <modelVersion>4.0.0</modelVersion>
    <artifactId>util</artifactId>

    <dependencies>
        <dependency>
            <groupId>org.hibernate</groupId>
            <artifactId>hibernate-c3p0</artifactId>
            <version>[4.2.6,4.2.9)</version>
        </dependency>
        <dependency>
            <groupId>org.hibernate</groupId>
            <artifactId>hibernate-entitymanager</artifactId>
            <version>[4.2.6,4.2.9)</version>
            <scope>test</scope>
        </dependency>
        <dependency>
            <groupId>com.mchange</groupId>
            <artifactId>c3p0</artifactId>
            <version>[0.9.2.1,)</version>
        </dependency>
    </dependencies>
</project>
```

---

[3]We want a nontransitive dependency because we don't want to force all of the modules that use the util project to include JPA support.

This adds the hibernate-entitymanager dependency to the previous version of the pom.xml. That is all we really need to do; we can now use JPA in this project. The dependency is scoped as "test" because, while we want it to be available to the compile and testing phases of the util project, we don't want it to be automatically (or *transitively*) included in modules that depend on this library.

The JPASessionUtil class

JPA uses the concept of "persistence units," which are named configurations. Every persistence configuration will have a unique name within a given deployment. Because the persistence units are named, we need to factor in the possibility of multiple persistence units for our utility class, as shown in Listing 7-2.

Listing 7-2. Our JPASessionUtil Class

```
package com.redhat.osas.jpa.util;

import org.hibernate.Session;

import javax.persistence.EntityManager;
import javax.persistence.EntityManagerFactory;
import javax.persistence.Persistence;
import java.util.Map;
import java.util.HashMap;

public class JPASessionUtil {
    static Map<String, EntityManagerFactory> persistenceUnits = new HashMap<>();
    /**
        Returns a JPA EntityManager given a valid persistence unit name.
    */
    public static synchronized EntityManager getEntityManager(String persistenceUnitName) {
        // have we already created this factory? If not, create it and save it.
        if (persistenceUnits.get(persistenceUnitName) == null) {
            persistenceUnits.put(persistenceUnitName,
                    Persistence.createEntityManagerFactory(persistenceUnitName));
        }
        return persistenceUnits.get(persistenceUnitName)
                .createEntityManager();
    }
    /**
        Returns the underlying Hibernate Session object for a valid JPA
        Persistence unit.
    */
    public static Session getSession(String persistenceUnitName) {
        return getEntityManager(persistenceUnitName).unwrap(Session.class);
    }
}
```

In this class, we're setting up a way to reuse EntityManagerFactory instances, looked up by name. If no EntityManagerFactory exists for a given name, we'll create it and save it. If no persistence unit exists for a given name, a javax.persistence.PersistenceException will be thrown.

The getSession() method provides access to the underlying implementation of the EntityManager. For Hibernate, this will be org.hibernate.Session; if the actual implementation isn't Hibernate, then you'll have a runtime exception thrown.

All this is useful, but let's get around to using it. Let's write some tests to show how this class should be used.

Testing JPASessionUtil

Our first tests simply try to acquire resources: one set of resources that are properly configured,[4] and another set of resources that do not. This will allow us to validate that the utility returns what it's expected to return, even when badly configured. Listing 7-3 shows the code for our first suite of tests; we're going to follow that up with a JPA configuration that these tests will use.

Listing 7-3. Testing Simple Resource Acquisition

```
@Test
public void getEntityManager() {
        EntityManager em = JPASessionUtil.getEntityManager("utiljpa");
        em.close();
}

@Test(expectedExceptions = {javax.persistence.PersistenceException.class})
public void nonexistentEntityManagerName() {
        JPASessionUtil.getEntityManager("nonexistent");
        fail("We shouldn't be able to acquire an EntityManager here");
}

@Test
public void getSession() {
        Session session = JPASessionUtil.getSession("utiljpa");
        session.close();
}

@Test(expectedExceptions = {javax.persistence.PersistenceException.class})
public void nonexistentSessionName() {
        JPASessionUtil.getSession("nonexistent");
        fail("We shouldn't be able to acquire a Session here");
}
```

You'll notice that the nonexistent tests do something odd: they declare expected Exceptions. Ordinarily, exceptions mean that a test has failed; in this case, we're saying that the test has *not* failed if a matching exception is thrown.

However, "not failing" isn't the same as "passing." For these tests, we actually want to fail *unless* we get an exception; therefore, we try to acquire the resource, and call fail() —and an exception will exit the method before fail() is executed, which means the test *passes*.

---

[4] Including the Platonic quality of, well, "existence." Each of us can decide on our own if this is a compliment to *The Republic* or not.

However, *none* of these tests will pass unless we include a JPA configuration file, which is placed in the classpath at /META-INF/persistence.xml, as shown in Listing 7-4:

Listing 7-4. util/src/test/resources/META-INF/persistence.xml

```xml
<persistence xmlns="http://java.sun.com/xml/ns/persistence"
             xmlns:xsi="http://www.w3.org/2001/XMLSchema-instance"
             xsi:schemaLocation="http://java.sun.com/xml/ns/persistence
                 http://java.sun.com/xml/ns/persistence/persistence_2_0.xsd"
             version="2.0">
    <persistence-unit name="utiljpa">
        <!-- This next node should be included for use of the Hibernate provider in
             A Java EE environment in which Hibernate is not the default. -->
        <!--
        <provider>org.hibernate.ejb.HibernatePersistence</provider>
        -->
        <properties>
            <!-- Properties prefixed with "javax" are part of the JPA specification.
                 Hibernate will use them as it can.
                 Properties prefixed with "hibernate" are passed to the Hibernate
                 provider, and map to the standard hibernate properties.
            -->
            <property name="javax.persistence.jdbc.driver"
                value="org.hsqldb.jdbcDriver"/>
            <property name="javax.persistence.jdbc.url"
                value="jdbc:hsqldb:utiljpa;shutdown=true"/>
            <property name="javax.persistence.jdbc.user" value="sa"/>
            <property name="javax.persistence.jdbc.password" value=""/>
            <property name="hibernate.dialect"
                value="org.hibernate.dialect.HSQLDialect"/>
            <property name="hibernate.hbm2ddl.auto" value="create-drop"/>
            <property name="hibernate.show_sql" value="true"/>
        </properties>
    </persistence-unit>
</persistence>
```

With this file created, we have a valid persistence unit, named "utiljpa"; we're now able to run our four tests. With their passing, you can see that JPASessionUtil returns an instance of EntityManager and Session when requested, and throws an exception when an invalid request is made.

However, our tests don't actually show the use of the persistence engine at all. Let's create an entity and a few tests that show some operations on it.

Before we do that, though, let's talk about boilerplate code.[5] So far, when we've seen code listings for entities, we usually have seen only part of the code: the class declaration (with an @Entity annotation), and a few attributes. We've been presuming that appropriate implementations of toString(), equals(), hashCode(), and various accessors and mutators have been present. This is a useful approach because usually such things are routine, and they are often automatically generated by a development environment.

However, there's a library that allows us to annotate an object simply and cleanly, such that we can display *all* of the code associated with the entity, with all of the boilerplate code removed even from the source. That library is called "Lombok," from Project Lombok (http://projectlombok.org).

---

[5]Specifically, let's talk about boilerplate code and how to avoid having to write so much of it.

Lombok provides a number of annotations that can generate all of the boilerplated methods we just mentioned, and more: toString(), equals(), hashCode(), mutators, accessors, and a no-argument constructor, among many others. Lombok is a compile-time dependency; we don't need the library to exist in anything that depends on the generated classes.

To use Lombok, all we need to do is add another nontransitive dependency to our pom.xml.

```
<dependency>
        <groupId>org.projectlombok</groupId>
        <artifactId>lombok</artifactId>
        <version>[1.12.2,)</version>
        <scope>test</scope>
</dependency>
```

Now, we can write an entity with this *full* source code, as shown in Listing 7-5:

Listing 7-5. A Lombok-annotated Entity for Our JPA test

```
package com.redhat.osas.util.model;

import lombok.*;

import javax.persistence.*;

@Entity
@NoArgsConstructor
@ToString
@EqualsAndHashCode
public class Thing {
    @Id
    @GeneratedValue(strategy = GenerationType.AUTO)
    @Getter
    @Setter
    Integer id;
    @Getter
    @Setter
    @Column
    String name;
}
```

The annotations tell Lombok what to generate; @NoArgsConstructor, @ToString, and @EqualsAndHashCode all apply to the class as a whole, and @Getter and @Setter apply to individual attributes, generating the appropriate utility methods, accessors, mutators, and constructors. The persistence annotations coexist peacefully with the Lombok annotations, such that this is our entire class's source, with no code elided for brevity's sake.

Of course, the proof's in the tests that *use* this class, as we see in Listing 7-6:

Listing 7-6. More Tests for JPASessionUtil

```
@Test
public void testEntityManager() {
    EntityManager em = JPASessionUtil.getEntityManager("utiljpa");
    em.getTransaction().begin();
    Thing t = new Thing();
```

```
        t.setName("Thing 1");
        em.persist(t);
        em.getTransaction().commit();
        em.close();

        em = JPASessionUtil.getEntityManager("utiljpa");
        em.getTransaction().begin();
        Query q = em.createQuery("from Thing t where t.name=:name");
        q.setParameter("name", "Thing 1");
        Thing result = (Thing) q.getSingleResult();
        assertNotNull(result);
        assertEquals(result, t);
        em.remove(result);
        em.getTransaction().commit();
        em.close();
    }

    @Test
    public void testSession() {
        Session session = JPASessionUtil.getSession("utiljpa");
        Transaction tx = session.beginTransaction();
        Thing t = new Thing();
        t.setName("Thing 2");
        session.persist(t);
        tx.commit();
        session.close();

        session = JPASessionUtil.getSession("utiljpa");
        tx = session.beginTransaction();
        org.hibernate.Query q =
        session.createQuery("from Thing t where t.name=:name");
        q.setParameter("name", "Thing 2");
        Thing result = (Thing) q.uniqueResult();
        assertNotNull(result);
        assertEquals(result, t);
        session.delete(result);
        tx.commit();
        session.close();
    }
```

Here, we see two functionally equivalent tests. In each one, we have two operations. In each, we acquire a class that offers persistence,[6] start a transaction, and persist a Thing entity, then commit the transaction; then we repeat the process, querying and then deleting the entity. The only difference between the two methods is the persistence API used; the testEntityManager() test uses JPA, and the testSession() uses the Hibernate API.

Most differences are fairly simple: instead of Session.delete(), JPA uses EntityManager.remove(), for example. The query types are different, although they are still functionally equivalent. Probably the most relevant change is in the usage of transactions, and that's been entirely voluntary. You could, for example, use the block shown in Listing 7-7 in the testSession() method, which makes it almost entirely identical to the JPA version:

---

[6]Something your author calls a "persistence actor," as in "something that acts on persistence," but that sounds irrepressibly stuffy.

Listing 7-7. Using Some of the `EntityManager`'s API with the Hibernate `Session`

```
Session session = JPASessionUtil.getSession("utiljpa");
session.getTransaction().begin();
Thing t = new Thing();
t.setName("Thing 2");
session.persist(t);
session.getTransaction().commit();
session.close();
```

It's important to note, however, that `Session` and `EntityManager` are *similar* but not identical; while Listing 7-7 would work if you were using `EntityManager` instead of `Session`, even in the small block of testing code `Session` uses `org.hibernate.Query` instead of the `javax.persistence.Query`.

So which one should you use? Well, it depends on what you need. If you need JPA compatibility, then you'll have to restrict yourself to the `EntityManager` and its capabilities; otherwise, use the one you prefer. The Hibernate API provides some fine-tuning features that JPA cannot; if you want to use them, you will want to use `Session`, but apart from that, the two APIs will be equivalent for most intents and purposes.

Lifecycle Events

The Java Persistence Architecture exposes certain events to a data model. These events allow the developer to implement additional functionality that the architecture itself might not easily offer. The events are specified through the use of annotations, and the event handlers can be embedded in an entity directly, or can be held in a separate entity listener class.

You could use the lifecycle in a few different ways: you could manually update a time stamp, for example, or perhaps you could write audit data, initialize transient data, or validate data before persisting it.

There are lifecycle events corresponding to object creation, reads, updates, and deletes. For each event type that makes sense in a persistence context, there are callback hooks for *before* and *after* the event occurs.

The event handlers are simple methods corresponding to one of seven lifecycle phases.

Table 7-1. *The Entity Lifecycle Annotations*

Lifecycle Annotation	When Methods Run
@PrePersist	Executes before the data is actually inserted into a database table. It is not used when an object exists in the database and an update occurs.
@PostPersist	Executes after the data is written to a database table.
@PreUpdate	Executes when a managed object is updated. This annotation is not used when an object is first persisted to a database.
@PostUpdate	Executes after an update for managed objects is written to the database.
@PreRemove	Executes before a managed object's data is removed from the database.
@PostRemove	Executes after a managed object's data is removed from the database.
@PostLoad	Executes after a managed object's data has been loaded from the database and the object has been initialized.

Listing 7-8 offers an entity, descriptively named "`LifecycleThing`," which offers hooks for the various lifecycle events. As with our earlier classes, this uses Lombok to hide the boilerplate, such that this is the actual entire source code listing.

Listing 7-8. An Entity with Hooks for Every Available Lifecycle Event

```
package chapter07.lifecycle;

import lombok.*;
import org.jboss.logging.Logger;

import javax.persistence.*;
import java.util.BitSet;

@Entity
@ToString
@NoArgsConstructor
@EqualsAndHashCode
public class LifecycleThing {
    static Logger logger = Logger.getLogger(LifecycleThing.class);
    static BitSet lifecycleCalls = new BitSet();

    @Id
    @GeneratedValue(strategy = GenerationType.AUTO)
    @Getter
    @Setter
    Integer id;
    @Getter
    @Setter
    @Column
    String name;

    @PostLoad
    public void postLoad() {
        log("postLoad", 0);
    }

    @PrePersist
    public void prePersist() {
        log("prePersist", 1);
    }

    @PostPersist
    public void postPersist() {
        log("postPersist", 2);
    }

    @PreUpdate
    public void preUpdate() {
        log("preUpdate", 3);
    }

    @PostUpdate
    public void postUpdate() {
        log("postUpdate", 4);
    }
```

```
    @PreRemove
    public void preRemove() {
        log("preRemove", 5);
    }

    @PostRemove
    public void postRemove() {
        log("postRemove", 6);
    }

    private void log(String method, int index) {
        lifecycleCalls.set(index, true);
        logger.errorf("%12s: %s (%s)", method, this.getClass()
            .getSimpleName(), this.toString());
    }
}
```

This class keeps track of the lifecycle calls made in a BitSet. When a lifecycle event occurs, it sets a bit in the BitSet; a test can (and will) examine the BitSet to make sure there are no gaps, which will give us a clearer picture of whether we have successfully executed each callback.

We could, of course, just use our eyes and examine the results visually. This works, of course (and is the backbone of most user testing, sadly), but we want objective, repeatable, and more verifiable results.

Our lifecycle test is shown in Listing 7-9. All it needs to do is create, read, update, and remove an entity; that will fire off each of our event handlers, and we can see the sequencing (if we watch the application logs) and have the test validate that no tests have been skipped (because it checks the BitSet). Along the way, we'll see the use of the alternative loader mechanism that we discussed near the end of Chapter 6.[7]

Listing 7-9. The Lifecycle Test Driver

```
package chapter07.lifecycle;

import com.redhat.osas.jpa.util.JPASessionUtil;
import org.hibernate.Session;
import org.hibernate.Transaction;
import org.testng.Reporter;
import org.testng.annotations.Test;

import static org.testng.Assert.*;

public class LifecycleTest {
    @Test
    public void testLifecycle() {
        Integer id;
        Session session = JPASessionUtil.getSession("chapter07");

        Transaction tx = session.beginTransaction();
        LifecycleThing thing1 = new LifecycleThing();
        thing1.setName("Thing 1");
```

---

[7]The "alternative loader mechanism" refers to the use of Session.byId().load().

```
            session.save(thing1);
            id = thing1.getId();

            tx.commit();
            session.close();

            session = JPASessionUtil.getSession("chapter07");
            tx = session.beginTransaction();
            LifecycleThing thing2 = (LifecycleThing) session
                    .byId(LifecycleThing.class)
                    .load(-1);
            assertNull(thing2);

            thing2 = (LifecycleThing) session.byId(LifecycleThing.class)
                    .getReference(id);
            assertNotNull(thing2);
            assertEquals(thing1, thing2);

            thing2.setName("Thing 2");

            tx.commit();
            session.close();

            session = JPASessionUtil.getSession("chapter07");
            tx = session.beginTransaction();
            LifecycleThing thing3 = (LifecycleThing) session
                    .byId(LifecycleThing.class)
                    .getReference(id);
            assertNotNull(thing3);
            assertEquals(thing2, thing3);

            session.delete(thing3);

            tx.commit();
            session.close();
            assertEquals(LifecycleThing.lifecycleCalls.nextClearBit(0), 7);
        }
}
```

There are three sections to this test, each using its own session and transaction. The first creates a LifecycleThing and persists it. The second attempts to load a nonexistent entity, and then an existing entity; it then updates the existing entity. The third section loads that same entity, and removes it. This means we have every lifecycle event in an object represented: creation, reads, updates, and deletes.

For each lifecycle event, a log message is produced (at too high a priority, realistically; it's just set this way to force output without extra configuration). At the same time, the internal BitSet is modified to track whether the lifecycle methods have been called; at the end of the test, the BitSet is checked to see that every bit up through 7 has been set. If the value is correct, then we know that every lifecycle method has been called at least once.

The result should be fairly obvious: in this case, prePersist() is called before the persistence takes place, and postPersist() runs after the persistence has occurred.

Exceptions can be tricky in lifecycle handlers. If an exception occurs in a lifecycle listener *before* the event—that is, @PrePersist, @PreUpdate, @PreRemove—it will get passed to the caller for handling. The transaction, however, remains valid. With that said, you will invalidate the transaction if an error occurs in the @PostPersist, @PostUpdate, @PostRemove, or @PostLoad code.

An exception in a postloading operation would be . . . interesting to have to handle. (It would indicate that the data in the database was invalid from the object's perspective.) It would probably have to be handled in the database itself, and you'd be well advised to avoid this possibility at all costs.

External Entity Listeners

The greatest weakness of the LifecycleThing (apart from the fact that it's a class whose sole purpose is illustrating the persistence lifecycle) is that all of the event listeners are embedded in the class itself. We can, instead, designate an external class as an entity listener, with the same annotations, through the use of the @EntityListeners annotation. Listing 7-10 shows a simple entity with an external entity listener, with all of the boilerplate removed.

Listing 7-10. An Entity with an External Event Listener

```
@Entity
@EntityListeners({UserAccountListener.class})
public class UserAccount {
    Integer id;
    String name;
    Integer salt;
    Integer passwordHash;
    @Transient
    String password;
}
```

Now, Listing 7-11 shows what a simple external listener might look like:

Listing 7-11. An External Entity Listener

```
public class UserAccountListener {
    @PrePersist
    void setPasswordHash(Object o) {
        UserAccount ua = (UserAccount) o;
        if (ua.getSalt() == null || ua.getSalt() == 0) {
            ua.setSalt((int) (Math.random() * 65535));
        }
        ua.setPasswordHash(
                ua.getPassword().hashCode() * ua.getSalt()
        );
    }
}
```

When the UserAccount is persisted, the UserAccountListener will set a hashed password, multiplied by a random salt; presumably, a user-supplied password could be tested by applying the same salt.[8] (This is not secure, by any means. Don't use this code as an example of security.)

---

[8]For more information on cryptographic salt, see http://en.wikipedia.org/wiki/Salt_(cryptography).

In this case, the listener only watches for one object type; it does no error checking. (It will throw an error if the incorrect type is passed to it.)

Event listeners factor in conveniently anywhere where you actually need access to the persistence lifecycle, especially when considering data validation.

Data Validation

Hibernate also offers a validation API, presently the reference implementation of Java's Bean Validation specification, version 1.1.[9] The Bean Validation specification allows your data model to enforce its own constraints, as opposed to the coders having to add their own data value checks throughout the application code.

Model-based validation should have obvious value: it means that you are able to trust the state of your model, no matter at what stage you're accessing data.

Consider the situation where data validation is applied in a web service; accessing that data apart from the web service might not have the validation applied, which means that you can trust the data accessed via the web service *more* than you can trust it if it's accessed from other environments. This is a bad thing.

Note that we already have *some* validation capabilities, as part of the JPA specification itself. We can, for example, specify that columns' values are unique (via @Id or @Column(unique=true); we can also specify that columns not be empty via @Column(nullable=false). Through the magic of the entity lifecycle, we can enforce data validation through callbacks and external listeners as well,[10] and it's worth noting that in some cases this is still a valuable, workable approach.

So let's see what we can do to try out some more powerful validation capabilities with Hibernate.

The first step is to add Hibernate Validator to our project. If you're using Validator in a Java SE project (a standalone application, for example, like our tests), then you need to add *four* dependencies; if you're deploying your application into a Java EE application server like Wildfly, you only need to add the Validator dependency itself.

The four dependencies for Maven look like what is shown in Listing 7-12:

Listing 7-12. Dependency Additions to Enable the Use of the Validator API

```
<dependency>
        <groupId>org.hibernate</groupId>
        <artifactId>hibernate-validator</artifactId>
        <version>5.1.0.Alpha1</version>
</dependency>
<!-- these are only necessary if not in a Java EE environment -->
<dependency>
        <groupId>org.hibernate</groupId>
        <artifactId>hibernate-validator-cdi</artifactId>
        <version>5.1.0.Alpha1</version>
</dependency>
<dependency>
        <groupId>javax.el</groupId>
        <artifactId>javax.el-api</artifactId>
        <version>2.2.4</version>
</dependency>
```

---

[9]See http://jcp.org/en/jsr/detail?id=349 for more details on this specification.
[10]A callback would be a validation applied through a lifecycle method; you might test a value in a method annotated with @PrePersist, for example. An external entity listener would do the same sort of thing.

```
<dependency>
        <groupId>org.glassfish.web</groupId>
        <artifactId>javax.el</artifactId>
        <version>2.2.4</version>
</dependency>
```

Now let's look at a class and a test that uses validation to ensure the correctness of our data. As we're using Lombok again, Listing 7-13 is the entire source code:

Listing 7-13. An Entity Using Hibernate Validator

```java
package chapter07.validated;

import lombok.*;
import lombok.experimental.Builder;

import javax.persistence.*;
import javax.validation.constraints.Min;
import javax.validation.constraints.NotNull;
import javax.validation.constraints.Size;

@Entity
@EqualsAndHashCode
@ToString
@Builder
@NoArgsConstructor
@AllArgsConstructor(access = AccessLevel.PACKAGE)
public class ValidatedSimplePerson {
    @Id
    @Getter
    @Setter
    @GeneratedValue(strategy = GenerationType.IDENTITY)
    Long id;
    @Column
    @NotNull
    @Size(min = 2, max = 60)
    @Getter
    @Setter
    String fname;
    @Column
    @NotNull
    @Size(min = 2, max = 60)
    @Getter
    @Setter
    String lname;
    @Column
    @Min(value = 13)
    @Getter
    @Setter
    Integer age;
}
```

We've actually added some things to this entity via Lombok. The first thing we should look into is the `@AllArgsConstructor` annotation, which creates a package-visible constructor with all attributes as parameters; it's as if we had created `ValidatedSimplePerson(Long id, String fname, String lname, Integer age)`. We set it to package-visible because we don't want any other classes using it, mostly because we're using another Lombok annotation, `@Builder`.

The `@Builder` annotation creates an inner class, accessible via a `builder()` method.[11] This inner class uses a fluent API[12] to provide a convenient way to construct classes; with the builder, we can use the following code to construct a `ValidatedSimplePerson`:

```
ValidatedSimplePerson person=ValidatedSimplePerson.builder()
    .age(15)
    .fname("Johnny")
    .lname("McYoungster").build();
```

Now let's look at the validation annotations we're using, and why. It's worth noting that we're not using all of the annotations Validator makes available to us–there are more than 25 currently documented, not counting the possibility of custom validators. These are just some of the validation annotations in common use.

The first one that stands out is `@NotNull`, used on the fname attribute. This is an analog to the `@Column(nullable=false)` annotation we've mentioned earlier, but is applied at a different point in the persistence lifecycle; if `@NotNull` is used, the column will still be set the same way (to not allow null values), but the validation occurs *before* persistence. If we use `@Column(nullable=false)`, the validation occurs in the database, and gives us a database constraint violation rather than a validation failure—which is a very slight semantic difference, but a difference nonetheless.

`@Size` can partially be emulated by using `@Column(length=60)`, but `@Column` has no way to enforce minimum size constraints, and again, the validation phase takes place before the persistence phase.

`@Min(value=13)` specifies that the integral value has a minimum value, as one might expect; there's a corresponding `@Max` annotation for maximum values.

One interesting thing about each of these is that they can actually affect the database definition.[13] `@Min` and `@Max`, for example, add table constraints if the database is able to support them, and `@NotNull` enforces the constraint both in code *and* at the database level. `@Size` will assign a maximum size to a database column, if the maximum size is given; minimum size isn't something the database can normally enforce.

Let's see what some of this looks like, in a test. What we'll do is write a series of objects into a Hibernate session, most of which will fail validation in some way. The actual persistence mechanism sounds like something for which we can write a method, so without further ado,[14] let's look at Listing 7-14 for the entire set of tests so we can see how validation is applied.

Listing 7-14. Testing Validation

```
private ValidatedSimplePerson persist(ValidatedSimplePerson person) {
    Session session = SessionUtil.getSession();
    Transaction tx = session.beginTransaction();
    session.persist(person);
    tx.commit();
    session.close();
    return person;
}
```

---

[11] As with most things, there's a limitation. Lombok cannot generate builders that are aware of a class hierarchy; this is caused by how Lombok works and is *very* difficult to get around.

[12] See http://en.wikipedia.org/wiki/Fluent_interface for more information on what a Fluent API is and what it can look like.

[13] The Validator documentation calls the level of effect on the database "Hibernate metadata impact," such that validations of which the database is unaware have no metadata impact, but validations like `@NotNull` are described as meaning "Column(s) are not nullable."

[14] Does *anyone* like lots of ado?

```java
@Test
public void createValidPerson() {
    persist(ValidatedSimplePerson.builder()
            .age(15)
            .fname("Johnny")
            .lname("McYoungster").build());
}

@Test(expectedExceptions = ConstraintViolationException.class)
public void createValidatedUnderagePerson() {
    persist(ValidatedSimplePerson.builder()
            .age(12)
            .fname("Johnny")
            .lname("McYoungster").build());
    fail("Should have failed validation");
}

@Test(expectedExceptions = ConstraintViolationException.class)
public void createValidatedPoorFNamePerson2() {
    persist(ValidatedSimplePerson.builder()
            .age(14)
            .fname("J")
            .lname("McYoungster2").build());
    fail("Should have failed validation");
}

@Test(expectedExceptions = ConstraintViolationException.class)
public void createValidatedNoFNamePerson() {
    persist(ValidatedSimplePerson.builder()
            .age(14)
            .lname("McYoungster2").build());
    fail("Should have failed validation");
}
```

Our first method in this listing—persist()—exercises the persistence cycle, to save code. Our test methods will create an object and pass it to this to execute the validation lifecycle.

Our four other methods create entities that match various single criteria: a valid entity, an entity whose fname is too short, an entity whose lname is too short, and an entity that's underage. In the case of the tests where we expect validation failures, we mark the methods as accepting an exception- and failing if the persist() method executes successfully. This works for us since we expect the persist() method to fail in these cases.

One thing you might notice, though, is that we have validations that encompass only single attributes. We can use the entity lifecycle to create our own custom validations, but Validator allows us to create our own validation annotations—including single-field validations (as we've seen used) and class-level validations.

Let's create a coordinate entity—and let's use, for the sake of example, a validation that ensures that a valid Coordinate isn't allowed to be in quadrant III in the Cartesian quadrant system. (Coordinates in quadrant III have negative x- and y- attributes.) Single-field validations wouldn't work here, because -5 is valid as an x-coordinate, as long as the y-coordinate isn't negative as well.

We actually have a number of options we can choose to build the validation. The most flexible option is an annotation that looks up the dependent fields—so a validation on X would contain a reference to Y and the attendant acceptable criteria, and vice versa. With that said, let's choose a simpler option, one very specific to our Coordinate class.[15]

First, let's *see* the Coordinate class, as shown in Listing 7-15. Then we'll create the tests that we expect to pass, and last, we'll take a look at the annotation that applies the validation. Much like the SimpleValidatedPerson entity, we're going to use Lombok fairly heavily to eliminate boilerplate code.

Listing 7-15. A Coordinate Class, Roughly Analogous to java.awt.Point

```
package chapter07.validated;

import lombok.*;
import lombok.experimental.Builder;

import javax.persistence.Entity;
import javax.persistence.GeneratedValue;
import javax.persistence.GenerationType;
import javax.persistence.Id;
import javax.validation.constraints.NotNull;

@Entity
@EqualsAndHashCode
@ToString
@NoArgsConstructor
@Builder
@AllArgsConstructor
@NoQuadrantIII
public class Coordinate {
    @Id
    @GeneratedValue(strategy = GenerationType.AUTO)
    @Getter
    @Setter
    Integer id;
    @Getter
    @Setter
    @NotNull
    Integer x;
    @Getter
    @Setter
    @NotNull
    Integer y;
}
```

Note that this class won't compile without our annotation being defined fully; that's coming up very shortly. First, though, let's look at our test code (shown in Listing 7-16), which creates five Coordinates and persists them all; the Coordinate objects that represent the origin as well as Quadrants I, II, and IV should all persist successfully, and the Coordinate for Quadrant III should fail.

---

[15]If you're interested in more detail about custom constraints—and you probably should be, if Validator interests you—see http://docs.jboss.org/hibernate/validator/5.0/reference/en-US/html/validator-customconstraints.html.

Listing 7-16. The Coordinate Validation Test

```
private Coordinate persist(Coordinate entity) {
    Session session = SessionUtil.getSession();
    Transaction tx = session.beginTransaction();
    session.persist(entity);
    tx.commit();
    session.close();
    return entity;
}

@DataProvider(name = "validCoordinates")
private Object[][] validCoordinates() {
    return new Object[][]{
        {1, 1},
        {1, 0},
        {-1, 1},
        {0, 1},
        {-1, 0},
        {0, -1},
        {1, -1},
        {0, 0}, // trailing comma is valid: see JLS 10.6
    };
}

@Test(dataProvider = "validCoordinates")
public void testValidCoordinate(Integer x, Integer y) {
    Coordinate c = Coordinate.builder().x(x).y(y).build();
    persist(c);
    // has passed validation, if we reach this point.
}

@Test(expectedExceptions = ConstraintViolationException.class)
public void testInvalidCoordinate() {
    testValidCoordinate(-1, -1);
    fail("Should have gotten a constraint violation");
}
```

Note the use of the @DataProvider annotation, which allows us to call testValidCoordinate() with a series of values instead of having separate methods. (The tests are all represented separately, so that this selection of code will result in nine separate tests being run, rather than two tests, one with a set of data.)

Now we finally get a chance to see the validation annotation itself. First, let's look at the annotation in Listing 7-17, and then we'll see how the annotation is implemented, as shown in Listing 7-18.

Listing 7-17. A Class-level Annotation

```
@Target({ElementType.TYPE, ElementType.ANNOTATION_TYPE})
@Retention(RetentionPolicy.RUNTIME)
@Constraint(validatedBy = {QuadrantIIIValidator.class})
@Documented
public @interface NoQuadrantIII {
    String message() default "Failed quadrant III test";
```

```
    Class<?>[] groups() default {};

    Class<? extends Payload>[] payload() default {};
}
```

Listing 7-18. The Validation Implementation, Used by Listing 7-17

```
public class QuadrantIIIValidator implements ConstraintValidator<NoQuadrantIII, Coordinate> {
    @Override
    public void initialize(NoQuadrantIII constraintAnnotation) {
    }

    @Override
    public boolean isValid(Coordinate value, ConstraintValidatorContext context) {
        return !(value.getX() < 0 && value.getY() < 0);
    }
}
```

With all of these classes as part of the compilation unit, we can now guarantee that any time Hibernate persists a Coordinate the Coordinate will not be written to the database unless it's not in Quadrant III.

A good exercise for the reader is to modify the annotation such that the coder can specify which quadrants should be used for the validation.

Summary

This chapter has covered the use of the standard Java Persistence Architecture configuration file, as well as how to access the persistence lifecycle and validation before persistence. It has also discussed the use of Lombok to help avoid boilerplate code, and shown how to use a data provider in TestNG to eliminate extra test code, as well.

In the next chapter, we will look at how a client application communicates with the database representation of the entities by using the Session object.

CHAPTER 8

■ ■ ■

Using the Session

You may have noticed that the Session object is the central point of access to Hibernate functionality. We will now look at what it embodies and what that implies about how you should use it.

Sessions

From the examples in the earlier chapters, you will have noticed that a small number of classes dominate our interactions with Hibernate. Of these, Session is the linchpin.

The Session object is used to create new database entities, read in objects from the database, update objects in the database, and delete objects from the database.[1] It allows you to manage the transaction boundaries of database access, and (in a pinch) to obtain a traditional JDBC connection object so that you can do things to the database that the Hibernate developers have not already considered in their existing design.

If you are familiar with the JDBC approach, it helps to think of a Session object as somewhat like a JDBC connection, and the SessionFactory, which provides Session objects, as somewhat like a ConnectionPool, which provides Connection objects. These similarities in roles are illustrated in Figure 8-1.

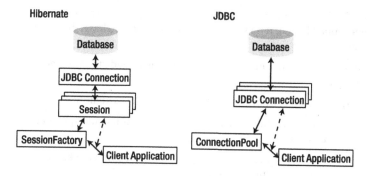

Figure 8-1. *Similarities between Hibernate and JDBC objects*

SessionFactory objects are expensive objects; needlessly duplicating them will cause problems quickly, and creating them is a relatively time-consuming process. Ideally, you should have a single SessionFactory for each database your application will access.

---

[1]Almost everything, which makes it linchpin-like. Go figure.

SessionFactory objects are threadsafe, so it is not necessary to obtain one for each thread. However, you will create numerous Session objects—at least one for each thread using Hibernate. Sessions in Hibernate are not threadsafe, so sharing Session objects between threads could cause data loss or deadlock. In fact, you will often want to create multiple Session instances even during the lifetime of a specific thread (see the "Threads" section for concurrency issues).

■ **Caution** The analogy between a Hibernate session and a JDBC connection only goes so far. One important difference is that if a Hibernate Session object throws an exception of any sort, you must discard it and obtain a new one. This prevents data in the session's cache from becoming inconsistent with the database.

We've already covered the core methods in Chapter 4, so we won't discuss all the methods available to you through the Session interface. For an exhaustive look at what's available, you should read the API documentation on the Hibernate website or in the Hibernate 4 download. Table 8-1 gives a broad overview of the various categories of methods available to you; despite its length, this is not an exhaustive list.

Table 8-1. *Hibernate Method Summary*

Method	Description
Create, Read, Update, and Delete	
save()	Saves an object to the database. This should not be called for an object that has already been saved to the database.
saveOrUpdate()	Saves an object to the database, or updates the database if the object already exists. This method is slightly less efficient than the save() method since it may need to perform a SELECT statement to check whether the object already exists, but it will not fail if the object has already been saved.
merge()	Merges the fields of a nonpersistent object into the appropriate persistent object (determined by ID). If no such object exists in the database, then one is created and saved.
Persist	Reassociates an object with the session so that changes made to the object will be persisted.
Get	Retrieves a specific object from the database by the object's identifier.
getEntityName	Retrieves the entity name (this will usually be the same as the fully qualified class name of the POJO).
getIdentifier	Determines the identifier—the object(s) representing the primary key—for a specific object associated with the session.
load()	Loads an object from the database by the object's identifier (you should use the get() methods if you are not certain that the object is in the database).
refresh()	Refreshes the state of an associated object from the database.
update	Updates the database with changes to an object.
delete()	Deletes an object from the database.

(continued)

Table 8-1. (*continued*)

Method	Description
createFilter()	Creates a filter (query) to narrow operations on the database.
enableFilter()	Enables a named filter in queries produced by createFilter().
disableFilter()	Disables a named filter.
getEnabledFilter()	Retrieves a currently enabled filter object.
createQuery()	Creates a Hibernate query to be applied to the database.
getNamedQuery()	Retrieves a query from the mapping file.
cancelQuery()	Cancels execution of any query currently in progress from another thread.
createCriteria()	Creates a criteria object for narrowing search results.
Transactions and Locking	
beginTransaction()	Begins a transaction.
getTransaction()	Retrieves the current transaction object. This does not return null when no transaction is in progress. Instead, the active property of the returned object is false.
lock()	Gets a database lock for an object (or can be used like persist() if LockMode.NONE is given).
Managing Resources	
contains()	Determines whether a specific object is associated with the database.
clear()	Clears the session of all loaded instances and cancels any saves, updates, or deletions that have not been completed. Retains any iterators that are in use.
evict()	Disassociates an object from the session so that subsequent changes to it will not be persisted.
flush()	Flushes all pending changes into the database—all saves, updates, and deletions will be carried out; essentially, this synchronizes the session with the database.
isOpen()	Determines whether the session has been closed.
isDirty()	Determines whether the session is synchronized with the database.
getCacheMode()	Determines the caching mode currently employed.
setCacheMode()	Changes the caching mode currently employed.
getCurrentLockMode()	Determines the locking mode currently employed.
setFlushMode()	Determines the approach to flushing currently used. The options are to flush after every operation, flush when needed, never flush, or flush only on commit.
setReadOnly()	Marks a persistent object as read-only (or as writable). There are minor performance benefits from marking an object as read-only, but changes to its state will be ignored until it is marked as writable.

(*continued*)

Table 8-1. (*continued*)

Method	Description
close()	Closes the session, and hence, the underlying database connection; releases other resources (such as the cache). You must not perform operations on the Session object after calling close().
getSessionFactory()	Retrieves a reference to the SessionFactory object that created the current Session instance.
The JDBC Connection	
connection()	Retrieves a reference to the underlying database connection.
disconnect()	Disconnects the underlying database connection.
reconnect()	Reconnects the underlying database connection.
isConnected()	Determines whether the underlying database connection is connected.

Transactions and Locking

Transactions and locking are intimately related: the locking techniques chosen to enforce a transaction can determine both the performance and the likelihood of success of the transaction. The type of transaction selected dictates, to some extent, the type of locking that it must use.

You are not obliged to use transactions if they do not suit your needs, but there is rarely a good reason to avoid them. If you decide to avoid them, you will need to invoke the flush() method on the session at appropriate points to ensure that your changes are persisted to the database.

Transactions

A transaction is a unit of work guaranteed to behave as if you have exclusive use of the database. Generally speaking, if you wrap your work in a transaction, the behavior of other system users will not affect your data. A transaction can be started, committed to write data to the database, or rolled back to remove all changes from the beginning onward (usually as the result of an error). To properly complete an operation, you obtain a Transaction object from the database (beginning the transaction) and manipulate the session as shown in the following code:

```
Session session = factory.openSession();
try {
  session.beginTransaction();

  // Normal session usage here...

  session.getTransaction().commit();
} catch (HibernateException e) {
  Transaction tx = session.getTransaction();
  if (tx.isActive()) tx.rollback();
} finally {
  session.close();
}
```

In the real world, it's not actually desirable for all transactions to be fully ACID (see the sidebar entitled "The ACID Tests") because of the performance problems that this can cause.

Different database suppliers support and permit you, to a lesser or greater extent, to break the ACID rules, but the degree of control over the isolation rule is actually mandated by the SQL-92 standard. There are important reasons that you might want to break this rule, so both JDBC and Hibernate also make explicit allowances for it.

THE ACID TESTS

- *Atomicity*: A transaction should be all or nothing. If it fails to complete, the database will be left as if none of the operations had ever been performed—this is known as a *rollback*.

- *Consistency*: A transaction should be incapable of breaking any rules defined for the database. For example, foreign keys must be obeyed. If for some reason this is impossible, the transaction will be rolled back.

- *Isolation*: The effects of the transaction will be completely invisible to all other transactions until it has completed successfully. This guarantees that the transaction will always see the data in a sensible state. For example, an update to a user's address should only contain a correct address (i.e., it will never have the house name for one location but the ZIP code for another); without this rule, a transaction could easily see when another transaction had updated the first part but had not yet completed.

- *Durability*: The data should be retained intact. If the system fails for any reason, it should always be possible to retrieve the database up to the moment of the failure.

The isolation levels permitted by JDBC and Hibernate are listed in Table 8-2.

Table 8-2. JDBC Isolation Levels

Level	Name	Transactional Behavior
0	None	Anything is permitted; the database or driver does not support transactions.
1	Read Uncommitted	Dirty, nonrepeatable, and phantom reads are permitted.
2	Read Committed	Nonrepeatable reads and phantom reads are permitted.
4	Repeatable Read	Phantom reads are permitted.
8	Serializable	The rule must be obeyed absolutely.

A *dirty read* may see the in-progress changes of an uncommitted transaction. As with the isolation example discussed in the preceding sidebar, it could see the wrong ZIP code for an address.

A *nonrepeatable read* sees different data for the same query. For example, it might determine a specific user's ZIP code at the beginning of the transaction and again at the end, and get a different answer both times without making any updates.

A *phantom read* sees different numbers of rows for the same query. For example, it might see 100 users in the database at the beginning of the query and 105 at the end without making any updates.

Hibernate treats the isolation as a global setting: you apply the configuration option hibernate.connection. isolation in the usual manner, setting it to one of the values permitted in Table 8-2. This is not always ideal, however. You will sometimes want to treat one particular transaction at a high level of isolation (usually Serializable), while permitting lower degrees of isolation for others. To do so, you will need to obtain the JDBC connection directly, alter the isolation level, begin the transaction, roll back or clean up the transaction as appropriate, and reset the isolation level to its original value before releasing the connection for general usage. Hibernate does not provide a more direct way to alter the isolation level of the connection in a localized way. The implementation of the createUser() method, shown in Listing 8-1, demonstrates the additional complexity that the connection-specific transaction isolation level involves.

Listing 8-1. Using a Specific Isolation Level

```
public static void createUser(String username)
    throws HibernateException
{
    Session session = factory.openSession();
    int isolation = -1;
    try {
    isolation = session.connection().getTransactionIsolation();
        session.connection().setTransactionIsolation(
            Connection.TRANSACTION_SERIALIZABLE);
        session.beginTransaction();

        // Normal usage of the Session here...
        Publisher p = new Publisher(username);
        Subscriber s = new Subscriber(username);
        session.saveOrUpdate(p);
        session.saveOrUpdate(s);

        // Commit the transaction
        session.getTransaction().commit();
    } catch (SQLException e1) {
        rollback(session);
        throw new HibernateException(e1);
    } catch (HibernateException e1) {
    rollback(session);
        throw e1;
    } finally {
        // reset isolation
        reset(session,isolation);

        // Close the session
    close(session);
    }
}
```

Fortunately, the normal case for a transaction using the global isolation level is much simpler. We provide a more standard implementation of the createUser() method for comparison in Listing 8-2.

Listing 8-2. Using the Global (Default) Isolation Level

```
public static void createUser(String username) throws HibernateException {
    Session session = factory.openSession();
    try {
        session.beginTransaction();
```

```
    // Normal usage of the Session here...
    Publisher p = new Publisher(username);
    Subscriber s = new Subscriber(username);
    session.saveOrUpdate(p);
    session.saveOrUpdate(s);

    // Commit the transaction
    session.getTransaction().commit();
  } catch (HibernateException e1) {
    rollback(session);
    throw e1;
  } finally {
    // Close the session
    close(session);
  }
}
```

Locking

A database can conform to these various levels of isolation in a number of ways, and you will need a working knowledge of locking to elicit the desired behavior and performance from your application in all circumstances.

To prevent simultaneous access to data, the database itself will acquire a lock on that data. This can be acquired for the momentary operation on the data only, or it can be retained until the end of the transaction. The former is called *optimistic locking* and the latter is called *pessimistic locking*.

The Read Uncommitted isolation level always acquires optimistic locks, whereas the Serializable isolation level will only acquire pessimistic locks. Some databases offer a feature that allows you to append the FOR UPDATE query to a select operation, which requires the database to acquire a pessimistic lock even in the lower isolation levels.

Hibernate provides some support for this feature when it is available, and takes it somewhat further by adding facilities that describe additional degrees of isolation obtainable from Hibernate's own cache.

The LockMode object controls this fine-grained isolation (see Table 8-3). It is only applicable to the get() methods, so it is limited; however, when possible, it is preferable to the direct control of isolation mentioned previously.

Table 8-3. Lock Modes

Mode	Description
NONE	Reads from the database only if the object is not available from the caches.
READ	Reads from the database regardless of the contents of the caches.
UPGRADE	Obtains a dialect-specific upgrade lock for the data to be accessed (if this is available from your database).
UPGRADE_NOWAIT	Behaves like UPGRADE, but when support is available from the database and dialect, the method will fail with a locking exception immediately. Without this option, or on databases for which it is not supported, the query must wait for a lock to be granted (or for a timeout to occur).

An additional lock mode, WRITE, is acquired by Hibernate automatically when it has written to a row within the current transaction. This mode cannot be set explicitly, but calls to getLockMode may return it.

Having discussed locking in general, we need to touch on some of the problems that locks can cause.

Deadlocks

Even if you have not encountered a deadlock (sometimes given the rather sordid name of "deadly embrace") in databases, you have probably encountered the problem in multithreaded Java code. The problem arises from similar origins.

Two threads of execution can get into a situation in which each is waiting for the other to release a resource that it needs. The most common way to create this situation in a database is shown in Figure 8-2.

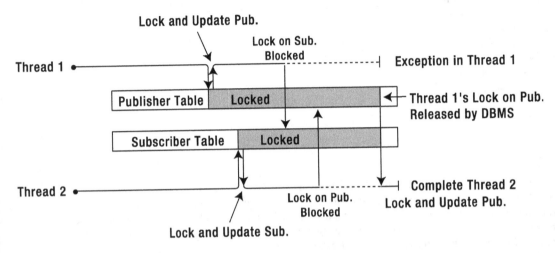

Figure 8-2. *The anatomy of a deadlock*

Each thread obtains a lock on its table when the update begins. Each thread proceeds until the table held by the other user is required. Neither thread can release the lock on its own table until the transaction completes—so something has to give.

A deadlock can also occur when a single thread of execution is carrying out an equivalent sequence of operations using two Session objects connected to the same database. In practice, the multiple-thread scenario is more common.

Fortunately, a database management system (DBMS) can detect this situation automatically, at which point the transaction of one or more of the offending processes will be aborted by the database. The resulting deadlock error will be received and handled by Hibernate as a normal HibernateException. Now you must roll back your transaction, close the session, and then (optionally) try again.

Listing 8-3 demonstrates how four updates from a pair of sessions can cause a deadlock. If you look at the output from the threads, you will see that one of them completes while the other fails, with a deadlock error.

Looking at the database after completion (shown in Listing 8-3), you will see that the test user has been replaced with either jeff or dave in both tables (you will never see dave from one thread and jeff from the other). Though it is not necessary here, because we close the session regardless, in a more extensive application it is important to ensure that the session associated with a deadlock or any other Hibernate exception is closed and never used again, because otherwise the cache may be left in a corrupted state.

It is worth building and running Listing 8-3 to ensure that you are familiar with the symptoms of a deadlock when they occur.

Listing 8-3. Code to Generate a Deadlock

```
package com.hibernatebook.session.deadlock;

import java.sql.Connection;
import java.sql.SQLException;
```

```java
import org.hibernate.HibernateException;
import org.hibernate.Query;
import org.hibernate.Session;
import org.hibernate.SessionFactory;
import org.hibernate.Transaction;
import org.hibernate.cfg.Configuration;

public class GenerateDeadlock {

    private static SessionFactory factory = new Configuration().configure()
        .buildSessionFactory();

    public static void createUser(String username) throws HibernateException {
        Session session = factory.openSession();
        try {
            session.beginTransaction();

            // Normal usage of the Session here...
            Publisher p = new Publisher(username);
            Subscriber s = new Subscriber(username);
            session.saveOrUpdate(p);
            session.saveOrUpdate(s);

            // Commit the transaction
            session.getTransaction().commit();
        } catch (HibernateException e1) {
            rollback(session);
            throw e1;
        } finally {
            // Close the session
            close(session);
        }
    }

    public static void reset(Session session, int isolation) {
        if (isolation >= 0) {
            try {
                session.connection().setTransactionIsolation(isolation);
            } catch (SQLException e) {
                System.err.println("Could not reset the isolation level: " + e);
            } catch (HibernateException e) {
                System.err.println("Could not reset the isolation level: " + e);
            }
        }
    }

    public static void close(Session session) {
        try {
            session.close();
```

```java
        } catch (HibernateException e) {
            System.err.println("Could not close the session: " + e);
        }
    }

    public static void rollback(Session session) {
        try {
            Transaction tx = session.getTransaction();
            if (tx.isActive())
                tx.rollback();
        } catch (HibernateException e) {
            System.err.println("Could not rollback the session: " + e);
        }
    }

    public static void main(String[] argv) {

        System.out.println("Creating test user...");
        createUser("test");

        System.out.println("Proceeding to main test...");
        Session s1 = factory.openSession();
        Session s2 = factory.openSession();

        try {
            s1.beginTransaction();
            s2.beginTransaction();

            System.out.println("Update 1");
            Query q1 = s1.createQuery("from Publisher");
            Publisher pub1 = (Publisher) q1.uniqueResult();
            pub1.setUsername("jeff");
            s1.flush();

            System.out.println("Update 2");
            Query q2 = s2.createQuery("from Subscriber");
            Subscriber sub1 = (Subscriber) q2.uniqueResult();
            sub1.setUsername("dave");
            s2.flush();

            System.out.println("Update 3");
            Query q3 = s1.createQuery("from Subscriber");
            Subscriber sub2 = (Subscriber) q3.uniqueResult();
            sub2.setUsername("jeff");
            s1.flush();

            System.out.println("Update 4");
            Query q4 = s2.createQuery("from Publisher");
            Publisher pub2 = (Publisher) q4.uniqueResult();
            pub2.setUsername("dave");
            s2.flush();
```

```
            s1.getTransaction().commit();
            s2.getTransaction().commit();

        } catch (RuntimeException e1) {
            e1.printStackTrace();
            // Run the boilerplate to roll back the sessions
            rollback(s1);
            rollback(s2);
            throw e1;
        } finally {
            // Run the boilerplate to close the sessions
            close(s1);
            close(s2);
        }
    }
}
```

Caching

Accessing a database is an expensive operation, even for a simple query. The request has to be sent (usually over the network) to the server. The database server may have to compile the SQL into a query plan. The query plan has to be run and is limited largely by disk performance. The resulting data has to be shuttled back (again, usually across the network) to the client, and only then can the application program begin to process the results.

Most good databases will cache the results of a query if it is run multiple times, eliminating the disk I/O and query compilation time. But this will be of limited value if there are large numbers of clients making substantially different requests. Even if the cache generally holds the results, the time taken to transmit the information across the network is often the larger part of the delay.

Some applications will be able to take advantage of in-process databases, but this is the exception rather than the rule—and such databases have their own limitations.

The natural and obvious answer is to have a cache at the client end of the database connection. This is not a feature provided or supported by JDBC directly, but Hibernate provides one cache (the first-level, or L1, cache) through which all requests must pass. A second-level cache (L2) is optional and configurable.

The L1 cache ensures that, within a session, requests for a given object from a database will always return the same object instance, thus preventing data from conflicting and preventing Hibernate from trying to load an object multiple times.

Items in the L1 cache can be individually discarded by invoking the evict() method on the session for the object that you wish to discard. To discard all items in the L1 cache, invoke the clear() method.

In this way, Hibernate has a major advantage over the traditional JDBC approach: with no additional effort from the developer, a Hibernate application gains the benefits of a client-side database cache.

Figure 8-3 shows the two caches available to the session: the compulsory L1 cache, through which all requests must pass, and the optional L2 cache. The L1 cache will always be consulted before any attempt is made to locate an object in the L2 cache. You will notice that the L2 cache is external to Hibernate; and although it is accessed via the session in a way that is transparent to Hibernate users, it is a pluggable interface to any one of a variety of caches that are maintained on the same JVM as your Hibernate application or on an external JVM. This allows a cache to be shared between applications on the same machine, or even among multiple applications on multiple machines.

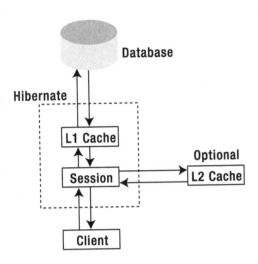

Figure 8-3. *The session's relationship to the caches*

In principle, any third-party cache can be used with Hibernate. An org.hibernate.cache.CacheProvider interface is provided, which must be implemented to provide Hibernate with a handle to the cache implementation. The cache provider is then specified by giving the implementation class name as the value of the hibernate.cache. provider_class property.

In practice, the four production-ready caches, which are already supported, will be adequate for most users (see Table 8-4).

Table 8-4. *L2 Cache Implementations Supported by Hibernate Out of the Box*

Cache Name	Description
EHCache	An in-process cache
Infinispan	Open source successor to JBossCache that provides distributed cache support
OSCache	An alternative in-process cache
SwarmCache	A multicast distributed cache

The type of access to the L2 cache can be configured on a per-session basis by selecting a CacheMode option (see Table 8-5) and applying it with the setCacheMode() method.

Table 8-5. *CacheMode Options*

Mode	Description
NORMAL	Data is read from and written to the cache as necessary.
GET	Data is never added to the cache (although cache entries are invalidated when updated by the session).
PUT	Data is never read from the cache, but cache entries will be updated as they are read from the database by the session.
REFRESH	This is the same as PUT, but the use_minimal_puts Hibernate configuration option will be ignored if it has been set.
IGNORE	Data is never read from or written to the cache (except that cache entries will still be invalidated when they are updated by the session).

The CacheMode setting does not affect the way in which the L1 cache is accessed.

The decision to use an L2 cache is not clear-cut. Although it has the potential to greatly reduce access to the database, the benefits depend on the type of cache and the way in which it will be accessed.

A distributed cache will cause additional network traffic. Some types of database access may result in the contents of the cache being flushed before they are used; in this case, it will be adding unnecessary overhead to the transactions.

The L2 cache cannot account for the changes in the underlying data, which are the result of actions by an external program that is not cache-aware. This could potentially lead to problems with stale data, which is not an issue with the L1 cache.

In practice, as with most optimization problems, it is best to carry out performance testing under realistic load conditions. This will let you determine if a cache is necessary and help you select which one will offer the greatest improvement.

Actually, configuring for cache usage is fairly simple. In order to set everything up, in this example, we will need to do the following:

1. Select a cache provider and add the dependency to Maven.

2. Configure Hibernate to use the cache provider for a second-level cache.

3. Alter our entities to mark them as cacheable.

We'll choose EhCache as a cache provider, as it's trivial to set up in a Java SE environment. The dependency block for Maven will look like this:

```
<dependency>
        <groupId>org.hibernate</groupId>
        <artifactId>hibernate-ehcache</artifactId>
        <version>4.2.8.Final</version>
</dependency>
```

Now, we need to add three properties to Hibernate that will tell it to use a second-level cache and which cache to use:

```
<property name="cache.use_second_level_cache">true</property>
<property name="hibernate.cache.use_query_cache">true</property>
<property name="hibernate.cache.region.factory_class">
        org.hibernate.cache.ehcache.SingletonEhCacheRegionFactory
</property>
```

The last thing we need to do is mark the entity as cacheable. In Listing 8-4, we'll create a simple Supplier entity (which we'll revisit in the next chapters) and show how it's used:

Listing 8-4. A Simple, Cacheable Supplier Entity

```
package chapter08.model;

import org.hibernate.annotations.Cache;
import org.hibernate.annotations.CacheConcurrencyStrategy;

import javax.persistence.*;
import java.io.Serializable;
```

```
@Entity
@Cacheable
@Cache(usage = CacheConcurrencyStrategy.READ_ONLY)
public class Supplier implements Serializable {
    @Id
    @GeneratedValue(strategy = GenerationType.AUTO)
    Integer id;
    @Column(unique = true)
    String name;
}
```

We're not showing the mutators, accessors, equals(), or hashCode() methods, of course.

Now, if we load a specific Supplier in one session, then immediately load the same Supplier in another session, the database will not (necessarily) be queried because it's being pulled from the second-level cache instead of from the database each time. Using different sessions is necessary because the Supplier instance would be cached in the first-level cache of each Session; the sessions share a second-level cache and not a first-level cache.

Threads

Having considered the caches available to a Hibernate application, you may now be concerned about the risk of a conventional Java deadlock if two threads of execution were to contend for the same object in the Hibernate session cache.

In principle, this is possible, and unlike database deadlocks, Java thread deadlocks do not time out with an error message. Fortunately, there is a very simple solution:

> Patient: Doctor, it hurts when I do this.

> Doctor: Don't do that, then.[2]

Do not share the Session object between threads. This will eliminate any risk of deadlocking on objects contained within the session cache.

The easiest way to ensure that you do not use the same Session object outside the current thread is to use an instance local to the current method. If you absolutely must maintain an instance for a longer duration, maintain the instance within a ThreadLocal object. For most purposes, however, the lightweight nature of the Session object makes it practical to construct, use, and destroy an instance, rather than to store a session.

Summary

In this chapter, we have discussed the nature of Session objects and how they can be used to obtain and manage transactions. We have looked at the two levels of caching that are available to applications, and how concurrent threads should manage sessions.

In the next chapter, we discuss the various ways in which you can retrieve objects from the database. We also show you how to perform more complicated queries against the database using HQL.

---

[2]For some reason, this is one of my favorite jokes. Another one is "Time flies like an arrow, fruit flies like a banana." Stop rolling your eyes, please.

CHAPTER 9

■ ■ ■

Searches and Queries

In the last chapter, we discussed how the Hibernate session is used to interact with the database. Some of the session's methods take query strings in their parameter lists or return Query objects. These methods are used to request arbitrary information from the database. In order to fully show how they're used, we must introduce the Hibernate Query Language (HQL), used to phrase these requests. As well as extracting information (with SELECT), HQL can be used to alter the information in the database (with INSERT, UPDATE, and DELETE). We cover all of this basic functionality in this chapter. Note: Hibernate's query facilities do not allow you to alter the database structure.

HQL is an object-oriented query language, similar to SQL, but instead of operating on tables and columns, HQL works with persistent objects and their properties. It is a superset of the JPQL, the Java Persistence Query Language; a JPQL query is a valid HQL query, but not all HQL queries are valid JPQL queries.

HQL is a language with its own syntax and grammar. It is written as strings, like from Product p–as opposed to Hibernate's criteria queries (discussed in the next chapter), which take the form of a conventional Java API. Ultimately, your HQL queries are translated by Hibernate into conventional SQL queries; Hibernate also provides an API that allows you to directly issue SQL queries.

Hibernate Query Language (HQL)

While most ORM tools and object databases offer an object query language, Hibernate's HQL stands out as complete and easy to use. Although you can use SQL statements directly with Hibernate (which is covered in detail in the "Using Native SQL" section of this chapter), we recommend that you use HQL (or criteria) whenever possible to avoid database portability hassles, as well as to take advantage of Hibernate's SQL-generation and caching strategies. In addition to its technical advantages over traditional SQL, HQL is a more compact query language than SQL because it can make use of the relationship information defined in the Hibernate mappings.

We realize that not every developer trusts Hibernate's generated SQL to be perfectly optimized. If you do encounter a performance bottleneck in your queries, we recommend that you use SQL tracing on your database during performance testing of your critical components. If you see an area that needs optimization, first try to optimize using HQL, and only later drop into native SQL. Hibernate provides statistics information through a JMX MBean, which you can use for analyzing Hibernate's performance. Hibernate's statistics also give you insight into how caching is performing.

■ **Note**   If you would like to execute HQL statements through a GUI-based tool, the Hibernate team provides a Hibernate console for Eclipse in the Hibernate Tools subproject. This console is a plug-in for recent versions of Eclipse, and the tool is described in detail in Appendix B.

Syntax Basics

HQL was inspired by SQL and is the inspiration for the Java Persistence Query Language (JPQL). The JPQL specification is included in the standard for JPA available from the Java Community Process web site (www.jcp.org/en/jsr/detail?id=220). HQL's syntax is defined as an ANTLR grammar; the grammar files are included in the grammar directory of the Hibernate core download. (ANTLR is a tool for building language parsers.)

As the ANTLR grammar files are somewhat cryptic, and as not every statement that is permissible according to the ANTLR grammar's rules can be used in Hibernate, we outline the syntax for the four fundamental HQL operations in this section. Note that the following descriptions of syntax are not comprehensive; there are some deprecated or more obscure usages (particularly for SELECT statements) that are not covered here.

UPDATE

UPDATE alters the details of existing objects in the database. In-memory entities, managed or not, will not be updated to reflect changes resulting from issuing UPDATE statements. Here's the syntax of the UPDATE statement:

```
UPDATE [VERSIONED]
    [FROM] path [[AS] alias] [, ...]
    SET property = value [, ...]
    [WHERE logicalExpression]
```

The fully qualified name of the entity or entities is path. The alias names may be used to abbreviate references to specific entities or their properties, and must be used when property names in the query would otherwise be ambiguous.

VERSIONED means that the update will update time stamps, if any, that are part of the entity being updated.

The property names are the names of properties of entities listed in the FROM path.

The syntax of logical expressions is discussed later, in the "Using Restrictions with HQL" section.

An example of the update in action might look like this:

```
Query query=session.createQuery("update Person set creditscore=:creditscore where name=:name");
query.setInteger("creditscore", 612);
query.setString("name", "John Q. Public");
int modifications=query.executeUpdate();
```

DELETE

DELETE removes the details of existing objects from the database. In-memory entities will not be updated to reflect changes resulting from DELETE statements. This also means that Hibernate's cascade rules will not be followed for deletions carried out using HQL. However, if you have specified cascading deletes at the database level (either directly or through Hibernate, using the @OnDelete annotation), the database will still remove the child rows. This approach to deletion is commonly referred to as "bulk deletion," since it is the most efficient way to remove large numbers of entities from the database. Here's the syntax of the DELETE statement:

```
DELETE
    [FROM] path [[AS] alias]
    [WHERE logicalExpression]
```

The fully qualified name of an entity is path. The alias names may be used to abbreviate references to specific entities or their properties, and must be used when property names in the query would otherwise be ambiguous.

In practice, deletes might look like this:

```
Query query=session.createQuery("delete from Person where accountstatus=:status");
query.setString("status", "purged");
int rowsDeleted=query.executeUpdate();
```

INSERT

An HQL INSERT cannot be used to directly insert arbitrary entities—it can only be used to insert entities constructed from information obtained from SELECT queries (unlike ordinary SQL, in which an INSERT command can be used to insert arbitrary data into a table, as well as insert values selected from other tables). Here's the syntax of the INSERT statement:

```
INSERT
    INTO path ( property [, ...])
    select
```

The name of an entity is path. The property names are the names of properties of entities listed in the FROM path of the incorporated SELECT query.

The select query is an HQL SELECT query (as described in the next section).

As this HQL statement can only use data provided by an HQL select, its application can be limited. An example of copying users to a purged table before actually purging them might look like this:

```
Query query=session.createQuery("insert into purged_users(id, name, status) "+
    "select id, name, status from users where status=:status");
query.setString("status", "purged");
int rowsCopied=query.executeUpdate();
```

SELECT

An HQL SELECT is used to query the database for classes and their properties. As noted previously, this is very much a summary of the full expressive power of HQL SELECT queries; however, for more complex joins and the like, you may find that using the Criteria API described in the next chapter is more appropriate. Here's the syntax of the SELECT statement:

```
[SELECT [DISTINCT] property [, ...]]
    FROM path [[AS] alias] [, ...] [FETCH ALL PROPERTIES]
    WHERE logicalExpression
    GROUP BY property [, ...]
    HAVING logicalExpression
    ORDER BY property [ASC | DESC] [, ...]
```

The fully qualified name of an entity is path. The alias names may be used to abbreviate references to specific entities or their properties, and must be used when property names used in the query would otherwise be ambiguous.

The property names are the names of properties of entities listed in the FROM path.

If FETCH ALL PROPERTIES is used, then lazy loading semantics will be ignored, and all the immediate properties of the retrieved object(s) will be actively loaded (this does not apply recursively).

When the properties listed consist only of the names of aliases in the FROM clause, the SELECT clause can be omitted in HQL. If you are using the JPA with JPQL, one of the differences between HQL and JPQL is that the SELECT clause is required in JPQL.

Named Queries

Hibernate (and JPA) provide named queries. Named queries are created via class-level annotations on entities; normally, the queries apply to the entity in whose source file they occur, but there's no absolute requirement for this to be true.

Named queries are created with the @NamedQueries annotation, which contains an array of @NamedQuery sets; each has a query and a name.

First, let's create an object model we can use as an example. Our object model will contain products and suppliers; it will also contain a specialized product ("Software") that adds an attribute to Product. One effect of the hierarchy we use here is that Lombok is no longer as usable as it has been,[1] so we're going to eliminate some of the boilerplate from the source code—namely, constructors, mutators, accessors, equals(), hashCode(), and toString(). The source code download for the book will have all of these methods, of course. This object model structure is shown in Listings 9-1, 9-2, and 9-3.

Listing 9-1. The Supplier Entity, with Boilerplate Removed

```
@Entity
public class Supplier implements Serializable {
    @Id
    @GeneratedValue(strategy = GenerationType.AUTO)
    Integer id;
    @Column(unique = true)
    @NotNull
    String name;
    @OneToMany(cascade = CascadeType.ALL, orphanRemoval = true,
            mappedBy = "supplier", targetEntity = Product.class)
    List<Product> products = new ArrayList<>();
}
```

Listing 9-2. The Basic Product Entity, with Boilerplate Removed

```
@Entity
public class Product implements Serializable {
    @Id
    @GeneratedValue(strategy = GenerationType.AUTO)
    Integer id;
    @ManyToOne(optional = false, fetch = FetchType.LAZY)
    Supplier supplier;
    @Column
    @NotNull
    String name;
    @Column
    @NotNull
    String description;
    @Column
    @NotNull
    Double price;
}
```

---

[1]Lombok works by analyzing Java source code. It does not walk a hierarchy; while this would be very useful, there are some real technical challenges to implementation. While someday Lombok may indeed be able to handle object hierarchies as conveniently as it handles simple objects, as of this writing it doesn't work well for object hierarchies, so we're not going to use it in this chapter.

Listing 9-3. The Software Entity, with Boilerplate Removed

```
@Entity
public class Software extends Product implements Serializable {
    @Column
    @NotNull
    String version;
}
```

Adding a named query is as simple as adding an annotation to one of the entities. For example, if we wanted to add a named query to retrieve all Supplier entities, we could do so by adding a @NamedQuery annotation to *any* of the entities, although it makes the most sense to put the query in Supplier's source code.

```
@NamedQuery(name = "supplier.findAll", query = "from Supplier s")
```

You can group queries together by adding a @NamedQueries annotation, and then embedding the named queries in an array as part of that annotation. This would look like this:

```
@NamedQueries({
        @NamedQuery(name = "supplier.findAll", query = "from Supplier s"),
        @NamedQuery(name = "supplier.findByName",
                query = "from Supplier s where s.name=:name"),
})
```

Using the named queries is very simple. Let's create a test that populates data before every test run, and clears it out after each test run, along with a test that uses our supplier.findAll query.[2] This test is shown in Listing 9-4.

Listing 9-4. A Test that Works with a Known Dataset

```
public class QueryTest {
    Session session;
    Transaction tx;

    @BeforeMethod
    public void populateData() {
        Session session = SessionUtil.getSession();
        Transaction tx = session.beginTransaction();

        Supplier supplier = new Supplier("Hardware, Inc.");
        supplier.getProducts().add(
                new Product(supplier, "Optical Wheel Mouse", "Mouse", 5.00));
        supplier.getProducts().add(
                new Product(supplier, "Trackball Mouse", "Mouse", 22.00));
        session.save(supplier);

        supplier = new Supplier("Supplier 2");
        supplier.getProducts().add(
```

---

[2]There are lots of ways to do this; we could use a technique we used earlier in the book, and create a new SessionFactory for each test, or we could use dbUnit (http://dbunit.sourceforge.net/). This just seems more direct.

```
                    new Software(supplier, "SuperDetect", "Antivirus", 14.95, "1.0"));
        supplier.getProducts().add(
                    new Software(supplier, "Wildcat", "Browser", 19.95, "2.2"));
        supplier.getProducts().add(
                    new Product(supplier, "AxeGrinder", "Gaming Mouse", 42.00));

        session.save(supplier);
        tx.commit();
        session.close();

        this.session = SessionUtil.getSession();
        this.tx = this.session.beginTransaction();
    }

    @AfterMethod
    public void closeSession() {
        session.createQuery("delete from Product").executeUpdate();
        session.createQuery("delete from Supplier").executeUpdate();
        if (tx.isActive()) {
            tx.commit();
        }
        if (session.isOpen()) {
            session.close();
        }
    }

    @Test
    public void testNamedQuery() {
        Query query = session.getNamedQuery("supplier.findAll");
        List<Supplier> suppliers = query.list();
        assertEquals(suppliers.size(), 2);
    }
}
```

The methods annotated with @BeforeMethod and @AfterMethod will run before and after each @Test method; this means that each test will have a consistent dataset upon entry, as well as an active transaction and session.

The actual test itself is very simple: it acquires a named query ("supplier.findAll") and executes it, making sure that we've retrieved all of the Supplier instances we expect to find.

We can, of course, create queries on the fly, as we've done many times through the book so far. Listing 9-5 is another example (for the sake of completeness) for querying all Products:

Listing 9-5. Creating a Query

```
@Test
public void testSimpleQuery() {
    Query query = session.createQuery("from Product");
    query.setComment("This is only a query for product");
    List<Product> products = query.list();
    assertEquals(products.size(), 5);
}
```

▨ **Note** Like all SQL syntax, you can write `from` in lowercase or uppercase (or mixed case). However, any Java classes or properties that you reference in an HQL query have to be specified in the proper case. For example, when you query for instances of a Java class named `Product`, the HQL query `from Product` is the equivalent of `FROM Product`. However, the HQL query `from product` is not the same as the HQL query `from Product`. Because Java class names are case-sensitive, Hibernate is case-sensitive about class names as well.

The `createQuery()` method takes a valid HQL statement and returns an `org.hibernate.Query` object. The Query class provides methods for returning the query results as a Java `List`, as an `Iterator`, or as a unique result. Other functionality includes named parameters, results scrolling, JDBC fetch sizes, and JDBC timeouts. You can also add a comment to the SQL that Hibernate creates, which is useful for tracing which HQL statements correspond to which SQL statements.

Logging and Commenting the Underlying SQL

Hibernate can output the underlying SQL behind your HQL queries into your application's log file. This is especially useful if the HQL query does not give the results you expect, or if the query takes longer than you wanted. You can run the SQL that Hibernate generates directly against your database in the database's query analyzer at a later date to determine the causes of the problem. This is not a feature you will have to use frequently, but it is useful should you have to turn to your database administrators for help in tuning your Hibernate application.

Logging the SQL

The easiest way to see the SQL for a Hibernate HQL query is to enable SQL output in the logs with the `show_sql` property. Set this property to `true` in your `hibernate.cfg.xml` configuration file,[3] and Hibernate will output the SQL into the logs. You do not need to enable any other logging settings, although setting logging for Hibernate to debug also outputs the generated SQL statements, along with a lot of other verbiage.

After enabling SQL output in Hibernate, you should rerun the previous example. Here is the generated SQL statement for the HQL statement `from Product`:

```
Hibernate: /* This is only a query for product */ select product0_.id as id1_0_, product0_.
description as descript2_0_, product0_.name as name3_0_, product0_.price as price4_0_, product0_.
supplier_id as supplier5_0_, product0_1_.version as version1_1_, case when product0_1_.id is not
null then 1 when product0_.id is not null then 0 end as clazz_ from Product product0_ left outer
join Software product0_1_ on product0_.id=product0_1_.id
```

As an aside, remember that the `Software` class inherits from `Product`, which complicates Hibernate's generated SQL for this simple query. When we select all objects from our simple `Supplier` class, the generated SQL for the HQL query `from Supplier` is much simpler:

```
select supplier0_.id as id1_2_, supplier0_.name as name2_2_ from Supplier supplier0_
```

When you look in your application's output for the Hibernate SQL statements, they will be prefixed with "Hibernate:". The previous SQL statement would look like this:

```
Hibernate: /* named HQL query supplier.findAll */ select supplier0_.id as id1_2_, supplier0_.name as
name2_2_ from Supplier supplier0_
```

---

[3]If you're using the JPA configuration, the property name is "`hibernate.show_sql`".

If you turn your log4j logging up to debug for the Hibernate classes, you will see SQL statements in your log files, along with lots of information about how Hibernate parsed your HQL query and translated it into SQL.

Commenting the Generated SQL

Tracing your HQL statements through to the generated SQL can be difficult, so Hibernate provides a commenting facility on the Query object that lets you apply a comment to a specific query. The Query interface has a setComment() method that takes a String object as an argument, as follows:

```
public Query setComment(String comment)
```

Hibernate will not add comments to your SQL statements without some additional configuration, even if you use the setComment() method. You will also need to set a Hibernate property, hibernate.use_sql_comments, to true in your Hibernate configuration.[4] If you set this property but do not set a comment on the query programmatically, Hibernate will include the HQL used to generate the SQL call in the comment. We find this to be very useful for debugging HQL.

Use commenting to identify the SQL output in your application's logs if SQL logging is enabled. For instance, if we add a comment to this example, the Java code would look like this:

```
String hql = "from Supplier";
Query query = session.createQuery(hql);
query.setComment("My HQL: " + hql);
List results = query.list();
```

The output in your application's log will have the comment in a Java-style comment before the SQL:

```
Hibernate: /*My HQL: from Supplier*/ select supplier0_.id as id, supplier0_.name ➡
as name2_ from Supplier supplier0_
```

This can be useful for identifying SQL in your logs, especially because the generated SQL is a little difficult to follow when you are scanning large quantities of it. (Running the example code from this test class serves as a great example; it's hundreds of lines' worth of output.)

The from Clause and Aliases

We have already discussed the basics of the from clause in HQL in the earlier section, "The First Example with HQL." The most important feature to note is the *alias*. Hibernate allows you to assign aliases to the classes in your query with the as clause. Use the aliases to refer back to the class inside the query. For instance, our previous simple example would be the following:

```
from Product as p
```

or the following:

```
from Product as product
```

---

[4]In case you're wondering, this was done in the runtime configuration before copying the logs for this chapter.

You'll see either alias-naming convention in applications. The as keyword is optional—you can also specify the alias directly after the class name, as follows:

```
from Product product
```

If you need to fully qualify a class name in HQL, just specify the package and class name. Hibernate will take care of most of this behind the scenes, so you really need this only if you have classes with duplicate names in your application. If you have to do this in Hibernate, use syntax such as the following:

```
from chapter09.model.Product
```

The from clause is very basic and useful for working directly with objects. However, if you want to work with the object's properties without loading the full objects into memory, you must use the select clause.

The select Clause and Projection

The select clause provides more control over the result set than the from clause. If you want to obtain the properties of objects in the result set, use the select clause. For instance, we could run a projection query on the products in the database that only returned the names, instead of loading the full object into memory, as follows:

```
select product.name from Product product
```

The result set for this query will contain a List of Java String objects. Additionally, we can retrieve the prices and the names for each product in the database, like so:

```
select product.name, product.price from Product product
```

This result set contains a List of Object arrays—each array represents one set of properties (in this case, a name and price pair).

If you're only interested in a few properties, this approach can allow you to reduce network traffic to the database server and save memory on the application's machine.

Using Restrictions with HQL

As with SQL, you use the where clause to select results that match your query's expressions. HQL provides many different expressions that you can use to construct a query. In the HQL language grammar, there are *many* possible expressions,[5] including:

- *Logic operators*: OR, AND, NOT

- *Equality operators*: =, <>, !=, ^=

- *Comparison operators*: <, >, <=, >=, like, not like, between, not between

- *Math operators*: +, -, *, /

- *Concatenation operator*: ||

---

[5]If you want to see them all and be amazed, see http://docs.jboss.org/hibernate/orm/4.2/manual/en-US/html/ch16.html #queryhql-expressions. There are a *lot*.

- *Cases*: Case when <logical expression> then <unary expression> else _<unary expression> end

- *Collection expressions*: some, exists, all, any

In addition, you may also use the following expressions in the where clause:

- *HQL named parameters*:, such as :date, :quantity

- *JDBC query parameter*: ?

- *Date and time SQL-92 functional operators*: current_time(), current_date(), current_timestamp()

- *SQL functions (supported by the database)*: length(), upper(), lower(), ltrim(), rtrim(), etc.

Using Named Parameters

Hibernate supports named parameters in its HQL queries. This makes writing queries that accept input from the user easy—and you do not have to defend against SQL injection attacks.

▪ **Note**   SQL injection is an attack against applications that create SQL directly from user input with string concatenation. For instance, if we accept a name from the user through a web application form, then it would be very bad form to construct an SQL (or HQL) query like this:

String sql = "select p from products where name = '" + name + "'";

A malicious user could pass a name to the application that contained a terminating quote and semicolon, followed by another SQL command (such as delete from products) that would let the user do whatever he wanted. He would just need to end with another command that matched the SQL statement's ending quote. This is a very common attack, especially if the malicious user can guess details of your database structure.[6]

You could escape the user's input yourself for every query, but it is much less of a security risk if you let Hibernate manage all of your input with named parameters. Hibernate's named parameters are similar to the JDBC query parameters (?) you may already be familiar with, but Hibernate's parameters are less confusing. It is also more straightforward to use Hibernate's named parameters if you have a query that uses the same parameter in multiple places.

When using JDBC query parameters, any time you add, change, or delete parts of the SQL statement, you need to update your Java code that sets its parameters, because the parameters are indexed based on the order in which they appear in the statement. Hibernate lets you provide names for the parameters in the HQL query, so you do not have to worry about accidentally moving parameters around in the query.

The simplest example of named parameters uses regular SQL types for the parameters:

```
String hql = "from Product where price > :price";
Query query = session.createQuery(hql);
query.setDouble("price",25.0);
List results = query.list();
```

---

[6]See http://xkcd.com/327/. You're welcome.

Normally, you do not know the values that are to be substituted for the named parameters; if you did, you would probably encode them directly into the query string. When the value to be provided will be known only at run time, you can use some of HQL's object-oriented features to provide objects as values for named parameters. The Query interface has a setEntity() method that takes the name of a parameter and an object.

Using this functionality, we could retrieve all the products that have a supplier whose object we already have:

```
String supplierHQL = "from Supplier where name='MegaInc'";
Query supplierQuery = session.createQuery(supplierHQL);
Supplier supplier = (Supplier) supplierQuery.list().get(0);

String hql = "from Product as product where product.supplier=:supplier";
Query query = session.createQuery(hql);
query.setEntity("supplier",supplier);
List results = query.list();
```

You can also use regular JDBC query parameters in your HQL queries. We do not particularly see any reason why you would want to, but they do work.

Paging Through the Result Set

Pagination through the result set of a database query is a very common application pattern. Typically, you would use pagination for a web application that returned a large set of data for a query. The web application would page through the database query result set to build the appropriate page for the user. The application would be very slow if the web application loaded all of the data into memory for each user. Instead, you can page through the result set and retrieve the results you are going to display one chunk at a time.

There are two methods on the Query interface for paging: setFirstResult() and setMaxResults(), just as with the Criteria interface. The setFirstResult() method takes an integer that represents the first row in your result set, starting with row 0. You can tell Hibernate to only retrieve a fixed number of objects with the setMaxResults() method. Your HQL is unchanged—you need only to modify the Java code that executes the query. Excuse our tiny dataset for this trivial example of pagination:

```
Query query = session.createQuery("from Product");
query.setFirstResult(1);
query.setMaxResults(2);
List results = query.list();
displayProductsList(results);
```

You can change the numbers around and play with the pagination. If you turn on SQL logging, you can see which SQL commands Hibernate uses for pagination. For the open-source HSQLDB database, Hibernate uses top and limit. For other databases, Hibernate uses the appropriate commands for pagination. For instance, Microsoft SQL Server does not support the limit command, so Hibernate uses only the top command. If your application is having performance problems with pagination, this can be very helpful for debugging.

If you only have one result in your HQL result set, Hibernate has a shortcut method for obtaining just that object.

Obtaining a Unique Result

HQL's Query interface provides a uniqueResult() method for obtaining just one object from an HQL query. Although your query may yield only one object, you may also use the uniqueResult() method with other result sets if you limit the results to just the first result. You could use the setMaxResults() method discussed in the previous section.

The uniqueResult() method on the Query object returns a single object, or null if there are zero results. If there is more than one result, then the uniqueResult() method throws a NonUniqueResultException.

The following short example demonstrates having a result set that would have included more than one result, except that it was limited with the setMaxResults() method:

```
String hql = "from Product where price>25.0";
Query query = session.createQuery(hql);
query.setMaxResults(1);
Product product = (Product) query.uniqueResult();
//test for null here if needed
```

Unless your query returns one or zero results, the uniqueResult() method will throw a NonUniqueResultException exception. Do not expect Hibernate just to pick off the first result and return it—either set the maximum results of the HQL query to 1, or obtain the first object from the result list.

Sorting Results with the order by Clause

To sort your HQL query's results, you will need to use the order by clause. You can order the results by any property on the objects in the result set: either ascending (asc) or descending (desc). You can use ordering on more than one property in the query, if you need to. A typical HQL query for sorting results looks like this:

```
from Product p where p.price>25.0 order by p.price desc
```

If you wanted to sort by more than one property, you would just add the additional properties to the end of the order by clause, separated by commas. For instance, you could sort by product price and the supplier's name, as follows:

```
from Product p order by p.supplier.name asc, p.price asc
```

HQL is more straightforward for ordering than the equivalent approach using the Criteria Query API.

Associations

Associations allow you to use more than one class in an HQL query, just as SQL allows you to use joins between tables in a relational database. You add an association to an HQL query with the join clause. Hibernate supports five different types of joins: inner join, cross join, left outer join, right outer join, and full outer join. If you use cross join, just specify both classes in the from clause (from Product p, Supplier s). For the other joins, use a join clause after the from clause. Specify the type of join, the object property to join on, and an alias for the other class.

You can use inner join to obtain the supplier for each product, and then retrieve the supplier name, product name, and product price, as so:

```
select s.name, p.name, p.price from Product p inner join p.supplier as s
```

You can retrieve the objects using similar syntax:

```
from Product p inner join p.supplier as s
```

We used aliases in these HQL statements to refer to the entities in our query expressions. These are particularly important in queries with associations that refer to two different entities with the same class—for instance, if we are doing a join from a table back to itself. Commonly, these types of joins are used to organize tree data structures.

Notice that Hibernate does not return Object objects in the result set; instead, Hibernate returns Object arrays in the results.[7] You will have to access the contents of the Object arrays to get the Supplier and the Product objects.

If you would like to start optimizing performance, you can use one query to ask Hibernate to fetch the associated objects and collections for an object. If you were using lazy loading with Hibernate, the objects in the collection would not be initialized until you accessed them. If you use fetch on a join in your query, you can ask Hibernate to retrieve the objects in the collection at the time the query executes. Add the fetch keyword after the join in the query, like so:

```
from Supplier s inner join fetch s.products as p
```

When you use fetch for a query like this, Hibernate will return only the Supplier objects, not the Product objects. This is because you are specifying the join, so Hibernate knows which objects to fetch (instead of using lazy loading). If you need to get the Product objects, you can access them through the associated Supplier object. You cannot use the properties of the Product objects in expressions contained in the where clause. Use of the fetch keyword overrides any settings you have in the mapping file for object initialization.

Aggregate Methods

HQL supports a range of aggregate methods, similar to SQL. They work the same way in HQL as in SQL, so you do not have to learn any specific Hibernate terminology. The difference is that in HQL, aggregate methods apply to the properties of persistent objects. The count(...) method returns the number of times the given column name appears in the result set. You may use the count(*) syntax to count all the objects in the result set, or count(product.name) to count the number of objects in the result set with a name property. Here is an example using the count(*) method to count all products:

```
select count(*) from Product product
```

The distinct keyword only counts the unique values in the row set—for instance, if there are 100 products, but 10 have the same price as another product in the results, then a select count(distinct product.price) from Product product query would return 90. In our database, the following query will return 2, one for each supplier:

```
select count(distinct product.supplier.name) from Product product
```

If we removed the distinct keyword, it would return 5, one for each product.

All of these queries return a Long object in the list. You could use the uniqueResult() method here to obtain the result.

The aggregate functions available through HQL include the following:

- avg(*property name*): The average of a property's value

- count(*property name* or *): The number of times a property occurs in the results

- max(*property name*): The maximum value of the property values

- min(*property name*): The minimum value of the property values

- sum(*property name*): The sum total of the property values

---

[7]This join results in a projection, thus the use of the Object arrays.

If you have more than one aggregate method, the result set List will contain an Object array with each of the aggregates you requested. Adding another aggregate to the select clause is straightforward:

```
select min(product.price), max(product.price) from Product product
```

You can also combine these with other projection properties in the result set.

Bulk Updates and Deletes with HQL

The Query interface contains a method called executeUpdate() for executing HQL UPDATE or DELETE statements.[8] The executeUpdate() method returns an int that contains the number of rows affected by the update or delete, as follows:

```
public int executeUpdate() throws HibernateException
```

HQL updates look as you would expect them to, being based on SQL UPDATE statements. Do not include an alias with the update; instead, put the set keyword right after the class name, as follows:

```
String hql = "update Supplier set name = :newName å
where name = :name";

Query query = session.createQuery(hql);
query.setString("name","SuperCorp");
query.setString("newName","MegaCorp");
int rowCount = query.executeUpdate();
System.out.println("Rows affected: " + rowCount);

//See the results of the update
query = session.createQuery("from Supplier");
List results = query.list();
```

After carrying out this query, any supplier previously named SuperCorp will be named MegaCorp. You may use a where clause with updates to control which rows get updated, or you may leave it off to update all rows. Notice that we printed out the number of rows affected by the query. We also used named parameters in our HQL for this bulk update.

Bulk deletes work in a similar way. Use the delete from clause with the class name you would like to delete from. Then use the where clause to narrow down which entries in the table you would like to delete. Use the executeUpdate() method to execute deletes against the database as well.

Be careful when you use bulk delete with objects that are in relationships. Hibernate will not know that you removed the underlying data in the database, and you can get foreign key integrity errors. To get around this, you could set the not-found attribute to ignore on your one-to-many and many-to-one mappings, which will make IDs that are not in the database resolve to null references. The default value for the not-found attribute is exception. Setting the not-found attribute to ignore also has the side effect of causing your associations to load eagerly and fetch all related records instead of using lazy loading. This can cause serious performance problems.

---

[8]Our test code uses a bulk delete to clear out the data, including the use of executeUpdate(), as mentioned earlier.

Our code surrounding the HQL DELETE statement is basically the same—we use named parameters, and we print out the number of rows affected by the delete:

```
String hql = "delete from Product where name = :name";
Query query = session.createQuery(hql);
query.setString("name","Mouse");
int rowCount = query.executeUpdate();
System.out.println("Rows affected: " + rowCount);

//See the results of the update
query = session.createQuery("from Product");
List results = query.list();
```

■ **Caution**   Using bulk updates and deletes in HQL works almost the same as in SQL, so keep in mind that these are powerful and can erase the data in your tables if you make a mistake with the where clause.

Using Native SQL

Although you should probably use HQL whenever possible, Hibernate does provide a way to use native SQL statements directly through Hibernate. One reason to use native SQL is that your database supports some special features through its dialect of SQL that are not supported in HQL. Another reason is that you may want to call stored procedures from your Hibernate application. We discuss stored procedures and other database-specific integration solutions in Appendix A. Rather than just providing an interface to the underlying JDBC connection, like other Java ORM tools, Hibernate provides a way to define the entity (or join) that the query uses. This makes integration with the rest of your ORM-oriented application easy.

You can modify your SQL statements to make them work with Hibernate's ORM layer. You do need to modify your SQL to include Hibernate aliases that correspond to objects or object properties. You can specify all properties on an object with {objectname.*}, or you can specify the aliases directly with {objectname.property}. Hibernate uses the mappings to translate your object property names into their underlying SQL columns. This may not be the exact way you expect Hibernate to work, so be aware that you do need to modify your SQL statements for full ORM support. You will especially run into problems with native SQL on classes with subclasses—be sure you understand how you mapped the inheritance across either a single table or multiple tables, so that you select the right properties off the table.

Underlying Hibernate's native SQL support is the org.hibernate.SQLQuery interface, which extends the org.hibernate.Query interface already discussed. Your application will create a native SQL query from the session with the createSQLQuery() method on the Session interface.

```
public SQLQuery createSQLQuery(String queryString) throws HibernateException
```

After you pass a string containing the SQL query to the createSQLQuery() method, you should associate the SQL result with an existing Hibernate entity, a join, or a scalar result. The SQLQuery interface has addEntity(), addJoin(), and addScalar() methods. For the entities and joins, you can specify a lock mode, which we discussed in Chapter 8. The addEntity() methods take an alias argument and either a class name or an entity name. The addJoin() methods take an alias argument and a path to join.

Using native SQL with scalar results is the simplest way to get started with native SQL. Our Java code looks like this:

```
String sql = "select avg(product.price) as avgPrice from Product product";
SQLQuery query = session.createSQLQuery(sql);
query.addScalar("avgPrice",Hibernate.DOUBLE);
List results = query.list();
```

Because we did not specify any entity aliases, Hibernate executes exactly the same SQL that we passed through:

```
select avg(product.price) as avgPrice from Product product
```

The SQL is regular SQL (we did not have to do any aliasing here). We created an SQLQuery object, and then added a scalar mapping with the built-in double type (from the org.hibernate._Hibernate class). We needed to map the avgPrice SQL alias to the object type. The results are a List with one object—a Double.

A bit more complicated than the previous example is the native SQL that returns a result set of objects. In this case, we will need to map an entity to the SQL query. The entity consists of the alias we used for the object in the SQL query and its class. For this example, we used our Supplier class:

```
String sql = "select {supplier.*} from Supplier supplier";
SQLQuery query = session.createSQLQuery(sql);
query.addEntity("supplier", Supplier.class);
List results = query.list();
```

Hibernate modifies the SQL and executes the following command against the database:

```
select Supplier.id as id0_, Supplier.name as name2_0_ from Supplier supplier
```

The special aliases allow Hibernate to map the database columns back to the object properties.

Summary

HQL is a powerful object-oriented query language that provides the power of SQL while taking advantage of Hibernate's object-relational mapping and caching. If you are porting an existing application to Hibernate, you can use Hibernate's native SQL facilities to execute SQL against the database. The SQL functionality is also useful for executing SQL statements that are specific to a given database and have no equivalents in HQL.

You can turn on SQL logging for Hibernate, and Hibernate will log the generated SQL that it executes against the database. If you add a comment to your HQL query object, Hibernate will display a comment in the log next to the SQL statement; this helps with tracing SQL statements back to HQL in your application.

■ ■ ■

CHAPTER 10

Advanced Queries Using Criteria

Hibernate provides three different ways to retrieve data. We have already discussed HQL and the use of native SQL queries; now we add criteria.

The Criteria Query API lets you build nested, structured query expressions in Java, providing a compile-time syntax checking that is not possible with a query language like HQL or SQL. The Criteria API also includes *query by example* (QBE) functionality. This lets you supply example objects that contain the properties you would like to retrieve instead of having to step-by-step spell out the components of the query. It also includes projection and aggregation methods, including counts.

In this chapter, we explore the use of the Criteria API, employing the sample object model established in the previous chapter. (We are, however, going to move it to a new package, from chapter09.model to chapter10.model).

Using the Criteria API

The Criteria API allows you to build up a criteria query object programmatically; the org.hibernate.Criteria interface defines the available methods for one of these objects. The Hibernate Session interface contains several createCriteria() methods. Pass the persistent object's class or its entity name to the createCriteria() method, and Hibernate will create a Criteria object that returns instances of the persistence object's class when your application executes a criteria query.

The simplest example of a criteria query is one with no optional parameters or restrictions—the criteria query will simply return every object that corresponds to the class.

```
Criteria crit = session.createCriteria(Product.class);
List<Product> results = crit.list();
```

When you run this example with our sample data, you will get all objects that are instances of the Product class. Note that this includes any instances of the Software class because they are derived from Product.

Moving on from this simple example, we will add constraints to our criteria queries so we can whittle down the result set.

Using Restrictions with Criteria

The Criteria API makes it easy to use restrictions in your queries to selectively retrieve objects; for instance, your application could retrieve only products with a price over $30. You may add these restrictions to a Criteria object with the add() method. The add() method takes an org.hibernate.criterion.Criterion object that represents an individual restriction. You can have more than one restriction for a criteria query.

Although you could create your own objects implementing the Criterion object, or extend an existing Criterion object, we recommend that you use Hibernate's built-in Criterion objects from your application's business logic. For instance, you could create your own factory class that returns instances of Hibernate's Criterion objects appropriately set up for your application's restrictions.

Use the factory methods on the org.hibernate.criterion.Restrictions class to obtain instances of the Criterion objects. To retrieve objects that have a property value that equals your restriction, use the eq() method on Restrictions, as follows:

```
public static SimpleExpression eq(String propertyName, Object value)
```

We would typically nest the eq() method in the add() method on the Criteria object. Here is an example of how this would look if we were searching for products with the name "Mouse":

```
Criteria crit = session.createCriteria(Product.class);
crit.add(Restrictions.eq("description","Mouse"));
List<Product> results = crit.list()
```

Next, we search for products that do *not* have the name "Mouse." For this, we would use the ne() method on the Restrictions class to obtain a not-equal restriction:

```
Criteria crit = session.createCriteria(Product.class);
crit.add(Restrictions.ne("description","Mouse"));
List<Product> results = crit.list();
```

■ **Tip** You cannot use the not-equal restriction to retrieve records with a NULL value in the database for that property (in SQL, and therefore in Hibernate, NULL represents the absence of data, and so cannot be compared with data). If you need to retrieve objects with NULL properties, you will have to use the isNull() restriction, which we discuss further on in the chapter. You can combine the two with an OR logical expression, which we also discuss later in the chapter.

Instead of searching for exact matches, we can retrieve all objects that have a property matching part of a given pattern. To do this, we need to create an SQL LIKE clause, with either the like() or the ilike() method. The ilike() method is case-insensitive. In either case, we have two different ways to call the method:

```
public static SimpleExpression like(String propertyName, Object value)
```

or

```
public static SimpleExpression like(String propertyName,
                                    String value,
                                    MatchMode matchMode)
```

The first like() or ilike() method takes a pattern for matching. Use the % character as a wildcard to match parts of the string, like so:

```
Criteria crit = session.createCriteria(Product.class);
crit.add(Restrictions.like("name","Mou%"));
List<Product> results = crit.list();
```

The second `like()` or `ilike()` method uses an `org.hibernate.criterion.MatchMode` object to specify how to match the specified value to the stored data. The `MatchMode` object (a type-safe enumeration) has four different matches:

- ANYWHERE: Anyplace in the string

- END: The end of the string

- EXACT: An exact match

- START: The beginning of the string

Here is an example that uses the `ilike()` method to search for case-insensitive matches at the end of the string:

```
Criteria crit = session.createCriteria(Product.class);
crit.add(Restrictions.ilike("description","ser", MatchMode.END));
List<Product> results = crit.list();
```

The `isNull()` and `isNotNull()` restrictions allow you to do a search for objects that have (or do not have) null property values. This is easy to demonstrate:

```
Criteria crit = session.createCriteria(Product.class);
crit.add(Restrictions.isNull("name"));
List<Product> results = crit.list();
```

Several of the restrictions are useful for doing math comparisons. The greater-than comparison is `gt()`, the greater-than-or-equal-to comparison is `ge()`, the less-than comparison is `lt()`, and the less-than-or-equal-to comparison is `le()`. We can do a quick retrieval of all products with prices over $25 like this, relying on Java's type promotions to handle the conversion to `Double`:

```
Criteria crit = session.createCriteria(Product.class);
crit.add(Restrictions.gt("price", 25.0));
List<Product> results = crit.list();
```

Moving on, we can start to do more complicated queries with the Criteria API. For example, we can combine AND and OR restrictions in logical expressions. When we add more than one constraint to a criteria query, it is interpreted as an AND, like so:

```
Criteria crit = session.createCriteria(Product.class);
crit.add(Restrictions.lt("price",10.0));
crit.add(Restrictions.ilike("description","mouse", MatchMode.ANYWHERE));
List<Product> results = crit.list();
```

If we want to have two restrictions that return objects that satisfy either or both of the restrictions, we need to use the `or()` method on the `Restrictions` class, as follows:

```
Criteria crit = session.createCriteria(Product.class);
Criterion priceLessThan = Restrictions.lt("price", 10.0);
Criterion mouse = Restrictions.ilike("description", "mouse", MatchMode.ANYWHERE);
LogicalExpression orExp = Restrictions.or(priceLessThan, mouse);
crit.add(orExp);
List<Product> results=crit.list();
```

The orExp logical expression that we have created here will be treated like any other criterion. We can therefore add another restriction to the criteria:

```
Criteria crit = session.createCriteria(Product.class);
Criterion price = Restrictions.gt("price",new Double(25.0));
Criterion name = Restrictions.like("name","Mou%");
LogicalExpression orExp = Restrictions.or(price,name);
crit.add(orExp);
crit.add(Restrictions.ilike("description","blocks%"));
List results = crit.list();
```

If we wanted to create an OR expression with more than two different criteria (for example, "price > 25.0 OR name like Mou% OR description not like blocks%"), we would use an org.hibernate.criterion.Disjunction object to represent a disjunction.[1] You can obtain this object from the disjunction() factory method on the Restrictions class. The disjunction is more convenient than building a tree of OR expressions in code. To represent an AND expression with more than two criteria, you can use the conjunction() method, although you can easily just add those to the Criteria object. The conjunction can be more convenient than building a tree of AND expressions in code. Here is an example that uses the disjunction:

```
Criteria crit = session.createCriteria(Product.class);
Criterion priceLessThan = Restrictions.lt("price", 10.0);
Criterion mouse = Restrictions.ilike("description", "mouse", MatchMode.ANYWHERE);
Criterion browser = Restrictions.ilike("description", "browser", MatchMode.ANYWHERE);
Disjunction disjunction = Restrictions.disjunction();
disjunction.add(priceLessThan);
disjunction.add(mouse);
disjunction.add(browser);
crit.add(disjunction);
List<Product> results = crit.list();
```

The last type of restriction is the SQL restriction sqlRestriction(). This restriction allows you to directly specify SQL in the Criteria API. It's useful if you need to use SQL clauses that Hibernate does not support through the Criteria API. Your application's code does not need to know the name of the table your class uses. Use {alias} to signify the class's table, as follows:

```
Criteria crit = session.createCriteria(Product.class);
crit.add(Restrictions.sqlRestriction("{alias}.description like 'Mou%'"));
List<Product> results = crit.list();
```

There are two other sqlRestriction() methods that permit you to pass JDBC parameters and values into the SQL statement. Use the standard JDBC parameter placeholder (?) in your SQL fragment.

---

[1] A disjunction represents data sets in which a data element fulfills one of a set of conditions, therefore an "or" construct. Given condition A (where value<4) and condition B (where value>9), and a data set consisting of 0, 5, and 10, a disjunction of A and B would give you 0 and 10.

A conjunction, conversely, represents an "and." A conjunction of A and B, with the same data set, would give you an empty set because no value is both less than 4 and greater than 9.

In practice, you'll probably never see these terms used outside of technical applications like this one. I can imagine the conversation now: "You could use a disjunction …" "No, thanks, I'd rather use an OR."

Paging Through the Result Set

One common application pattern that criteria can address is pagination through the result set of a database query. When we say pagination, we mean an interface in which the user sees part of the result set at a time, with navigation to go forward and backward through the results. A naïve pagination implementation might load the entire result set into memory for each navigation action, and would usually lead to atrocious performance.[2] Both of us have worked on improving performance for separate projects suffering from exactly this problem. The problem appeared late in testing because the sample data set that developers were working with was trivial, and they did not notice any performance problems until the first test data load.

If you are programming directly to the database, you will typically use proprietary database SQL or database cursors to support paging. Hibernate abstracts this away for you: behind the scenes, Hibernate uses the appropriate method for your database.

There are two methods on the Criteria interface for paging, just as there are for Query: setFirstResult() and setMaxResults(). The setFirstResult() method takes an integer that represents the first row in your result set, starting with row 0. You can tell Hibernate to retrieve a fixed number of objects with the setMaxResults() method. Using both of these together, we can construct a paging component in our web or Swing application. We have a very small data set in our sample application, so here is an admittedly trivial example:

```
Criteria crit = session.createCriteria(Product.class);
crit.setFirstResult(1);
crit.setMaxResults(2);
List<Product> results = crit.list();
```

As you can see, this makes paging through the result set easy. You can increase the first result you return (for example, from 1, to 21, to 41, etc.) to page through the result set. If you have only one result in your result set, Hibernate has a shortcut method for obtaining just that object.

Obtaining a Unique Result

Sometimes you know you are going to return only zero or one object from a given query. This could be because you are calculating an aggregate (like COUNT, which we discuss later) or because your restrictions naturally lead to a unique result—when selecting upon a property under a unique constraint, for example. You may also limit the results of any result set to just the first result, using the setMaxResults() method discussed earlier. In any of these circumstances, if you want obtain a single Object reference instead of a List, the uniqueResult() method on the Criteria object returns an object or null. If there is more than one result, the uniqueResult() method throws a HibernateException.

The following short example demonstrates having a result set that would have included more than one result, except that it was limited with the setMaxResults() method:

```
Criteria crit = session.createCriteria(Product.class);
Criterion price = Restrictions.gt("price",new Double(25.0));
crit.setMaxResults(1);
Product product = (Product) crit.uniqueResult();
```

Again, we stress that you need to make sure that your query returns only one or zero results if you use the uniqueResult() method. Otherwise, Hibernate will throw a NonUniqueResultException exception, which may not be what you would expect—Hibernate does not just pick the first result and return it.[3]

---

[2]When naïve pagination would *not* lead to atrocious performance, chances are the result set is small enough that you wouldn't need pagination in the first place.

[3]Thus, it's about a *unique* result and not just a single result. You have to enforce uniqueness if it's not already present.

Sorting the Query's Results

Sorting the query's results works much the same way with criteria as it would with HQL or SQL. The Criteria API provides the org.hibernate.criterion.Order class to sort your result set in either ascending or descending order, according to one of your object's properties.

Create an Order object with either of the two static factory methods on the Order class: asc() for ascending or desc() for descending. Both methods take the name of the property as their only argument. After you create an Order, use the addOrder() method on the Criteria object to add it to the query.

This example demonstrates how you would use the Order class:

```
Criteria crit = session.createCriteria(Product.class);
crit.add(Restrictions.gt("price",10.0));
crit.addOrder(Order.desc("price"));
List<Product> results = crit.list();
```

You may add more than one Order object to the Criteria object. Hibernate will pass them through to the underlying SQL query. Your results will be sorted by the first order, then any identical matches within the first sort will be sorted by the second order, and so on. Beneath the covers, Hibernate passes this on to an SQL ORDER BY clause after substituting the proper database column name for the property.

Associations

To add a restriction on a class that is associated with your criteria's class, you will need to create another Criteria object. Pass the property name of the associated class to the createCriteria() method, and you will have another Criteria object. You can get the results from either Criteria object, although you should pick one style and be consistent for readability's sake. We find that getting the results from the top-level Criteria object (the one that takes a class as a parameter) makes it clear what type of object is expected in the results.

The association works when going from either one-to-many or from many-to-one. First, we will demonstrate how to use one-to-many associations to obtain suppliers who sell products with a price over $25. Notice that we create a new Criteria object for the products property, add restrictions to the products' criteria we just created, and then obtain the results from the supplier Criteria object:

```
Criteria crit = session.createCriteria(Supplier.class);
Criteria prdCrit = crit.createCriteria("products");
prdCrit.add(Restrictions.gt("price",25.0));
List<Supplier> results = crit.list();
```

Going the other way, we obtain all the products from the supplier MegaInc using many-to-one associations:

```
Criteria crit = session.createCriteria(Product.class);
Criteria suppCrit = crit.createCriteria("supplier");
suppCrit.add(Restrictions.eq("name","Hardware Are We"));
List<Product> results = crit.list();
```

Although we can use either Criteria object to obtain the results, it makes a difference which criteria we use for ordering the results. In the following example, we are ordering the supplier results by the supplier names:

```
Criteria crit = session.createCriteria(Supplier.class);
Criteria prdCrit = crit.createCriteria("products");
prdCrit.add(Restrictions.gt("price",25.0));
crit.addOrder(Order.desc("name"));
List<Supplier> results = prdCrit.list();
```

If we wanted to sort the suppliers by the descending price of their products, we would use the following line of code. This code would have to replace the previous addOrder() call on the supplier Criteria object.

```
prdCrit.addOrder(Order.desc("price"));
```

Although the products are not in the result set, SQL still allows you to order by those results. If you get mixed up about which Criteria object you are using and pass the wrong property name for the sort-by order, Hibernate will throw an exception.

Distinct Results

If you would like to work with distinct results from a criteria query, Hibernate provides a result transformer for distinct entities, org.hibernate.transform.DistinctRootEntityResultTransformer, which ensures that no duplicates will be in your query's result set. Rather than using SELECT DISTINCT with SQL, the distinct result transformer compares each of your results using their default hashCode() methods, and only adds those results with unique hash codes to your result set. This may or may not be the result you would expect from an otherwise equivalent SQL DISTINCT query, so be careful with this. An additional performance note: the comparison is done in Hibernate's Java code, not at the database, so non-unique results will still be transported across the network.

Projections and Aggregates

Instead of working with objects from the result set, you can treat the results from the result set as a set of rows and columns, also known as a *projection* of the data. This is similar to how you would use data from a SELECT query with JDBC; also, Hibernate supports properties, aggregate functions, and the GROUP BY clause.

To use projections, start by getting the org.hibernate.criterion.Projection object you need from the org.hibernate.criterion.Projections factory class. The Projections class is similar to the Restrictions class in that it provides several static factory methods for obtaining Projection instances. After you get a Projection object, add it to your Criteria object with the setProjection() method. When the Criteria object executes, the list contains object references that you can cast to the appropriate type.

The row-counting functionality provides a simple example of applying projections. The code looks similar to the restrictions examples we were working with earlier in the chapter:

```
Criteria crit = session.createCriteria(Product.class);
crit.setProjection(Projections.rowCount());
List<Long> results = crit.list();
```

The results list will contain one object, a Long that contains the results of executing the COUNT SQL statement. Other aggregate functions available through the Projections factory class include the following:

- avg(String propertyName): Gives the average of a property's value

- count(String propertyName): Counts the number of times a property occurs

- countDistinct(String propertyName): Counts the number of unique values the property contains

- max(String propertyName): Calculates the maximum value of the property values

- min(String propertyName): Calculates the minimum value of the property values

- sum(String propertyName): Calculates the sum total of the property values

We can apply more than one projection to a given Criteria object. To add multiple projections, get a projection list from the projectionList() method on the Projections class. The org.hibernate.criterion.ProjectionList object has an add() method that takes a Projection object. You can pass the projections list to the setProjection() method on the Criteria object because ProjectionList implements the Projection interface. The following example demonstrates some of the aggregate functions, along with the projection list:

```
Criteria crit = session.createCriteria(Product.class);
ProjectionList projList = Projections.projectionList();
projList.add(Projections.max("price"));
projList.add(Projections.min("price"));
projList.add(Projections.avg("price"));
projList.add(Projections.countDistinct("description"));
crit.setProjection(projList);
List<Object[]> results = crit.list();
```

When you execute multiple aggregate projections, you get a List with an Object array as the first element. The Object array contains all of your values, in order. For this projection, you'll have three Double references, and then a Long reference for the count.

Another use of projections is to retrieve individual properties, rather than entities. For instance, we can retrieve just the name and description from our product table, instead of loading the entire object representation into memory. Use the property() method on the Projections class to create a Projection for a property. When you execute this form of query, the list() method returns a List of Object arrays. Each Object array contains the projected properties for that row. The following example returns just the contents of the name and description columns from the Product data. Remember, Hibernate is polymorphic, so this also returns the name and description from the Software objects that inherit from Product.[4]

```
Criteria crit = session.createCriteria(Product.class);
ProjectionList projList = Projections.projectionList();
projList.add(Projections.property("name"));
projList.add(Projections.property("description"));
crit.setProjection(projList);
List<Object[]> results = crit.list();
```

Use this query style when you want to cut down on network traffic between your application servers and your database servers. For instance, if your table has a large number of columns, this can slim down your results. In other cases, you may have a large set of joins that would return a very wide result set, but you are only interested in a few columns. Lastly, if your clients have limited memory, this can save you trouble with large data sets. But make sure you don't have to retrieve additional columns for the entire result set later, or your optimizations may actually decrease performance.

You can group your results (using SQL's GROUP BY clause) with the groupProperty projection. The following example groups the products by name and price:

```
Criteria crit = session.createCriteria(Product.class);
ProjectionList projList = Projections.projectionList();
projList.add(Projections.groupProperty("name"));
projList.add(Projections.groupProperty("price"));
crit.setProjection(projList);
crit.addOrder(Order.asc("price"));
List<Object> results = crit.list();
```

---

[4]This kind of projection is supported by JPA, via JPQL, as well.

As you can see, projections open up aggregates to the Criteria API, which means that developers do not have to drop into HQL for aggregates. Projections offer a way to work with data that is closer to the JDBC result set style, which may be appropriate for some parts of your application.

Query By Example (QBE)

In this section, because of the confusing terminology, we will refer to excerpts from our demonstration code as "samples" rather than "examples," reserving "example" for its peculiar technical meaning in the context of QBE.

In QBE, instead of programmatically building a Criteria object with Criterion objects and logical expressions, you can partially populate an instance of the object. You use this instance as a template and have Hibernate build the criteria for you based upon its values. This keeps your code clean and makes your project easier to test. The org.hibernate.criterion.Example class contains the QBE functionality. Note that the Example class implements the Criterion interface, so you can use it like any other restriction on a criteria query.

For instance, if we have a user database, we can construct an instance of a user object, set the property values for type and creation date, and then use the Criteria API to run a QBE query. Hibernate will return a result set containing all user objects that match the property values that were set. Behind the scenes, Hibernate inspects the Example object and constructs an SQL fragment that corresponds to the properties on the Example object.

To use QBE, we first need to construct an Example object. Then we need to create an instance of the Example object, using the static create() method on the Example class. The create() method takes the Example object as its argument. You add the Example object to a Criteria object just like any other Criterion object.

The following basic example searches for suppliers that match the name on the example Supplier object:

```
Criteria crit = session.createCriteria(Supplier.class);
Supplier supplier = new Supplier();
supplier.setName("MegaInc");
crit.add(Example.create(supplier));
List<Supplier> results = crit.list();
```

When Hibernate translates our Example object into an SQL query, all the properties on our Example objects get examined. We can tell Hibernate which properties to ignore; the default is to ignore null-valued properties. To search our products or software in the sample database with QBE, we need either to specify a price or to tell Hibernate to ignore properties with a value of zero, because we used a double primitive for storage instead of a Double object. The double primitive initializes to zero, while a Double would have been null; and so, left to its own devices, the QBE logic will assume that we are specifically searching for prices of zero, whereas we want it to ignore this default value.

We can make the Hibernate Example object exclude zero-valued properties with the excludeZeroes() method. We can exclude properties by name with the excludeProperty() method, or exclude nothing (compare for null values and zeroes exactly as they appear in the Example object) with the excludeNone() method. This sample applies the excludeZeroes() method to ignore the default zero prices:

```
Criteria crit = session.createCriteria(Product.class);
Product exampleProduct = new Product();
exampleProduct.setName("Mouse");
Example example = Example.create(exampleProduct);
example.excludeZeroes();
crit.add(example);
List<Product> results = crit.list();
```

Other options on the Example object include ignoring the case for strings with the ignoreCase() method and enabling use of SQL's LIKE for comparing strings, instead of just using equals().

We can also use associations for QBE. In the following sample, we create two `Example` objects: one for the product and one for the supplier. We use the technique explained in the "Associations" section of this chapter to retrieve objects that match both criteria.

```
Criteria prdCrit = session.createCriteria(Product.class);
Product product = new Product();
product.setName("M%");
Example prdExample = Example.create(product);
prdExample.excludeProperty("price");
prdExample.enableLike();
Criteria suppCrit = prdCrit.createCriteria("supplier");
Supplier supplier = new Supplier();
supplier.setName("SuperCorp");
suppCrit.add(Example.create(supplier));
prdCrit.add(prdExample);
List<Product> results = prdCrit.list();
```

We also ignore the price property for our product, and we use LIKE for object comparison, instead of equals.

The QBE API works best for searches in which you are building the search from user input. The Hibernate team recommends using QBE for advanced searches with multiple fields because it's easier to set values on business objects than to manipulate restrictions with the Criteria API.

JPA 2 AND THE TYPE-SAFE CRITERIA API

In addition to the Hibernate Criteria API described in this chapter, Hibernate 4.2 includes a new type-safe Criteria API based on the JPA 2 standard. The advantage of this new API is that if you use it, you will not have any errors related to typos in the Criteria restrictions, such as "prduct". Rather than relying on strings in Criteria, there is a new metamodel class for each JPA entity. You would use the references to properties in these metamodel classes in your criteria restrictions, but you would use the javax.persistence criteria classes. Hibernate can generate the metamodel classes for you from the annotations in your existing classes.

The JPA 2 type-safe criteria does not replace the Hibernate Criteria API covered in this chapter. Both criteria APIs will accomplish the same thing for building a query. In this book, we covered the Hibernate way of doing things. Using the JPA 2 Criteria API is similar to the Hibernate Criteria API, but references to fields as strings are replaced with references to fields on generated metamodel classes.

In our example for this chapter, we would run the Hibernate Static Metamodel Generator against our annotated classes to generate the metamodel class files. The Metamodel Generator is a Java 6 annotation processor, so your existing build tools should automatically create the generated metamodel classes. Depending on how you have your source repository and project layout arranged, you will have to decide where to put the generated classes.

Summary

Using the Criteria API is an excellent way to get started developing with HQL. The developers of Hibernate have provided a clean API for adding restrictions to queries with Java objects. Although HQL isn't too difficult to learn, some developers prefer the Criteria Query API, as it offers compile-time syntax checking—although column names and other schema-dependent information cannot be checked until run time.

In the next chapter, we discuss the use of Hibernate filters to restrict the range of data against which queries are applied.

CHAPTER 11

■ ■ ■

Filtering the Results of Searches

Your application will often need to process only a subset of the data in the database tables. In these cases, you can create a Hibernate *filter* to eliminate the unwanted data. Filters provide a way for your application to limit the results of a query to data that passes the filter's criteria. Filters are not a new concept—you can achieve much the same effect using SQL database views or, well, named queries—but Hibernate offers a centralized management system for them.

Unlike database views, Hibernate filters can be enabled or disabled during a Hibernate session. In addition, Hibernate filters are parameterized, which is particularly useful when you are building applications on top of Hibernate that use security roles or personalization.

Filters are particularly useful when you have many similar queries with generalizable selection clauses. Filters allow you to use a generalized query, adding criteria for the query as needed.

When to Use Filters

As an example, consider an application that uses users and groups. A user has a status indicating whether that user is active or inactive, and a set of memberships; if your application needs to manage users based on status and/or group membership, you're looking at four separate queries (or a wildcard query, which seems silly). The wildcard query could indeed work, but it would add a burden on the database that shouldn't be there, especially if one set of wildcards was very common.

If we were to use four different queries ("all users," "all users with *this* status," "all users in *this* group," and "all users with *this* status and in *this* group"), not only would we have four queries to test and maintain but we'd also have to have a way of keeping track of which query we were supposed to be using at any given time.

We could also use custom queries for each execution (building the query as needed, instead of storing a set of queries). It's doable, but not entirely efficient, and it pollutes your services with query data.[1]

Filters allow us to define sets of restrictions. Instead of custom queries or sets of similar queries, we can create a filter and apply it when we query the database, such that our actual *query* doesn't change, even though the data set does.

The advantage to using Hibernate filters is that you can programmatically turn filters on or off in your application code, and your filters are defined in consistent locations for easy maintainability. The major disadvantage of filters is that you cannot create new filters at run time. Instead, any filters your application requires need to be specified in the proper Hibernate annotations or mapping documents. Although this may sound somewhat limiting, the fact that filters can be parameterized makes them pretty flexible. For our user status filter example, only one filter would need to be defined in the mapping document (albeit in two parts). That filter would specify that the status column must match a named parameter. You would not need to define the possible values of the status column in the Hibernate annotations or mapping documents—the application can specify those parameters at run time.

---

[1] Query data are the methods that retrieved users would have to keep track of the specific criteria in question. To some degree, this is going to be necessary anyway, but we'd prefer the impact be as small as possible.

Although it is certainly possible to write applications with Hibernate that do not use filters, we find them to be an excellent solution to certain types of problems—notably security and personalization.

Defining and Attaching Filters

Your first step is to create a filter definition. A filter definition is like metadata for a filter, including parameter definitions; it's not the filter itself, but it serves as a starting point.[2] After you have the filter definition, you create the filter itself; this contains the actual filter specification. Using the filter is a simple matter of enabling the filter by name and populating the parameters, if any.

What's the reason for having a filter definition separate from the filter itself? It's that the filter definitions are often written for a specific database, and thus they trend to being nonportable. If the filters and their definitions were unified, it'd be much more difficult to keep them portable; with a separated definition, it's easy to put a filter in a separately included resource.

Let's look at some filters, to make their usage clear.

Filters with Annotations

To use filters with annotations, you will need to use the @FilterDef, @ParamDef, and @Filter annotations. The @FilterDef annotation defines the filter and belongs to either the class or the package. To define a filter on a class, add an @FilterDef annotation after the @Entity annotation.

After you have defined your filters, you can attach them to classes or collections with the @Filter annotation. The @Filter annotation takes two parameters: name and condition. The name references a filter definition that we have previously described in an annotation. The condition parameter is an HQL WHERE clause. The parameters in the condition are denoted with colons, similar to named parameters in HQL. The parameters have to be defined on the filter definition. Here is a skeleton example of the filter annotations:

```
@Entity
@FilterDef(name = "byStatus", parameters = @ParamDef(name = "status", type = "boolean"))
@Filter(name = "byStatus", condition = "active = :status")
public class User {
    // other fields removed for brevity's sake
    boolean status;
}
```

■ **Note** Defining filters on each class is simple, but if you use filters in multiple classes, you will have a lot of duplication. To define any annotation at a package level, you will need to create a Java source file named package-info.java in the package. The package-info.java class should only include the package-level annotations and then declare the package immediately afterward. It is not meant to be a Java class. You will also need to tell Hibernate to map the package when you configure Hibernate, either through the addPackage() method on AnnotationConfiguration or in your Hibernate configuration XML.

---

[2] In this, it's like JNDI; you refer to a name in the filter definition, but the filter itself is defined elsewhere.

Filters with XML Mapping Documents

For the XML mapping documents, use the <filter-def> XML element. These filter definitions must contain the name of the filter and the names and types of any filter parameters. You specify filter parameters with the <filter-param> XML element. Here is an excerpt from a mapping document with a filter called latePaymentFilter defined:

```
<?xml version='1.0' encoding='utf-8'?>
<!DOCTYPE hibernate-mapping
    PUBLIC "-//Hibernate/Hibernate Mapping DTD//EN"
    "http://hibernate.sourceforge.net/hibernate-mapping-3.0.dtd">

<hibernate-mapping>
  <class ...

  </class>
  <filter-def name="latePaymentFilter">
    <filter-param name="dueDate" type="date"/>
  </filter-def>
</hibernate-mapping>
```

Once you have created the filter definitions, you need to attach the filters to class or collection mapping elements. You can attach a single filter to more than one class or collection. To do this, you add a <filter> XML element to each class and/or collection. The <filter> XML element has two attributes: name and condition. The name references a filter definition (for instance: latePaymentFilter). The condition represents a WHERE clause in HQL. Here's an example:

```
<class ...
  <filter name="latePaymentFilter" condition=":dueDate = paymentDate"/>
</class>
```

Each <filter> XML element must correspond to a <filter-def> element.

Using Filters in Your Application

Your application programmatically determines which filters to activate or deactivate for a given Hibernate session. Each session can have a different set of filters with different parameter values. By default, sessions do not have any active filters—you must explicitly enable filters programmatically for each session. The Session interface contains several methods for working with filters, as follows:

- public Filter enableFilter(String filterName)

- public Filter getEnabledFilter(String filterName)

- public void disableFilter(String filterName)

These are pretty self-explanatory—the enableFilter(String filterName) method activates the specified filter, the disableFilter(String filterName) method deactivates the method, and if you have already activated a named filter, getEnabledFilter(String filterName) retrieves that filter.

The org.hibernate.Filter interface has six methods. You are unlikely to use validate(); Hibernate uses that method when it processes the filters. The other five methods are as follows:

- public Filter setParameter(String name, Object value)

- public Filter setParameterList(String name, Collection values)

- public Filter setParameterList(String name, Object[] values)

- public String getName()

- public FilterDefinition getFilterDefinition()

The setParameter() method is the most useful. You can substitute any Java object for the parameter, although its type should match the type you specified for the parameter when you defined the filter. The two setParameterList() methods are useful for using IN clauses in your filters. If you want to use BETWEEN clauses, use two different filter parameters with different names. Finally, the getFilterDefinition() method allows you to retrieve a FilterDefinition object representing the filter metadata (its name, its parameters' names, and the parameter types).

Once you have enabled a particular filter on the session, you do not have to do anything else to your application to take advantage of filters, as we demonstrate in the following example.

A Basic Filtering Example

Because filters are very straightforward, a basic example allows us to demonstrate most of the filter functionality, including activating filters and defining filters in mapping documents.

We're going to create a User entity, with an active status and membership in groups. We're going to define three filters: one very simple filter with no parameters (just to show how), and then two parameterized filters, which we'll apply in various combinations.

We're going to stick with the annotation configuration, as we're using a single database (HSQL), and it simplifies our example drastically.[3] We're going to also revert to using Lombok, because that will shorten our example code, as shown in Listing 11-1.

Listing 11-1. User.java

```
package chapter11.model;

import lombok.*;
import lombok.experimental.Builder;
import org.hibernate.annotations.*;

import javax.persistence.*;
import javax.persistence.Entity;
import java.util.Arrays;
import java.util.HashSet;
import java.util.Set;

@Entity
@NoArgsConstructor
@Builder
@AllArgsConstructor
```

---

[3]We could anticipate multiple database engines, but most environments use the same databases for testing and production, as they should. It's a good habit to follow.

```java
@EqualsAndHashCode
@ToString
@FilterDefs({
        @FilterDef(name = "byStatus",
            parameters = @ParamDef(name = "status", type = "boolean")),
        @FilterDef(name = "byGroup",
            parameters = @ParamDef(name = "group", type = "string")),
        @FilterDef(name = "userEndsWith1")
})
@Filters({
        @Filter(name = "byStatus", condition = "active = :status"),
        @Filter(name = "byGroup",
         condition = ":group in ( select ug.groups from user_groups ug where ug.user_id = id)"),
        @Filter(name = "userEndsWith1", condition = "name like '%1'")
})
public class User {
    @Id
    @GeneratedValue(strategy = GenerationType.AUTO)
    Integer id;
    @Getter
    @Setter
    @Column(unique = true)
    String name;
    @Getter
    @Setter
    boolean active;
    @Getter
    @Setter
    @ElementCollection
    Set<String> groups;

    public void addGroups(String... groupSet) {
        if (getGroups() == null) {
            setGroups(new HashSet<String>());
        }
        getGroups().addAll(Arrays.asList(groupSet));
    }

}
}
```

There are a few things about this that stand out, especially with regard to groups.

First, groups are defined as a Set, annotated with @ElementCollection. This will create a table, USER_GROUPS, that will contain a user ID and a single column, with the various group names in a column named after the collection (thus, "groups" and not "group.").

Then, the filter that selects by group uses a subselect to limit the users returned. This condition is database-specific and uses knowledge of the actual table structure; filters do some introspection, but not as much as they could. Be prepared to do some analysis to work out exactly what the filter condition should be.

Now let's create a test class in Listing 11-2, FilterTests.java, that runs a simple query to make sure we have a basic framework in place. We'll add various test methods to this class to show the filters in action.

Listing 11-2. Our basic test framework, FilterTests.java

```java
public class FilterTests {
    Session session;
    Transaction tx;
    Query query;
    List<User> users;

    @BeforeMethod
    public void setupTest() {
        session = SessionUtil.getSession();
        tx = session.beginTransaction();
        User user = User.builder().name("user1").active(true).build();
        user.addGroups("group1", "group2");
        session.save(user);
        user = User.builder().name("user2").active(true).build();
        user.addGroups("group2", "group3");
        session.save(user);
        user = User.builder().name("user3").active(false).build();
        user.addGroups("group3", "group4");
        session.save(user);
        user = User.builder().name("user4").active(true).build();
        user.addGroups("group4", "group5");
        session.save(user);
        tx.commit();
        session.close();

        session = SessionUtil.getSession();
        tx = session.beginTransaction();
        query = session.createQuery("from User");
    }

    @AfterMethod
    public void endTest() {
        if (session.isOpen()) {
            if (tx.isActive()) {
                tx.commit();
            }
            tx = session.beginTransaction();
            session.disableFilter("byGroup");
            session.disableFilter("byStatus");
            session.createSQLQuery("DELETE FROM USER_GROUPS").executeUpdate();
            session.createSQLQuery("DELETE FROM USER").executeUpdate();
            tx.commit();
            session.close();
        }
        session = null;
        tx = null;
        query = null;
        users = null;
    }
```

```
@Test
public void testSimpleQuery() {
    users = (List<User>) query.list();
    assertEquals(users.size(), 4);
}
}
```

This creates a set of users, some active, some inactive, and with membership in various groups. It also runs a basic query ("from User") and validates that it retrieved all of the users.

First, let's test the simplest filter we have in Listing 11-3, which is named "userEndsWith1" – a filter that is constructed solely for the sake of showing a non-parameterized filter.[4]

Listing 11-3. Using a non-parameterized filter

```
@Test
public void testNoParameterFilter() {
    session.enableFilter("userEndsWith1");
    List<User> users = query.list();
    assertEquals(users.size(), 1);
    assertEquals(users.get(0).getName(), "user1");
}
```

This test enables a filter for the session, and then runs our basic query (which is "from User," as you'll recall). With no other configuration or specification, our data set returns only those users whose name ends with a "1" –and since we created only one user like that, that's the user that's returned.

Now let's see how to use a parameter in a filter with two tests, shown in Listing 11-4.

Listing 11-4. A filter using a parameter

```
@Test
public void testActivesFilter() {
    session.enableFilter("byStatus").setParameter("status", Boolean.TRUE);
    users = (List<User>) query.list();
    assertEquals(users.size(), 3);
}

@Test
public void testInactivesFilter() {
    session.enableFilter("byStatus").setParameter("status", Boolean.FALSE);
    users = (List<User>) query.list();
    assertEquals(users.size(), 1);
}
```

Here, we try both of our status conditions, first enabling the filter and then setting a parameter on the filter reference. Again, we're relying on our known data set.

We can combine filters, as well. We're going to include two more tests, in Listing 11-5; the first will test our group filter, and the second will combine the two filters for a single query.

---

[4] A better example *might* have been a constant status, instead of "name ends with a 1", but the status is ideally parameterized as well. The data model would have been polluted without a contrived example, so that's what we have.

Listing 11-5. Combining filters

```
@Test
public void testGroupFilter() {
    session.enableFilter("byGroup").setParameter("group", "group4");
    users = (List<User>) query.list();
    assertEquals(users.size(), 2);
    session.enableFilter("byGroup").setParameter("group", "group1");
    users = (List<User>) query.list();
    assertEquals(users.size(), 1);
    // should be user 1
    assertEquals(users.get(0).getName(), "user1");
}

@Test
public void testBothFilters() {
    session.enableFilter("byGroup").setParameter("group", "group4");
    session.enableFilter("byStatus").setParameter("status", Boolean.TRUE);
    List<User> users = query.list();
    assertEquals(users.size(), 1);
    assertEquals(users.get(0).getName(), "user4");
}
```

It's worth noting again that our query has not changed for *any* of this code; we're reusing the same query definition, over and over again, while getting different data sets from it.

You can see here that it's trivial to concatenate criteria via filters, allowing us to use simpler (and fewer) queries, and applying simple criteria.

Summary

Filters are a useful way to separate some database concerns from the rest of your code. A set of filters can cut back on the complexity of the HQL queries used in the rest of your application, at the expense of some run-time flexibility. Instead of using views (which must be created at the database level), your applications can take advantage of dynamic filters that can be activated as and when they are required.

CHAPTER 12

■ ■ ■

Leaving the Relational Database Behind: NoSQL

Hibernate doesn't limit you to using purely relational databases; Hibernate OGM stands as a project that can carry an object model into the realm of the NoSQL datastore, allowing developers to use a familiar mechanism to access multiple types of storage.

Relational databases are tabular in nature; sets of data ("tables") are homogenous and regular, often described in terms of rows and columns. Relationships are fixed; a table can require that the value of one column be represented as a column or set of columns in another table. Rows cannot change shape or form (or size); the row and column sizes are generally fixed.

NoSQL datastores are more easily described in negative terms: they're typically *not* tabular, data structures are *not* fixed, relationships are *not* enforced, data types for a given attribute are *not* consistent. That's not to say that NoSQL data stores can't have these characteristics. It just means that NoSQL datastores tend to be able to turn the rules of traditional databases on their heads. This can yield massive scalability or flexibility. Scalability in this context can refer to speed *or* size; Cassandra, for example, can use a cell concept, distributed among rows and columns–such that if you wanted, you could theoretically have a single row with two *billion* pieces of data.[1]

Flexible data structures mean that you can represent your data as a tree, or a set of trees, just as correctly as you can represent your data as a map, a set of values associated with a single key.[2]

The biggest problem with NoSQL is the object/data impedance mismatch. With a relational database, if your table has four columns in it, you can easily model that with an object. Each column would map to an object attribute, and that attribute's type is presumably easily derived from the database metadata. However, most NoSQL databases don't follow a mandated structure.[3] A single item of a given type might have four attributes, but another item of the same type might have 15 attributes, or 70, or 400.

Because of the lack of mandated structure, objects can be difficult to design well, if at all,[4] and many NoSQL Java APIs either ignore object design altogether (where information is represented simply as a stream of data) or enforce regular structures on a data storage system where regular structures aren't the norm. As a result, migrating an application to NoSQL can be a problem to address.

---

[1] This is not a good idea. 64,000 columns, sure. Two billion is a *bit* much.

[2] Many caches are now billing themselves as forms of NoSQL. Whether this is true or not tends to depend on how persistent the cache really is.

[3] The Java Content Repository (JCR) can manage both; nodes in JCR can have an enforced schema or be freeform. Most adherents strongly advocate the freeform aspect.

[4] The shrieks of horror you're hearing are from all the advocates of good design, wondering how one can ever create an application where objects aren't designed, but just happen.

In the end, NoSQL is not necessarily *better than* a relational database as much as it's merely different. NoSQL datastores have their own challenges and strengths, and whether you can leverage them properly or not depends on the specific use case you have and your own expertise. Contrast that with relational systems, which are well known and much understood in terms of strengths and weaknesses; looking at the well of experience, we find for most problems SQL is by far the most appropriate solution, if only because so many people know what SQL can do and how to do it.

This chapter will not be able to tell you everything you will ever need to know about NoSQL. One of the strengths and weaknesses of the NoSQL landscape is that it's not restricted by the definition of SQL, such that a NoSQL implementation can target specific use cases very well, being a master of one aspect of data rather than a jack of all trades, as the relational model is.

Where Is Hibernate When it Comes to NoSQL?

Hibernate can serve as a mapper for nonrelational datastores too, through Hibernate OGM. OGM is an adaptive layer between a strict object model and NoSQL's typically rather flexible object model.

From the Java coder's perspective, usage of Hibernate is fairly typical,[5] in most respects; one defines objects annotated with @Entity, and interaction is through a standard Hibernate Session or JPA EntityManager object.

There are exceptions to the seamless integration, which range from minor to severe. This is unavoidable, because of the mismatch of features between SQL and NoSQL. Most of the exceptions center on queries, because NoSQL databases typically index and query differently from how SQL does. Hibernate provides a query language layer for NoSQL, but there's no guarantee of feature completeness between SQL and NoSQL. This is less of a problem than it could be, because accessing a NoSQL datastore as if it were a SQL database can have negative performance implications. You don't necessarily *want* to have an exact correspondence between feature sets.

So let's get started.

Basic CRUD Operations

What we'd like to do is see a set of operations done with Hibernate, with a few NoSQL backends. We'll test writes, reads, updates, and deletes, with some queries thrown in for good measure. Our object model will be very simple, because mapping from Java to a nonrelational backing store really should be tuned for each NoSQL implementation. There's no good generalized solution here.[6]

Our project has a unique set of dependencies. Obviously, we need to include OGM and drivers for the specific NoSQL backends we're using. The project file can be seen in Listing 12-1.

Listing 12-1. The OGM Project's pom.xml

```xml
<?xml version="1.0" encoding="UTF-8"?>
<project xmlns="http://maven.apache.org/POM/4.0.0"
         xmlns:xsi="http://www.w3.org/2001/XMLSchema-instance"
         xsi:schemaLocation="http://maven.apache.org/POM/4.0.0
             http://maven.apache.org/xsd/maven-4.0.0.xsd">
    <groupId>com.redhat.osas.books.hibernate</groupId>
    <artifactId>chapter12</artifactId>
    <version>1.0-SNAPSHOT</version>
    <modelVersion>4.0.0</modelVersion>
```

---

[5] This is by far the most important sentence in this chapter, in terms of how powerful Hibernate can be.

[6] It's possibly a bit unfair to say that there's no generalized solution; there may be.

```xml
<dependencies>
    <dependency>
        <groupId>org.hibernate.ogm</groupId>
        <artifactId>hibernate-ogm-mongodb</artifactId>
        <version>[4.0.0.Beta4,4.1.0)</version>
    </dependency>
    <dependency>
        <groupId>org.hibernate.ogm</groupId>
        <artifactId>hibernate-ogm-infinispan</artifactId>
        <version>[4.0.0.Beta4,)</version>
    </dependency>
    <dependency>
        <groupId>org.hibernate.javax.persistence</groupId>
        <artifactId>hibernate-jpa-2.0-api</artifactId>
        <version>1.0.1.Final</version>
    </dependency>
    <dependency>
        <groupId>org.jboss.spec.javax.transaction</groupId>
        <artifactId>jboss-transaction-api_1.1_spec</artifactId>
        <version>1.0.0.Final</version>
        <scope>provided</scope>
    </dependency>
    <dependency>
        <groupId>org.hibernate</groupId>
        <artifactId>hibernate-search</artifactId>
        <version>4.4.2.Final</version>
    </dependency>
    <dependency>
        <groupId>org.jboss.jbossts</groupId>
        <artifactId>jbossjta</artifactId>
        <version>4.16.4.Final</version>
    </dependency>
    <dependency>
        <groupId>org.testng</groupId>
        <artifactId>testng</artifactId>
        <version>[6.8.7,)</version>
    </dependency>
    <dependency>
        <groupId>org.mongodb.morphia</groupId>
        <artifactId>morphia</artifactId>
        <version>[0.105,)</version>
    </dependency>
</dependencies>
<build>
    <plugins>
        <plugin>
            <groupId>org.apache.maven.plugins</groupId>
            <artifactId>maven-compiler-plugin</artifactId>
            <version>3.1</version>
```

```
            <configuration>
                <source>1.7</source>
                <target>1.7</target>
            </configuration>
        </plugin>
    </plugins>
  </build>
</project>
```

Listing 12-2 shows our entire object model, a Person object, containing an ID, a name, and a balance. We're going to eliminate the boilerplate methods again; Lombok could help, but let's keep the listing more focused.

Listing 12-2. The Object Model forOour NoSQL Venture, in src/main/java/chapter12/Person.java

```
package chapter12;

import org.hibernate.search.annotations.Analyze;
import org.hibernate.search.annotations.Field;
import org.hibernate.search.annotations.Indexed;

import javax.persistence.*;

@Entity
@Indexed
public class Person {
    @Id
    @GeneratedValue(strategy = GenerationType.AUTO)
    @Field(name = "id")
    Integer id;
    @Field(analyze = Analyze.NO)
    @Column
    String name;
    @Field(analyze = Analyze.NO)
    @Column
    Integer balance;

    public Person() {
    }

    public Person(String name, int balance) {
        this.name = name;
        this.balance = balance;
    }
    // We're not showing the mutators, accessors, or equals()/hashCode()
}
```

We've introduced some new annotations: @Indexed and @Field. These will be important for searching our data, in the event that HQL isn't supported or doesn't fit our needs. These annotations come from Hibernate Search, which provides a bridge between an object model and a search engine (Lucene, in this case); the annotations tell Hibernate Search what factors to use for searching and how the elements should be used.

We're going to configure two persistence units via JPA for our examples; the persistence.xml file looks like Listing 12-3.

Listing 12-3. The two NoSQL Persistence Units, Both Using the Same Object Model

```xml
<?xml version="1.0"?>
<persistence xmlns="http://java.sun.com/xml/ns/persistence"
             xmlns:xsi="http://www.w3.org/2001/XMLSchema-instance"
             xsi:schemaLocation="http://java.sun.com/xml/ns/persistence
                 http://java.sun.com/xml/ns/persistence/persistence_2_0.xsd"
             version="2.0">

    <persistence-unit name="chapter12-mongo" transaction-type="RESOURCE_LOCAL">
        <!-- Use Hibernate OGM provider: configuration will be transparent -->
        <provider>org.hibernate.ogm.jpa.HibernateOgmPersistence</provider>
        <class>chapter12.Person</class>
        <properties>
            <property name="hibernate.ogm.datastore.provider"
                value="org.hibernate.ogm.datastore.mongodb.impl.MongoDBDatastoreProvider"/>
            <property name="hibernate.ogm.mongodb.database" value="chapter12"/>
            <property name="hibernate.transaction.jta.platform"
                value="org.hibernate.service.jta.platform.internal.JBossStandAloneJtaPlatform"/>
        </properties>
    </persistence-unit>

    <persistence-unit name="chapter12-ispn" transaction-type="RESOURCE_LOCAL">
        <provider>org.hibernate.ogm.jpa.HibernateOgmPersistence</provider>
        <class>chapter12.Person</class>
        <properties>
            <property name="hibernate.ogm.datastore.provider"
                value="org.hibernate.ogm.datastore.infinispan.impl.InfinispanDatastoreProvider"/>
            <property name="hibernate.transaction.jta.platform"
                value="org.hibernate.service.jta.platform.internal.JBossStandAloneJtaPlatform"/>
        </properties>
    </persistence-unit>
</persistence>
```

The code to acquire a working EntityManager from this is trivial. If we want the chapter12-ispn persistence unit, we could use the following snippet of code:

```java
EntityManagerFactory factory = null;
public synchronized EntityManager getEntityManager() {
    if (factory == null) {
        factory = Persistence.createEntityManagerFactory("chapter12-ispn");
    }
    return factory.createEntityManager();
}
```

The Tests

Since we have two persistence units, we could create an abstract base class for the tests that contains the actual tests themselves, with extending classes providing specific custom information for the test–like the persistence unit name. Listing 12-4 shows a skeleton BaseOGMTest.java, to which we'll add some tests as we progress.

Listing 12-4. BaseOGMTest.java Skeleton

```java
public abstract class BaseOGMTest {

    abstract String getPersistenceUnitName();

    EntityManagerFactory factory = null;

    public synchronized EntityManager getEntityManager() {
        if (factory == null) {
            factory = Persistence.createEntityManagerFactory(getPersistenceUnitName());
        }
        return factory.createEntityManager();
    }
}
```

Extending classes would provide a definition for getPersistenceUnitName(), and any methods annotated with @Test in either class can be executed.

Testing Create and Read

Listing 12-5 shows our first test; this test creates a Person, persists it, and then reads it. After we see the code, we'll create an InfinispanTest class that extends BaseOGMTest, which will give us enough to actually run our code.

Listing 12-5. The testCR Method, Which Tests Creates and Reads

```java
@Test
public void testCR() {
    EntityManager em = getEntityManager();
    em.getTransaction().begin();
    Person person = new Person("user 1", 1);
    em.persist(person);
    em.getTransaction().commit();
    em.close();

    em = getEntityManager();
    Person p2 = em.find(Person.class, person.getId());
    em.close();
    System.out.println(p2);
    assertNotNull(p2);
    assertEquals(p2, person);
}
```

One thing that stands out about this code is that it is idiomatic normal Java persistence. We're not using anything here that would indicate that we weren't using a standard JPA entity manager.

As we see in Listing 12-6, the InfinispanTest class is very simple, but it provides the persistence unit name we'll be using for Infinispan:

Listing 12-6. The Full Definition for InfinispanTest.java

```java
public class InfinispanTest extends BaseOGMTest {
    @Override
    String getPersistenceUnitName() {
        return "chapter12-ispn";
    }
}
```

Testing Updates

Now let's take a look at test for updates, in Listing 12-7; this will also follow the standard JPA idiom.

Listing 12-7. Testing NoSQL Updates with JPA

```java
@Test
public void testUpdate() {
    EntityManager em = getEntityManager();
    em.getTransaction().begin();
    Person person = new Person("user 2", 1);
    em.persist(person);
    em.getTransaction().commit();
    em.close();

    em = getEntityManager();
    em.getTransaction().begin();
    Person p2 = em.find(Person.class, person.getId());
    p2.setBalance(2);
    em.getTransaction().commit();
    em.close();

    em = getEntityManager();
    em.getTransaction().begin();
    Person p3 = em.find(Person.class, person.getId());
    em.getTransaction().commit();
    em.close();

    assertEquals(p3, p2);
}
```

As usual, we acquire the EntityManager; we start a transaction; we load a managed Person reference, update it, and commit the transaction. This is very much the same process that we use for *any* such updates; from the coder's perspective, we don't know if we're using PostgreSQL or Infinispan as a datastore.[7]

---

[7] From a runtime perspective, we would notice; PostgreSQL is very fast, but an in-memory datagrid like Infinispan will typically run circles around a relational database.

Testing Removal

As one might expect, removing entities remains idiomatic as well, as Listing 12-8 shows:

Listing 12-8. Removing Entities with JPA

```
@Test
public void testDelete() {
    EntityManager em = getEntityManager();
    em.getTransaction().begin();
    Person person = new Person("user 3", 1);
    em.persist(person);
    em.getTransaction().commit();
    em.close();

    em = getEntityManager();
    em.getTransaction().begin();
    Person p2 = em.find(Person.class, person.getId());
    em.remove(p2);
    em.getTransaction().commit();
    em.close();

    em = getEntityManager();
    em.getTransaction().begin();
    Person p3 = em.find(Person.class, person.getId());
    em.getTransaction().commit();
    em.close();

    assertNull(p3);
}
```

Querying in OGM

That leaves queries, which is where we finally see a divergence from idiomatic JPA.

As of this writing, Hibernate OGM does *not* support the use of JP-QL, the standard query language for JPA. It *does*, however, support the use of some HQL, depending on which NoSQL datastore you're using. Thus, to use a query language with NoSQL, we're going to need to break idiom and use the Session underneath the EntityManager we've been using.

Note, also, that the full HQL language is not likely to be available. Basic operations are likely to be supported; the more advanced your HQL gets, the less likely that OGM will support it.

The lack of full HQL is inconvenient, but not necessarily a terrible thing; providing SQL-like concepts across a nonrelational database can cripple performance. Since HQL provides features that are likely to be kinder to the datastores, you can usually use what capabilities are provided without wondering if you're brutalizing performance too much.

Listing 12-9 shows how we populate our data set. We not only persist data but also preserve the entities in a Map so we can validate the returned data. Listing 12-10 shows an HQL query that uses this data.

Listing 12-9. Populating Some Data for Our HQL Tests

```
Map<Integer, Person> people = new HashMap<>();
EntityManager em = getEntityManager();
em.getTransaction().begin();

for (int i = 4; i < 7; i++) {
    people.put(i, new Person("user " + i, i));
    em.persist(people.get(i));
}

em.getTransaction().commit();
em.close();
```

Listing 12-10. A Simple HQL Query

```
em = getEntityManager();
em.getTransaction().begin();
Session session = em.unwrap(Session.class);
Query q = session.createQuery("from Person p where p.balance = :balance");
q.setInteger("balance", 4);
Person p = (Person) q.uniqueResult();
System.out.println(p);
assertEquals(p, people.get(4));
em.getTransaction().commit();
em.close();
```

As you can see, we unwrap the `Session` from our `EntityManager` so that we can use Hibernate's query language instead of JPA's query language. Apart from that, the usage of the query is idiomatic; we don't have to do much to our code yet.[8]

Our selection statement (the "where clause") can combine elements, as shown in Listing 12-11:

Listing 12-11. Using AND in a "Where Clause" in HQL

```
em = getEntityManager();
em.getTransaction().begin();
session = em.unwrap(Session.class);
q = session.createQuery("from Person p where p.balance = :balance and p.name=:name");
q.setInteger("balance", 4);
q.setString("name", "user 4");
p = (Person) q.uniqueResult();
assertEquals(p, people.get(4));
em.getTransaction().commit();
em.close();
```

Lastly, we can use comparison operators too, although here we'll see yet another potential difference between SQL and NoSQL.

---

[8] Unless, of course, you consider dropping back to HQL to be "much."

The concept of uniqueness in NoSQL isn't quite the same as it is in relational models; it's possible, depending on the datastore, to retrieve multiple copies of the same entity for a given query.[9] As a result, we *might* get two values from our simple query, even though it should return only one; here, we're adding the list of results into a Set<Person>, which will trim duplicates and give us single references for each entity. Our code is shown in Listing 12-12.

Listing 12-12. Using More Comparison Operators in HQL

```
em = getEntityManager();
em.getTransaction().begin();
session = em.unwrap(Session.class);
q = session.createQuery("from Person p where p.balance > :balance");
q.setInteger("balance", 4);
// we use a Set because NoSQL's concept of uniqueness is.. difficult
Set<Person> peopleList = new HashSet<Person>(q.list());
assertEquals(peopleList.size(), 2);
em.getTransaction().commit();
em.close();
```

This leads us to Hibernate Search, which provides a programmatic interface to Apache Lucene. If an entity is indexed, its fields will be stored in a Lucene directory, which means they're available for full-text queries.

To mark an entity as being indexed for Lucene, one simply adds the @Indexed annotation to the class, as we did for Person. The fields are annotated with @Field; the default is to have the fields analyzed, which makes them appropriate for use in a full-text, fuzzy search.[10] If we want to use the fields verbatim for searches, we want to turn analysis off, which is done with @Field(analyze = Analyze.NO).

Actually executing the query involves creating a FullTextEntityManager, then building a Lucene query with that; one then converts the Lucene query into something that Hibernate can use to return entities. Lucene is even more prone to returning single entities multiple times, so one has to trim the result set for uniqueness here as well. Listing 12-13 shows an example of querying on a simple value with Hibernate Search, including populating data:

Listing 12-13. A Simple Hibernate Search Example

```
@Test
public void testQueryLucene() {
    Map<Integer, Person> people = new HashMap<>();
    EntityManager em = getEntityManager();
    em.getTransaction().begin();

    for (int i = 7; i < 9; i++) {
        people.put(i, new Person("user " + i, i));
        em.persist(people.get(i));
    }

    em.getTransaction().commit();
    em.close();

    em = getEntityManager();
    em.getTransaction().begin();
    FullTextEntityManager ftem = Search.getFullTextEntityManager(em);
```

---

[9] We'll see this again when we look at the Hibernate Search facility.
[10] In a fuzzy search, it's possible to get a hit on "gives" with "give" as a search term, and vice versa. Verbatim searches wouldn't return a hit on "give" with "gives."

```
//Optionally use the QueryBuilder to simplify Query definition:
QueryBuilder b = ftem.getSearchFactory()
        .buildQueryBuilder()
        .forEntity(Person.class)
        .get();
org.apache.lucene.search.Query lq =
        b.keyword().onField("id").matching(people.get(7).getId()).createQuery();

//Transform the Lucene Query in a JPA Query:
FullTextQuery ftQuery = ftem.createFullTextQuery(lq, Person.class);
//This is a requirement when using Hibernate OGM instead of ORM:
ftQuery.initializeObjectsWith(ObjectLookupMethod.SKIP,
        DatabaseRetrievalMethod.FIND_BY_ID);

Set<Person> resultList = new HashSet<Person>(ftQuery.getResultList());
// lucene can return multiple results for a given query!
Set<Person> personSet = new HashSet<>();
personSet.addAll(resultList);
assertEquals(personSet.size(), 1);
em.getTransaction().commit();
em.close();
}
```

This looks like a lot of code to accomplish something very simple, but it's worth noting that we're also able to execute full-text queries with similar code. Full-text and fuzzy queries aren't trivial; the Hibernate Search code isn't entirely trivial either, but it's fairly simple.

All of this code runs against Infinispan fairly well, but what happens if we switch to another datastore, such as MongoDB?

MongoDB

MongoDB (http://www.mongodb.org) is an open-source document database using JSON as a serialization format. It can shard well, has full indexing, and performs atomic operations for single documents; it's also incredibly fast.

Installing mongodb is very easy.

- On Windows, it's as simple as downloading the appropriate Windows installer and running it.

■ **Note** The same process works for other operating systems, as well, but the Linux and MacOSX package managers have mongodb available.

- On Linux, Fedora users can install the mongodb server packages by using sudo yum install mongodb-server; Ubuntu users can do the same with sudo apt-get install mongodb-server.
- MacOSX users can install it with brew install mongodb.

Once mongodb is installed, you can start mongo for our tests by going to a temporary working directory and executing the following command:

```
mongod --dbpath . --noauth
```

This will run through a few steps for initialization, then wait for connection.

For us to use mongodb as a backend datastore instead of Infinispan, all we need to do is provide the mongodb persistence unit's name. Listing 12-14 is our example MongoTest.java code:

Listing 12-14. Using mongodb Instead of Infinispan for Our Datastore

```java
public class MongoTest extends BaseOGMTest {
    @Override
    String getPersistenceUnitName() {
        return "chapter12-mongo";
    }
}
```

Apart from that, all of our tests should run cleanly. We have preserved the benefit of using a library for persistence, even while giving ourselves the chance to leverage the features that NoSQL datastores offer us.

Summary

Hibernate OGM is a library that offers a bridge from Hibernate to nonrelational datastores, allowing easy and convenient usage of data grids or other document storage mechanisms. The code can be unusual compared to idiomatic Java persistence code, largely because of impedance mismatches between storage models.

■ ■ ■

More Advanced Features

In this appendix, we discuss some of the features that, strictly speaking, lie outside the scope of this book, but that you should be aware of if you go on to use Hibernate in more depth.

Managed Versioning and Optimistic Locking

While we have saved versioning for this appendix's discussion of advanced features, it is actually quite straightforward to understand and apply. Consider the following scenario:

- Client A loads and edits a record.

- Client B loads and edits the same record.

- Client A commits its edited record data.

- Client B commits its differently edited record data.

While the scenario is simple, the problems it presents are not. If Client A establishes a transaction, then Client B may not be able to load and edit the same record. Yet in a Web environment, it is not unlikely that Client A will close a browser window on the open record, never committing or canceling the transaction, so that the record remains locked until the session times out. Clearly this is not a satisfactory solution. Usually, you will not want to permit the alternative scenario, in which no locking is used, and the last person to save a record wins!

The solution, versioning, is essentially a type of optimistic locking (see Chapter 8). When any changes to an entity are stored, a version column is updated to reflect the fact that the entity has changed. When a subsequent user tries to commit changes to the same entity, the original version number will be compared against the current value—if they differ, the commit will be rejected.

The Hibernate/JPA 2 annotation mappings and the Hibernate XML-based mappings both provide a simple syntax for indicating which field should be used for storing the managed version information. The annotation for this field is shown in Listing A-1.

Listing A-1. Marking the Version Attribute Using Annotations

```
@Version
protected int getVersionNum() {
   return versionNum;
}
```

The default optimistic locking strategy for Hibernate is versioning, so if you provide a column annotated with @Version in your object model, this will be used as long as you have enabled dynamic updates (as shown in Listing A-2).

Listing A-2. Marking the Version Attribute Using XML Mappings

```
@Entity
public class MyObject {
    @Version
    @Column
    Integer version;
    ...
}
```

The version attribute is defined in a very similar way to the normal property configuration. The version can be of type long, integer, short, timestamp, or calendar.

You can modify the default lock mode for a given managed object by using Session.load() and include a LockMode, or Session.lock(); or–if you're accessing the managed objects through a Query–through Query.setLockMode().

If you elect not to use versioning, dirty checking offers an alternative form of optimistic locking. Here, the values of the entities are themselves checked to see if they have changed since the entity was originally obtained. As with versioning-based optimistic locking, the check against the database is carried out when the changes are committed. If an optimistic lock type of dirty is selected, then only those fields that have changed since the persistent entity was obtained will be checked (the Session keeps track of the appropriate state information). If an optimistic lock type of all is selected, then all the fields making up the entity will be checked for changes. If the fields being checked have changed prior to the commit, then the commit will fail.

Versioning is generally a simpler and more reliable approach, so we suggest that you use this whenever you need optimistic locking features.

Limitations of Hibernate

First and foremost, Hibernate wants every entity to be identifiable with a primary key. Ideally, it would like this to be a *surrogate key* (a single column distinct from the fields of the table). Hibernate will accept a primary key that is not a surrogate key. For example, the username column might be used to uniquely identify an entry in the user table. Hibernate will also accept a composite key as its primary key, so that the username and hostname might be used to form the primary key if the username alone does not serve to identify the row.

In the real world, things do not really work like that. Any database that has been around the block a few times is likely to have at least one table for which the primary key has been omitted. For instance, the contents of the table may not have needed to be involved in any relations with other tables. While this is still bad database design, the error is only exposed when Hibernate tries to map objects to data. It may be that adding a suitable surrogate key column is an option—when this is the case, we urge you to do so. In practice, however, the fundamental schema may not be under the developer's control, or other applications may break if the schema is radically changed.

In most scenarios, a developer will be able to arrange the creation of views or stored procedures. It may be possible to create the appearance of a suitable primary key using these if no other options present themselves, but you should consult with your database administrators, since a table for which no true primary key can be obtained is likely to cause long-term corruption of your data.

Finally, if you can neither change a broken schema nor add views or stored procedures to ameliorate its effects, you have the option of obtaining a pure JDBC connection (see Listing A-3) from the session to the database, and carrying out traditional connected database access. This is the option of last resort, and is only truly of value when you anticipate being able to correct the faulty schema at some future time.

Listing A-3. Obtaining a JDBC Connection from Hibernate

```
SessionFactory factory =
       new Configuration().configure().buildSessionFactory();
Session session = factory.openSession();
Connection connection = session.getConnection();
```

Hand-Rolled SQL

While Hibernate cannot operate upon entities that lack primary keys, it is also extremely awkward to use Hibernate when there is a poor correspondence between the tables and the classes of your object model.

Using a Direct Mapping

Figure A-1 presents a fairly typical example of a valid database model that may be painful to represent in our mapping files.

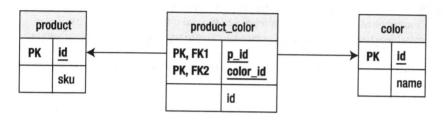

Figure A-1. *A problematic but legal schema*

Here, the `product` table represents a product (for example, a flashlight). The `color` table represents the colors in which it is sold. The link table named `product_color` then allows us to identify a product by stock keeping unit (SKU), and identify the colors in which it is available.

If we do not mind the `Product` object retaining a set of colors (representing the colors in which it can be sold), then we have no problem; but if we want to distinguish between a red flashlight and a green one, things become more difficult (see Listing A-4).

Listing A-4. A Fairly Direct Representation of the Product as an XML Mapping

```
<class name="com.hibernatebook.legacy.Product" table="product_color">

  <composite-id
    class="com.hibernatebook.legacy.ProductKey"
    name="key">

    <key-property type="int" name="id" column="product_id"/>
    <key-property type="int" name="colorId" column="color_id"/>

  </composite-id>

  <many-to-one
    name="color"
    class="com.hibernatebook.legacy.Color"
    column="color_id"
    insert="false"
    update="false"/>
```

```
<many-to-one
    name="data"
    class="com.hibernatebook.legacy.ProductData"
    column="product_id"
    insert="false"
    update="false"/>
```

```
</class>
```

There are several dissatisfying aspects to the mapping in Listing A-5. First, rather than mapping our product table, we have mapped the link table. This makes sense when you consider that the primary key formed from the two columns of this table uniquely identifies a "colored product," which the product table alone cannot do.

Second, we are obliged to create a number of distinct objects to represent the class: the Product class itself, a class to represent the primary key (inevitable where a composite id occurs), a class to represent the other attributes of the product, and the Color class.

Last, the use of the columns more than once within the mapping requires us to flag them so that they cannot be written—this is a *read-only mapping*.

Using a View

Fortunately, most databases provide a simple mechanism for manipulating a schema so that it better matches the business requirements. A database view will allow you to put together a join that appears to be a table. By a suitable choice of columns from the existing tables, you can construct a view that is much easier to map (see Listing A-5).

Listing A-5. A View on the Product Tables

```
create view vwProduct (ProductKey,ColorKey,Id,SKU,ColorId)
AS
    select
        p.id as ProductKey,
        c.id as ColorKey,
        p.id as Id,
        p.sku as SKU,
        c.id as ColorId
    from
        product p,
        product_color pc,
        color c
    where
        p.id = pc.product_id
    and
        pc.color_id = c.id;
```

This view effectively reformats our table so that it has a correct (composite) primary key formed from the link table's two columns. It makes the SKU data available directly, and it retains the foreign key into the color table.

Listing A-6 is a much more natural mapping.

Listing A-6. The Revised Mapping

```xml
<class name="com.hibernatebook.legacy.Product" table="vwProduct">
   <composite-id
       class="com.hibernatebook.legacy.ProductKey"
       name="key">
       <key-property
           type="int"
           name="id"
           column="ProductKey"/>
       <key-property
           type="int"
           name="colorId"
           column="ColorKey" />
   </composite-id>

   <property
       name="id"
       type="int"
       column="id"
       insert="false"
       update="false"
       unique="true"/>

   <property
       name="SKU"
       type="int"
       column="sku"
       insert="false"/>

   <many-to-one
       name="color"
       class="com.hibernatebook.legacy.Color"
       column="ColorId"/>
</class>
```

The behavior of the composite primary key is unchanged, but the SKU now becomes a simple property. The color entity is mapped as before.

The caveat for this approach is the problem of writing data to the mapping. Some databases (for example, versions 4 and lower of MySQL) do not support writable views, and others may have only limited support for them. To avoid views in these circumstances, we must abandon complete portability in favor of database-specific SQL inserted directly into the mapping file.

Putting SQL into an Annotation or Mapping

Hibernate provides three annotations and several XML tags that can be used to override the default behavior when writing to the database. Instead of accepting the SQL generated by Hibernate from the information in the mapping file, you can dictate exactly how changes to an entity should be enforced. The disadvantage is that you will lose Hibernate's guarantee of cross-database platform portability. The advantage is that you can carry out operations that are not explicitly described in the mapping, such as calculating and inserting values in the process of carrying out an insert.

The annotations are @SQLInsert, @SQLUpdate, and @SQLDelete; while the XML mapping elements are `<sql-insert>`, `<sql-update>`, and `<sql-delete>`. All of these work in the same way.

If you take a look at the DDL script for this example, you will see that our client table includes seven fields, the last of which is the country field, as shown in Listing A-7.

Listing A-7. The DDL Script to Create the Client Table

```
create table client (
    id int not null primary key,
    name varchar(32) not null,
    number varchar(10),
    streetname varchar(128),
    town varchar(32),
    city varchar(32),
    country varchar(32)
);
```

We will, however, ignore the country field in our mapping file. We would like this to be automatically set to UK whenever a client entity is persisted.

Depending on the database, this could be implemented as part of the view's support for writing operations, or as a trigger invoked when the other fields are written—but we use the @SQLInsert annotation or `<sql-insert>` tag to specify the operation to perform.

The necessary ordering of the parameters can be determined by running Hibernate with logging enabled for the org.hibernate.persister.entity level. You must do this before you add the mapping. Listing A-8 shows a suitably formatted `<sql-insert>` element with the parameters suitably ordered. Note that the identifier field id is in the last position—not the first, as you might have expected.

Listing A-8. The Mapping File Using Explicit SQL to Update the Tables

```
<class name="com.hibernatebook.legacy.Client" table="Client">
    <id type="int" name="id" column="id">
        <generator class="native"/>
    </id>
    <property type="text" name="name" column="name"/>
    <property type="text" name="number" column="number"/>
    <property type="text" name="streetname" column="streetname"/>
    <property type="text" name="town" column="town"/>
    <property type="text" name="city" column="city"/>

    <sql-insert>
    insert into client(name,number,streetname,town,city,id,country)
    values (?,?,?,?,?,?,'UK');
    </sql-insert>
</class>
```

In addition to the three SQL terms for writing to the database, you can specify hand-rolled SQL for reading. This is appended as `<sql-query>` tags outside the class tag (see Listing A-9). They are not intrinsically a part of the mapping. However, you *can* specify that one of them should be used as the default loader for your class.

Listing A-9. An Alternative Mapping File Defining a Default Loader

```
...
<hibernate-mapping>
    <class name="com.hibernatebook.legacy.Client"
            table="Client">
        <id type="int" name="id" column="id">
            <generator class="native"/>
        </id>
        <property name="name"/>
        <property name="number"/>
        <property name="streetname"/>
        <property name="town"/>
        <property name="city"/>

        <loader query-ref="DefaultQuery"/>
    </class>

<sql-query name="DefaultQuery">
    <return alias="c"
            class="com.hibernatebook.legacy.Client"/>
    SELECT
        id as {c.id},
        'NOT SPECIFIED' as {c.name},
        number as {c.number},
        streetname as {c.streetname},
        town as {c.town},
        city as {c.city}
    FROM
        Client
    WHERE
        id = ?
</sql-query>

</hibernate-mapping>
```

■ **Tip** Unfortunately, this technique is not quite as sophisticated as you might hope—the custom SQL will not be invoked in general terms. Only if the `id` is explicitly supplied, as is the case when calling the `Session` class's `get()` method, will the default handling be overridden in favor of the loader query.

Invoking Stored Procedures

Data outlives application logic. This is a general rule of thumb, and as we can attest, it holds true in practice. The natural lifespan of a database will tend to see multiple applications. The lifespan of some of these applications will, in turn, tend to overlap, so that at any one time we expect substantially different code bases to be accessing the same data.

To resolve such issues, databases usually provide their own programming language to allow complex business rules to be expressed and enforced within the boundary of the database itself. These languages are expressed in stored procedures—essentially an API to the database. Often, free-form SQL access to such a database is denied, and only access through stored procedures is permitted. Barring errors in the code of the stored procedures themselves, this removes any risk of corruption.

One final advantage of using stored procedures is that when a substantial calculation is required, the use of a stored procedure can reduce the network traffic involved. For example, if you invoke a stored procedure to calculate the grand total of a table of accounts, only the request and the result figure would need to traverse the network. The equivalent client-side implementation would need to acquire the value to be totaled from every row!

Taking the client example from the "Putting SQL into a Mapping" section, we could replace the SQL logic in the <sql-insert> tag with a call to a suitable stored procedure. The callable attribute is set to true to indicate that Hibernate needs to issue a call to a stored procedure instead of a standard query (see Listing A-10).

Listing A-10. Mapping a Call to the Stored Procedure

```
<sql-insert callable="true">
    {call insertClient(?,?,?,?,?,?)}
</sql-insert>
```

In the stored procedure definition (see Listing A-11), you will note that the order of the parameters to be passed in has been tailored to match the order in which they will be provided by Hibernate.

Listing A-11. The Logic of the Stored Procedure

```
CREATE PROCEDURE
    insertClient( p_name varchar(32),
                  p_number varchar(10),
                  p_streetname varchar(128),
                  p_town varchar(32),
                  p_city varchar(32),
                  p_id int)
AS
BEGIN
    INSERT INTO client
        (id,name,number,streetname,town,city,country)
    VALUES
        (:p_id,:p_name,:p_number,:p_streetname,:p_town,:p_city,'UK');
END
```

By obtaining a JDBC connection from the session, it is of course possible to invoke stored procedures directly; however, you must be aware that the Hibernate session cache cannot track these updates.

Overriding the Default Constructor

Occasionally, you will find that it is necessary to persist a POJO that has no default constructor. Usually you will have access to the source code, and should just make the change directly. Occasionally, however, you may find that you are working with classes for which the source code is not available—or that you are working with large bodies of generated objects for which it is extremely inconvenient to manage changes made to the source code. In these circumstances, it is possible to use an interceptor to replace the default object-creation logic.

This technique can be used as long as you have some way of obtaining or applying default values for the parameters of the POJO's non-default constructor. Listing A-12 shows an example of the use of this technique to instantiate a POJO whose only constructor demands a String parameter.

Listing A-12. Invoking a Non-Default Constructor

```
private static class OverrideCtor implements Interceptor {

    public Object instantiate(
        String entityName,
        EntityMode entityMode,
        Serializable id)
            throws CallbackException
    {
        if( entityName.equals(MissingDefaultCtorClass.class.getName())) {
            // My call to CTor
            return new MissingDefaultCtorClass("NOT SET");
        } else {
            // Some other class - continue to default handling
            return null;
        }
    }

    // ... the remaining default method declarations...
}
```

Summary

In this appendix, we have looked at alternative mechanisms for accessing Hibernate entities, and we have shown how SQL and stored procedures can be integrated into the Hibernate environment.

Index

A

Annotations
  Hibernate mappings, 81, 195
  Hibernate-specific persistence annotations
    Immutable annotation, 109
    natural ID, 110
  Hibernate XML configuration file, 108
  JPA 2 persistence (*see* JPA 2 persistence annotations)

B

Basic annotation, 94
BeforeSuite method, 15

C

CacheMode setting, 147
CacheProvider interface, 146
Column annotation, 93, 95
Criteria query API, 160
  aggregate functions, 171
  createCriteria() methods, 165
  groupProperty projection, 172
  JPA 2, 174
  many-to-one associations, 170
  one-to-many associations, 170
  pagination, 169
  projections, 171–172
  QBE, 173–174
  restrictions
    conjunction() method, 168
    disjunction() factory method, 168
    eq() method, 166
    factory methods, 166
    like() or ilike() method, 166
    ne() method, 166
    or() method, 167
    sqlRestriction() methods, 168

setMaxResults() method, 169
sorting, 170
SQL DISTINCT query, 171
uniqueResult() method, 169

D

Database management system (DBMS), 142
DiscriminatorColumn annotation, 102

E

ElementCollection annotation, 105
Entities
  annotation, 84
  associations
    bidirectional, 46–48
    corrected email class, 48–49
    corrected message class, 48
    email class, 45
    mappingBy attribute, 50
    message class, 45
    misleading behavior, 49–50
    owner, 50
    relationship management, 44
    types, 44
  delete() method, 61
  loading
    basic load() methods, 56
    getEntityName() method, 57
    get() methods, 57
    lock mode, 56–57
    supplier ID, 57–58
  mappings, 42
  merging, 58–59
  refresh() methods, 59–60
  save method
    entityName argument, 51
    object updation, 53–54

Entities (*cont.*)
    session interface, 51
    simple object, 51
    testSaveLoad() method, 52
    testSavingEntitiesTwice() method, 52–53
    updation, 60–61

■ F

Filters
    activating filters, 178
    advantage of, 175
    annotations, 176
    application, 177
    combining filters, 182
    custom queries, 175
    definition, 176
    ElementCollection, 179
    FilterTests.java, 179
    Lombok, 178
    non-parameterized filter, 181
    parameter, 181
    wildcard query, 175
    XML mapping documents, 177
Flush() method, 138

■ G

GeneratedValue annotation, 85
getReference() test, 113
getSession() method, 118

■ H

Hibernate
    API, 1
    binary download
    cache.provider_class property, 146
    criteria API (*see* Criteria query API)
    default constructor, 202–203
    hand-rolled SQL
        annotation/mapping, 199–201
        direct mapping, 197–198
        views, 198–199
    integration and configuration
        C3P0, 17
        concept, 9
        database driver and libraries, 10
        Java Application, 10
        JDBC connection management, 16
        JNDI, 17–18
        Maven installation (*see* Maven installation)
    invoking stored procedures, 201–202
    JDBC, 5–6

JPA integration (*see* Java persistence
    architecture (JPA))
life cycle (*see* Life cycle)
limitations, 196
mappings, 6, 81 (*see also* Mapping; Annotations)
message object, 7
NoSQL datastore (*see* NoSQL datastores)
object model design (*see* Object model design)
object/relational mapping, 3–4
origins, 3–4
persistence solution, 4–5
POJO (*see* Plain Old Java Objects (POJOs))
searches and queries
    filters (*see* Filters)
    HQL (*see* Hibernate Query Language (HQL))
session object (*see* Session object)
versioning and optimistic locking
    annotations, 195
    dirty checking, 196
    scenario, 195
    XML mappings, 196
Hibernate Query Language (HQL), 6
    aggregate methods, 161
    alias, 156
    associations, 160
    basic syntax
        ANTLR grammar, 150
        DELETE, 150
        INSERT, 151
        SELECT, 151
        UPDATE, 150
    bulk deletes, 162
    bulk updates, 162
    commenting SQL, 156
    definition, 149
    executeUpdate() method, 162
    from clause, 156
    JMX MBean, 149
    logging the SQL, 155
    named parameters, 158
    named queries
        Basic Product entity, 152
        class-level annotations, 152
        createQuery() method, 155
        software entity, 153
        supplier entity, 152
        test method, 153
    native SQL, 163
    object model design (*see* Object model design)
    pagination, 159
    query's expressions, 157
    select clause and projection, 157
    sorting, 160
    uniqueResult() method, 159

■ I

Id annotation, 84
Immutable annotation, 109

■ J, K

J2EE Connector Architecture (JCA), 10
Java Database Connectivity (JDBC), 1, 3, 6, 10, 196
Java Management Extensions (JMX), 10
Java Naming and Directory
       Interface (JNDI), 10
Java persistence architecture (JPA)
    data validation
       AllArgsConstructor annotation, 129
       Bean Validation specification, 127
       class-level annotation, 132
       coordinate validation test, 132
       hibernate validator, 128
       implementation, 133
       persist() method, 130
       SimpleValidatedPerson entity, 131
       testing, 129
       validator API, 127
    external entity listeners, 126
    JPASessionUtil class, 117
    lifecycle events
       lifecycle phases, 122
       lifecycle test driver, 124
       LifecycleThing, 122–123
    project object model, 116
    Testing JPASessionUtil
       EntityManager.remove(), 121
       Lombok-annotated Entity, 120
       testSession() method, 121
Java Persistence Query
       Language (JPQL), 150
Java Runtime Environment (JRE), 83
JPA 2 persistence annotations
    Basic annotation, 94
    Book class, unannotated, 83
    column annotation, 95
    compound primary keys
       DDL, 92
       Embeddable annotations, 88, 91
       Id annotation, 88, 91
    element collections, 105
    entity annotation, 84
    inheritance
       joined table, 103
       joined-table approach, 104
       single table, 102
       table-per-class approach, 104
    Lob annotation, 105
    many-to-many association, 101

MappedSuperclass, 105
one-to-one association
    cascading operations, 98
    conventional, 97
    Embedded annotation, 97
    OrderColumn annotation, 99
OrderColumn
    NamedNativeQuery annotation, 107
    NamedQueries, 106
primary keys
    GeneratedValue annotation, 85
    Id annotation, 84
    property access, 85
    SequenceGenerator, 86
    TableGenerator, 86
SecondaryTable annotation, 93
Table annotation, 93
temporal data, 104
Transient annotation, 95

■ L

Life cycle
    cascading operations
       configuration option, 63
       Failed save(), 62
       Java Persistence Architecture, 62
       library object, 65
       orphan removal, 63–65
    detached objects, 42
    entities (see Entities)
    identifiers, 43
       artificial, 43
       columns, 43
       Id annotation, 43–44
       natural, 43
    lazy loading, 66
    object equality and identity, 54–56
    persistent objects, 41–42
    querying objects, 67
    removed objects, 42
    transient objects, 41
Lob annotation, 105
LockMode object, 141

■ M

MappedSuperclass, 105
Mapping
    annotations, 195
    associations
       entity relationship, 75
       many-to-many association, 78
       many-to-one association, 77–78
       one-to-many association, 77–78

Mapping (*cont.*)
    one-to-one association, 75, 77
    public customer, 74
  column types and sizes, 79
  email object acquiring, 69
  inheritance relationships, 79
  lazy loading
    data subset selection, 73
    email, 73
    userId and username, 73
  mandatory and
    unique constraints, 80
  object-oriented association, 69
  primary keys, 80
    ambiguous table updation, 73
    row identification, 71–72
    string object, 72
    user and usernumber, 72
  relational association, 69–70
  SQL formula–based properties, 80
  user class
    customer and email classes, 70
    customer and email table, 71
    password field, 70
    tool design, 71
Maven installation
  Assert.fail(), 15
  BeforeSuite method, 15
  child projects, 13
  dialect, 16
  PersistenceTest.java, 13
  pom.xml file, 13
  project object model, 11
  SessionFactory, 15
  src/test/java directory, 13
  src/test/resource/hibernate.cfg.xml, 15
  @Test, 15
  UNIX users, 11
MongoDB, 193

■ **N**

NamedQuery annotations, 107
NoSQL datastores
  BaseOGMTest.java Skeleton, 188
  flexible data, 183
  Hibernate Search, 192–193
  HQL query, 191
  @Indexed and @Field, 186
  InfinispanTest.java, 189
  Lucene directory, 192
  MongoDB, 193
  object model, 186
  OGM Project's pom.xml, 184–186

  persistence.xml file, 187
  removing entities, 190
  scalability, 183
  testCR Method, 188
  testing updates, 189
  "Where Clause" statement, 191

■ **O**

Object model design
  data reading
    findPerson() method, 24
    "name" attribute, 24
    person instance, 24
    ranking instance, 24
    ranking object, 26
    ranking operation testing, 25
  data removing, 27–28
  data updation, 26–27
  data writing
    data model, 21–22
    initialization, 23
    object finding, 23
    person entity, 22–23
    person object, 22
    query mechanism, 24
  entities, 19
  persistence contexts, 27
  ranking, 19
    data reading and writing, 20
    entity relationship diagram, 20
    ignore simple mutators, 20
    JavaBean, 20
    person's skill, 20–21
  sample application writing
    application server, 29
    object model, 29
    ranking, 31
    ranking (*see* Ranking)
    session retrieving, 30
    SessionUtil Class test, 30
    user interactions, 29
  sessions management, 28
  transactions, 28–29
Object/relational
    mapping (ORM), 1, 3–4
Optimistic locking, 141
  annotations, 195
  dirty checking, 196
  scenario, 195
  XML mappings, 196
OrderColumn annotation, 99
org.hibernate.persister.
    entity level, 200

■ P

PersistenceTest.java, 13
Pessimistic locking, 141
Plain Old Java Objects (POJOs), 6, 202
    constraints, 2
    default constructor, 3
    Java application, 2
    mapping annotations, 6–7
    retrieving
        Hibernate approach, 5–6
        JDBC approach, 3–4
    rose-rinted view, 1–2
Primary key, 196
Product class, 198
Product object, 197
Product table, 197–198
Project object model, 11

■ Q

Query by example (QBE), 173–174

■ R

Ranking
    addition
        getRankingFor() method, 32–33
        internal method, 33
        public and private mechanisms, 32
        RankingService Interface, 31–32
        test, 31
    average, 35
    findings
        control-break mechanism, 37
        highest ranked subject, 38, 40
        service methods, 37
        test code, 36
    removal, 35
    updation
        service's code, 34
        tests, 33–34
Read-only mapping, 198

■ S

SecondaryTable annotation, 93
SequenceGenerator, 86
Session object
    caching
        CacheMode options, 146
        database server, 145
        implementations, 146
        L1 and L2 cache, 145–146
        properties, 147
        supplier entity, 147
        usage, 147
    deadlocks, 142
    hibernate method, 136
    JDBC approach, 135
    locking, 141
    SessionFactory objects, 136
    threads, 148
    transactions
        ACID tests, 139
        createUser() method, 140
        database and
            manipulate, 138
        dirty read, 139
        JDBC isolation levels, 139
        nonrepeatable read, 139
        phantom read, 139
setCacheMode() method, 146
setParameter() method, 178
Stock keeping
    unit (SKU), 197
String parameter, 202
Surrogate key, 196

■ T, U, V, W, X, Y, Z

Table annotation, 93
TableGenerator, 86
Transient annotation, 95

Get the eBook for only $10!

Now you can take the weightless companion with you anywhere, anytime. Your purchase of this book entitles you to 3 electronic versions for only $10.

This Apress title will prove so indispensible that you'll want to carry it with you everywhere, which is why we are offering the eBook in 3 formats for only $10 if you have already purchased the print book.

Convenient and fully searchable, the PDF version enables you to easily find and copy code—or perform examples by quickly toggling between instructions and applications. The MOBI format is ideal for your Kindle, while the ePUB can be utilized on a variety of mobile devices.

Go to www.apress.com/promo/tendollars to purchase your companion eBook.